WORLD WAR II · TIME-LIFE INTERNATIONAL (NEDERLAND) B.V.

BY NICHOLAS BETHELL

AND THE EDITORS OF TIME-LIFE BOOKS

RUSSIA BESIEGED

WORLD WAR II

Editorial Staff for *Russia Besieged*:
Editor: William K. Goolrick
Picture Editor/Designer: Thomas S. Huestis
Text Editors: Jim Hicks, Anne Horan
Staff Writers: Susan Bryan, Richard W. Flanagan,
Henry P. Leifermann, Teresa M. C. Redd,
Henry Woodhead
Researchers: Christine M. Bowie,
Josephine G. Burke, Barbara Fleming,
Henry Wiencek, Frances G. Youssef
Art Assistant: Daniel J. McSweeney
Editorial Assistant: Dolores Morrissy

Correspondents: Elisabeth Kraemer (Bonn);
Margot Hapgood, Dorothy Bacon (London); Susan
Jonas, Lucy T. Voulgaris (New York); Maria
Vincenza Aloisi (Paris); Ann Natanson (Rome).
Valuable assistance was also provided by: Helga
Kohl, Heidi Sanford; Felix Rosenthal (Moscow);
Carolyn T. Chubet (New York).

Cover: Moving to the front to help defend Moscow in
late 1941, a Russian cavalry column wends its way
across snow-encrusted fields near the city. In an age of
motorized warfare the Red Army's cavalry, more than
200,000 strong, proved invaluable—especially when
weather immobilized mechanized vehicles.

The Author: NICHOLAS BETHELL, a former staff
member of *The Times Literary Supplement* and the
Drama Department of the BBC, has translated several Russian books, including Alexander Solzhe-
nitsyn's *Cancer Ward*. He wrote *The War Hitler
Won*, an account of the outbreak of war in September 1939, and *The Last Secret*, the story of the
postwar repatriation of Soviet citizens by British
and American troops.

Introduction: MICHAEL FOOT was educated at
Oxford and was elected President of the Oxford Union
in 1933. After a period as assistant editor of the Left-
wing weekly, *Tribune*, and then as editor of the
London *Evening Standard*, he began his parliamentary
career in 1945 as Labour MP for Devonport. He was
elected Deputy Leader of the Labour Party in 1976
and served as Lord President of the Council and
Leader of the House of Commons from 1976 to 1979.
He is the author of *Armistice 1918-39* and *The Trial of
Mussolini*, and co-author of *Guilty Men*, a study of the
pre-war appeasers.

The Consultants: COL. JOHN R. ELTING, USA
(Ret.), is a military historian, author of *The Battle
of Bunker's Hill, A Military History* and *Atlas of
the Napoleonic Wars*. He edited *Military Uniforms in North America: The Revolutionary Era*
and was associate editor of *The West Point Atlas
of American Wars*.

HANS-ADOLF JACOBSEN, Director of the Semi-
nar for Political Science at the University of Bonn,
is the co-author of *Anatomy of the S.S.*, and editor of *Decisive Battles of World War II: The German View*.

THOMAS W. WOLFE is a senior staff member of
The Rand Corporation and a member of the faculty
of the Institute for Sino-Soviet Studies, George
Washington University. He is a graduate of the
Russian Institute, Columbia University. During his
military career, Dr. Wolfe served as Air Attaché at
the American Embassy in Moscow in 1956-1958. He
is the author of *Soviet Strategy at the Crossroads*
and *Soviet Power and Europe: 1945-1970* and co-
author of other books on Soviet defense and foreign policy.

ISBN 7054 0527 3

Other Publications:
THE SEAFARERS
WORLD WAR II
THE GOOD COOK
THE TIME-LIFE ENCYCLOPAEDIA
OF GARDENING
HUMAN BEHAVIOUR
THE GREAT CITIES
THE ART OF SEWING
THE OLD WEST
THE WORLD'S WILD PLACES
THE EMERGENCE OF MAN
LIFE LIBRARY OF PHOTOGRAPHY
THIS FABULOUS CENTURY
TIME-LIFE LIBRARY OF ART
FOODS OF THE WORLD
GREAT AGES OF MAN
LIFE SCIENCE LIBRARY
LIFE NATURE LIBRARY
YOUNG READERS LIBRARY
LIFE WORLD LIBRARY
THE TIME-LIFE BOOK OF BOATING
TECHNIQUES OF PHOTOGRAPHY
LIFE AT WAR
LIFE GOES TO THE MOVIES
BEST OF LIFE

Previous World War II volumes:
Prelude to War
Blitzkrieg
The Battle of Britain
The Rising Sun
The Battle of the Atlantic

CONTENTS

INTRODUCTION TO THE BRITISH EDITION

For the whole Western world, and for the people of Britain in particular, the moment when Hitler let loose his super-blitzkrieg against the Soviet Union was the most fateful of the century. Great events often conceal their significance from the contemporary eye, or later judgements may emerge to blur the first hasty verdicts. But the flash of lightning which illumined the heavens in the early hours of June 22, 1941, became a flaming sun whose radiance is scarcely dimmed even today. The following account, first published in the United States, explains how the conflict came to assume such earth-shattering significance.

For the people of London, who had survived the Battle of Britain, the first winter of bombing, and a springtime of devastating military news from almost every corner of the globe, there was a special sense of relief in knowing that we were no longer alone in the fight against Hitler. The defiance of the past two years had bred an exhilaration and buoyancy, yet it was hard to discern a coherent design for the future. No one would accept defeat, but who could believe in victory? Then, from the blackest sky, came the transformation of all our lives.

I have my own peculiar recollection of that Sunday morning in June. I was a socialist journalist employed by the aggressively non-socialist newspaper proprietor, Lord Beaverbrook, who at that tempestuous period had transferred his energies from Fleet Street to the War Cabinet. I was spending the weekend at his country house in Surrey, along with the assortment of newspapermen and politicians of every persuasion which he normally collected and encouraged to argue with one another to the top of their bent.

I was the first in that company to hear on the early morning radio the authentic news of the German attack. So I leapt out of bed, ran downstairs, and routed out from Beaverbrook's collection of gramophone records the one I knew he possessed of the socialist hymn, beloved by the communists, the *Internationale*. The whole place was awakened and, as they poured downstairs, I was happy to inform Beaverbrook's bleary-eyed household, guests and butlers alike, that they were now allies of the Soviet Union.

No one greeted the news more joyously than Beaverbrook himself. His newspaper had been among the very few in the previous 12 months which had not become possessed by the anti-Soviet delirium, and he had also sought to keep open a line of intelligent communication with Ivan Maisky, the highly perceptive and Anglophile Soviet Ambassador in London. (Ironically, during Britain's finest but most dangerous hour of 1940, the Soviet Ambassador had persisted in believing in Britain's survival, while the American Ambassador, Joseph Kennedy, had reached a contrary conclusion.)

More than any other member of the War Cabinet, Beaverbrook seemed to appreciate just how great was the opportunity presented by Russia's participation in the war. He left at once to confer with the Prime Minister at Chequers, and made his contribution to Churchill's famous broadcast that same night, in which the new Anglo-Soviet alliance was proclaimed with true Churchillian eloquence and magnanimity.

During the weeks, months and, indeed, years which followed, the overwhelming sentiment and resolve of the British people was to act in the spirit of that speech: to make the alliance work, to ward off attacks upon it, never to lose sight of the fact that defeat for Russia would mean defeat for Britain. It was this mood which gave birth and impetus to the so-called Second Front Campaign. At a series of great public meetings up and down the country, the call was made for an Allied return to the Continent, to relieve the Russian armies and thus forestall the possibility of a triumphant Germany once more turning its attention exclusively westward.

No doubt it was absurd to suppose that a Second Front, in any real sense of the term, could have been launched in 1941. (Any argument about 1942 and 1943 is in a different category and is not directly relevant to the period covered by this volume.) Hitler's Europe at that time was not fortified, as Churchill chose to claim in his notes to Stalin; and Churchill himself toyed with the idea of extensive raids on Norway and elsewhere. Even so, the case against such action, on the facts available now, is overwhelming: resources, landing craft and men in sufficient numbers were just not available.

But this does not end the debate. Surely the whole strategy of the war should have been remodelled to take account of the new, stupendous event in the East. Surely this was the deduction to be drawn, without a day's delay, from Churchill's historic broadcast of June 22. Yet, incredibly, this was not the view of Churchill's advisers—or even of Churchill himself. They were convinced that the Russians could not survive. Sir Stafford Cripps, the British Ambassador in Moscow, was reported to have said that the Germans would go through the Russians like a hot knife through butter, and the phrase was common in some circles at the time.

Was it not only two years previously that the British War Office had regarded Poland as a more valuable ally than the Soviet Union? "Almost all responsible military opinion," wrote Churchill in later years, "held that the Russian armies would soon be defeated and largely destroyed." The Service Departments wanted as little interference with their previous plans as possible, and persuading them to send aid to Russia was, in Churchill's own words, "like flaying off pieces of their skin".

Churchill's memoirs are littered with indications that, in his heart, he too regarded the Eastern war as no more than a temporary affair. "It is right to make it clear," he wrote, "that for more than a year after Russia was involved in the war she presented herself to our minds as a burden and not as a help." This was the prevalent view in British ruling circles, both in the defence ministries and at No. 10 Downing Street, which contrasted so fiercely with emotions outside, and which so outraged Beaverbrook. He believed that the official British conception of the war had become "completely obsolete on the day when Russia was attacked".

The view of our own military was shared by Hitler. Six months before, he had grandiloquently announced to his generals that, when Operation *Barbarossa* was finally unveiled, "the world will hold its breath and make no comment", while the Soviets would collapse "like a soap bubble". Never could there have been such a misleading prophecy, and yet how nearly it came true!

Before the end of June, great Russian armies had been tricked, encircled and destroyed. By the beginning of October the whole Red Army had, according to Hitler, been "struck down, never to rise again". By the end of that month, the Soviet Union itself had, in Churchill's phrase, been reduced to "a second-rate military power". By November, the gross production of the areas that remained within Soviet Government control had been halved; 40 per cent of the Soviet population had been lost to the enemy, along with two thirds of the country's coal and iron, and nearly half its grain fields and railways.

Never had any great nation suffered such a defeat and survived—unless the Russians themselves may be said to have achieved a similar feat in 1812. It might have been wiser for the statesmen to consult Tolstoy rather than their military advisers. "It was not Napoleon alone," he wrote in *War and Peace*, "who had the nightmare feeling that his own mighty army was stricken powerless; all the generals, all the soldiers of the French Army, after all their experiences of previous battles (when, after one tenth of the effort, the enemy had always run), showed the feelings of horror before this foe, who, after losing *one half* of the army, still stood its ground as dauntless at the end as at the beginning of the battle."

In 1941, as in 1812, the centre of the storm swirled around Moscow. In December the Red Army launched a surprise counter-offensive that swept the invaders from the outskirts of the Soviet capital and first dented the myth of German invincibility. The Russian success was due to many factors: the conflicting strategies of the Führer and his generals; the "surprisingly early winter" of which Hitler complained, and which reduced the mightiest and most triumphant army in history to freezing immobility; the nerve and courage which Stalin recovered after the setbacks of the summer; the appearance of the Russian T-34 tank, which could keep going in the worst weather and which was so heavily armoured that the German anti-tank shells bounced harmlessly off it; the arrival of Siberian reserves released from the Eastern border by Japan's decision to attack the United States instead of the Soviet Union.

Transcending all these factors, however, was something Tolstoy would have needed no second glance to recognize: the spirit of the Russian people. No matter what crimes and follies may have led them to their life-and-death struggle with the legions of the Third Reich, they provided an example of fortitude and endurance without parallel.

Michael Foot

THE LAST BLITZKRIEG

German soldiers, part of an invading force of 152 divisions poised on the Russian border, wait in a morning fog for the attack on the Soviet Union to begin.

A SCHEME OF CONQUEST CALLED BARBAROSSA

At 2 a.m. on Sunday, June 22, 1941, the last train from the east chugged across the River Bug and puffed its way toward the German side of the Russo-German frontier. The atmosphere was one of summer calm, attended by the plaintive croaking of frogs farther down the river. An hour later, a terrifyingly different sound filled the air, as German artillery and mortar shells screamed across the Russian border. The war on the Eastern Front had begun, and so had a grandiose scheme of conquest called Operation *Barbarossa*.

From attack points in East Prussia and Poland, three million German soldiers—using everything from tanks to bicycles—swarmed into the U.S.S.R. to launch the largest attack in the history of warfare and the last of the German blitzkriegs. Even as Hitler's proclamation of the invasion was broadcast to the German nation at 7 o'clock that morning *(left)*, panzer spearheads were ripping through the Russian defenses. By sundown tanks were more than 50 miles inside the Soviet Union.

In the ensuing days, success followed success, cloaking the attacking force in an aura of invincibility not enjoyed by any invading army since Napoleon's time. Thousands of Russian soldiers lay dead in the wake of the onslaught and many more thousands were captured. So sudden was the attack that in one encounter German motorcyclists came upon a group of Red Army recruits while they were still undergoing drill instruction.

Despite the exhausting pace of the invasion, the victorious Germans pressed ahead, flushed with what appeared to be a repetition on a vast scale of their earlier triumphs in Poland, the Lowlands and France. Infantrymen marched as many as 30 miles a day, while engineers threw up bridges in less than nine hours. So quickly did the advance go that news of the front was hard to come by; it was passed to the troops largely by word of mouth from long-distance transport drivers riding back and forth on the roads. By July 10, with some units more than 300 miles from their starting points and poised to strike at Smolensk, many of the invaders had concluded that final victory was only days away.

Hitler's proclamation of war on the Soviet Union is read over the radio to the German homeland by Minister of Propaganda Joseph Goebbels.

In one of the first photographs of the invasion, German shock troops hurry through the gray light of dawn to cross an undefended bridge on the Russian border.

A German Panzer III, one of the work horses of Operation Barbarossa, clambers up a Russian riverbank. The logs behind the tank were for climbing muddy banks.

A section of horse-drawn German field artillery crosses a stream during the advance in the southern Ukraine. The German Army used 750,000 horses in its

artillery and supply units in the Russian campaign.

German soldiers paddle across the Russian border as engineers rebuild a bridge for vehicular use.

13

A German motorcyclist and his dispatch rider glance anxiously backward as two low-flying Soviet fighter planes head toward them during the push to Smolensk in early July, 1941. Russian air attacks were too infrequent to slow the advance of the Germans.

German engineers hastily construct a bridge over the Berezina River for their onrushing army.

Belching fire, a German 150mm howitzer lobs a high-explosive shell into nearby Russian positions.

A group of panzer grenadiers, leaving the safety of

their armored half-tracks, rush forward to clean out Soviet sharpshooters who had taken refuge in a farmhouse during the Germans' advance on Smolensk.

Weary SS soldiers, fighting in the Ukraine, grab some sleep in their vehicle during a pause in the advance. Entire SS divisions fought in Russia, manning their own tanks and field artillery, and providing troops for punitive operations against suspected partisans in the rear areas.

As the Russian city of Vitebsk burns around them, conquering German soldiers pause to rest and eat—and refresh their spirits with vodka. Before withdrawing from the town, Russian troops went from house to house setting fires as part of a scorched earth policy, shooting any owners who resisted.

On the evening of June 18, 1941, a telephone rang in the office of Colonel Ivan I. Fedyuninsky, commander of a Red Army infantry corps that was stationed in the western Ukraine, near the frontier of German-occupied Poland. An excited officer of the border guard was on the line. "A German soldier has just come over to our side," he said. "He is giving us very important information. I don't know whether he can be believed."

"Wait for me," Fedyuninsky said, and went immediately to the post where the German was being held. "Ask him why he came over to us," he told an interpreter. The young German explained. He had got drunk and struck an officer. He was going to be court-martialed. He had always liked the Russians, and his father was a Communist. "Will my life be spared?" he asked.

It was a strange question. Why should the Russians want to kill an ordinary soldier in the army of a friendly nation with which their government had signed a nonaggression pact less than two years previously? They asked him. "Because war is going to start soon," the deserter said, "and the German army will be the enemy of Russia." At 4 a.m. on June 22, he continued, Hitler's soldiers would invade along the entire length of the 2,000-mile frontier, from the Arctic to the Black Sea.

Fedyuninsky found the information "incredible." It was true that rumors of war had been circulating in the western Ukraine—to the obvious satisfaction of many Ukrainians, who believed German rule would be less onerous than that of Russian Communists. But only four days earlier, on the 14th of June, the official Soviet news agency TASS had issued a communiqué stating unequivocally that rumors of an imminent German attack were "completely without foundation"; it had labeled them "clumsy propaganda by forces hostile to the U.S.S.R. and Germany interested in an extension of the War"—in other words, Great Britain and the United States. "Germany," it concluded, "is unswervingly observing the conditions of the Non-Aggression Pact, just as the U.S.S.R. is doing."

The colonel was understandably skeptical of the deserter's story. But the German was insistent: "If at 5 a.m. on June 22 you see that there is no invasion, I ask you to please shoot me!" Fedyuninsky phoned Major General M. I. Potapov who was commander of the Russian Fifth Army. Pota-

THE THRUST TO VICTORY

pov was not impressed. "You should not believe provocations like that," he said. "A German in fear of his life would babble anything."

That same day the Kremlin received an almost identical warning. A Soviet secret agent in Switzerland named Alexander Foote had obtained a report on a military operation the German High Command was calling *Barbarossa*, a surprise invasion designed to destroy the Red Army in a swift campaign and make Hitler ruler of all Soviet territory west of the Urals. So complete was Foote's information that it had taken him four days to transmit all the details to Moscow by radio. The crux of the message was received June 18. It read: "General attack on territories occupied by Russians dawn of Sunday 22 June 3:15 a.m."

These reports were only the latest of dozens of similar warnings the government had received in recent months. In mid-February, a German printer, perhaps inspired by anti-Nazi sympathies, had given the Soviet Embassy in Berlin a German-Russian phrase book that his employer was producing in large quantity. It instructed the German reader how to say in Russian such phrases as: "Are you a Communist?" "Take me to the collective farm chairman." "What is the name of the secretary of the local party committee?" and "Hands up or I shoot!" The embassy promptly forwarded the book to Moscow.

At about the same time, the embassy started relaying reports of large-scale movements of German troops and war matériel from west to east. By March, said an embassy official, these transfers had swelled to a "ceaseless stream of trains with tanks, artillery and ammunition."

In March the United States gave Konstantin A. Oumansky, the Soviet Ambassador in Washington, a copy of Hitler's invasion plans that had been received from the American commercial attaché in Berlin, Sam Edison Woods. Woods had been in Berlin since 1934 and had developed reliable, secret relationships with anti-Nazis, one of whom had given him the plans. Secretary of State Cordell Hull said that when the plans were handed to Oumansky, the Russian diplomat turned pale.

A month later, Winston Churchill dispatched a top-secret message to the British Embassy in Moscow to be personally delivered to Stalin by the ambassador, Sir Stafford Cripps. It said Hitler had told Prince Paul of Yugoslavia that Germany would attack the Soviet Union on June 30. But Cripps was unable to see Stalin—or even Foreign Minister Vyacheslav Molotov. After a two-week delay, Churchill's message was accepted by a low-ranking Soviet foreign office official who passed it up to Stalin.

What should have been the most convincing warning of all came from a brilliant Soviet secret agent in Tokyo named Richard Sorge. Ostensibly a loyal Nazi working for the German Ambassador, Sorge ran a Red spy ring that included informants high in the Japanese government. In early May, Hitler revealed to Japanese officials his blueprint for conquering the Soviet Union (he wanted Japan to attack simultaneously from the east), and Sorge soon heard about it. On May 12 the spy informed Moscow that some 150 German divisions would invade Russia on June 20. Three days later he corrected the date: the invasion would begin on June 22.

Within the Soviet Union itself there were undeniable signs that something momentous was about to happen. More and more German planes were spotted flying reconnaissance missions over Soviet territory. In mid-May, German diplomats' wives and children started packing their valuables and leaving for home. In Leningrad, officials of the German consulate canceled orders to their Russian tailors. And on the 11th of June, Stalin learned that officials of the German Embassy were burning documents and getting ready to depart. Three or four days later Admiral N. G. Kuznetsov, Commissar of the Navy, told Molotov that German ships were pulling out of Soviet ports in a hurry. "Only a fool would attack us," Molotov replied.

More amazing than the reports was Stalin's refusal to believe them. His obduracy is especially puzzling in the light of the fact that the Führer's basic intentions regarding Russia had been public knowledge for more than a decade. In *Mein Kampf* (My Struggle), the bible of the Nazi party, written in the 1920s, Hitler had exposed his obsessive hunger for *Lebensraum* (living space) "to guarantee to the German nation the soil and the territory to which it is entitled on this earth," and when speaking of new lands, he had stated, "we are bound to think first of Russia and her border states."

It was not only Russia's prized resources and great expanses of rich agricultural land that had drawn Hitler's eyes eastward. Here was an "inferior race" for the Germans to exploit. Slavs, racially "degenerated" by centuries of mixing with Mongoloid stock, "are a mass of born slaves," Hitler believed. Furthermore, the country's political system was hateful; Bolshevism, he said, was a Jewish plot. "Any cooperation with Russia is out of the question," he wrote to a fellow Nazi in 1932, "for there on a Slav-Tartar body is set a Jewish head."

Hitler frequently reiterated his eastern ambitions. In 1933, a short while after he became Chancellor, he told Germany's senior commanders that, once the nation had regained its military strength, his primary goal was going to be "the conquest of new living space in the East and its ruthless Germanization."

Still, he did not allow his disdain for the Russians and his designs on their land to stand in the way of his signing a nonaggression pact with their government in the summer of 1939. It had served his aims well by enabling him to take what he wished of Poland and to pursue another dream, the conquest of Western Europe, without having to worry about what his giant neighbor to the east might be up to. A concomitant trade agreement with the Soviet Union also assured Germany of supplies of food and raw materials needed for war. But Hitler had never intended the pact to last. On August 22, 1939, the very day his Foreign Minister, Joachim von Ribbentrop, flew to Moscow to sign the docu-

ment, Hitler told a jubilant conference of leading Nazis: "My pact was only meant to stall for time. We will crush the Soviet Union."

If he had a compeer in the practice of such cynical treachery, it was, of course, Stalin, whose wily opportunism and pitiless suppression of opposition—and imagined opposition—kept him firmly in control of his people and party. Stalin's approval of the pact—which bewildered his people, who were accustomed to virulent anti-Hitler propaganda—was no act of friendship toward Germany. Besides protecting his western frontier while he extricated himself from a little-noticed but sizable border war with Japan in the Soviet Union's Far East, it gave more immediate gratification to his own yearnings for territorial aggrandizement than it did to Hitler's. While in the public part of the pact the two nations simply pledged not to attack each other, a secret protocol outlined a carve-up of Eastern Europe. Each was to get a share of Poland. Finland and the small Baltic states of Latvia, Estonia and Lithuania were allotted to the Soviet Union's "sphere of influence," except for a strip of Lithuania that was specifically reserved for German hegemony. Stalin was authorized to take the province of Bessarabia away from Rumania.

Once the Germans were thoroughly involved in the West, Stalin took even more than the deal actually allowed him. After settling his dispute with Japan, he collected his agreed

THE SECRET AGENT WHOM STALIN IGNORED

Printed in Japanese, the press pass of German journalist Richard Sorge served as a cover for one of Russia's most successful spies. As a reporter, Sorge became a confidant of Tokyo's German Ambassador, and he heard about Hitler's plan to invade Russia while having a drink with a German military attaché. Sorge wired the details to Moscow but his message was ignored.

The son of an engineer, Sorge spent his childhood in Berlin and fought in the German Army in the First World War. After shrapnel had torn through both his legs, he became a dedicated Communist, committed to stopping wars and opposing capitalism at any cost. By the time Sorge reached Japan in 1933, he was a veteran of spying missions in Scandinavia, Britain and China. In Tokyo, he ran a five-man ring that spied on the Japanese as well as the Germans. Arrested five months after relaying his warning to Stalin, Sorge was hanged by the Japanese in 1944.

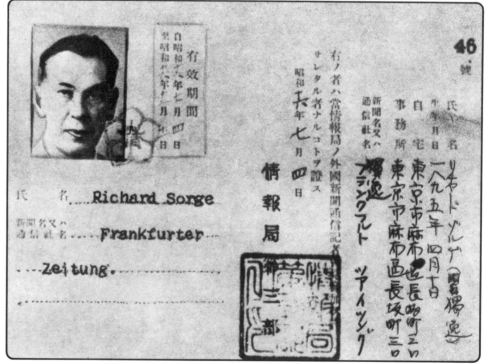

Sorge's Japanese press pass identifies the spy as a writer for the German paper Frankfurter Zeitung.

share of Poland in mid-September, 1939. Instead of merely exerting influence over Finland, the Soviet Union—after smothering Finnish resistance in the hard-fought Winter War of 1939-1940—annexed great chunks of Finnish territory, including the country's second largest city, in March 1940. Hitler did not like this one bit, but he was preoccupied with preparations for his invasion of France and could do nothing about it.

As soon as the Germans launched their blitzkrieg in the West, Stalin also rushed to incorporate Latvia, Estonia and Lithuania—including Germany's piece of Lithuania—into the Soviet Union. The U.S.S.R. then hastened to absorb not only Bessarabia, but also Rumania's North Bukovina region, which was not part of the deal. Thus in less than a year after the pact took effect Stalin added some 175,000 square miles and 20 million people to the U.S.S.R.

As soon as France was defeated, Hitler looked east again. First, to discourage further Soviet ambitions in Finland, he made a treaty with the Finns that eventually led to the presence of German troops there. Then he ordered 20 German divisions to the Lithuanian border, a move that led Stalin to offer compensation for Germany's share of the small Baltic state. Finally, Hitler turned to Rumania, which provided much of the oil that fueled his war machine. Stalin, not satisfied with annexing Bessarabia and North Bukovina, had moved his troops to the Rumanian border and was talking about guaranteeing that country's security. Hitler moved first. With the compliance of the Rumanian government, he guaranteed Rumanian security and dispatched soldiers to the country.

As relations with the U.S.S.R. worsened, Hitler decided the time had come for the ultimate action. In July 1940 he instructed his top generals to prepare for an invasion of the Soviet Union, to be launched no later than spring of the following year. "The sooner Russia is crushed," he announced, "the better."

Some of his startled generals objected. They reminded him that he himself had often cited the lesson of World War I as proof that Germany should never again fight on two fronts at once. Hitler insisted that he still embraced that principle, and had decided to invade Russia for just that reason: to avoid a two-front war. Britain, he contended, was

reeling from German blows at the moment, but would only grow stronger with increasing American assistance. In the years ahead the Soviet Union, too, would develop its military muscle and, when powerful enough, would strike at Germany in concert with Britain. At the moment, Russia was so weak it could be conquered in eight to 10 weeks. "Just kick in the door," Hitler told one of his doubting generals, "and the whole rotten structure will collapse." If Russia was conquered, he was sure a demoralized Britain would sue for peace.

The Führer was accustomed to browbeating his commanders into submission. He and the old-line German officers held each other in contempt. High-ranking professionals sneered—behind his back—at the upstart Austrian corporal. Hitler scorned them for lacking imagination, for being "imprisoned in their technical knowledge." He saw himself as a "creative genius" who could reduce military problems "to their simplest foundations." He had demonstrated this in Austria, in Poland, in the Lowlands, in France. Few could gainsay his successes, but his generals were still concerned about the Russian adventure. But when Field Marshal Wilhelm Keitel, Chief of the German High Command, counseled caution the Führer retorted that he had not created his magnificent army "only to let it rot."

Planning for the invasion of the Soviet Union got under way. But until he was ready to strike, Hitler kept smiling at his intended victim.

In November he invited Molotov to Berlin to talk about having the Soviet Union join the Axis nations—Germany, Italy and Japan—in a four-power alliance. The first secretary of the Soviet Embassy in Berlin, V. M. Berezhkov, later recalled the meeting. When the Russians were ushered into Hitler's presence the Führer rose, raised his arm in a Nazi salute, and then shook hands with all the visitors without saying a single word. "His clammy palm reminded me of the touch of a frog," Berezhkov wrote. Hitler immediately launched into an hour-long monologue. The War was virtually over, he said. It was now time to discuss dividing the spoils. What part of the British Empire would the Soviet Union like to have?

When his time came to speak, the Soviet Foreign Minister ignored the Führer's words completely and instead demanded to know why Germany had put troops in Finland

and Rumania without first consulting Moscow in compliance with the terms of the nonaggression pact. The Führer tried to steer the discussion back to his original theme, and over the course of the talks pretended to keep the Soviet Union's interests in mind.

"England is beaten," Hitler said, although he conceded that "a little still remains to be done." The British Empire was "a block of forty million square kilometers in a gigantic auction." Would Russia be interested in claiming part of the Indian subcontinent as its share? Molotov refused to respond to the question. Germany must withdraw from Finland and Rumania, he insisted, and recognize Russian influence in the Balkans and Scandinavia. Both sides might as well have been addressing brick walls.

On the last night of the conference in Berlin, Molotov and Ribbentrop took refuge in an air-raid shelter as sirens signaled the arrival of British bombers over the city. "If England is beaten," Molotov wondered out loud to Ribbentrop while bombs exploded outside, then "why are we sitting in this shelter?"

On November 12, while Molotov was still in Berlin, Hitler issued a directive to his generals: "Irrespective of the results of these discussions all preparations for the East which have been verbally ordered will be continued."

Within a month of the meeting, the invasion plans were ready, and on December 18, Hitler set them in motion with an order to his generals that was labeled Directive No. 21. "The German Army must be prepared to crush Soviet Russia in a quick campaign," it began. Armored wedges were to be driven deep into the Soviet Union to trap and destroy the Red Army, taking care to prevent any retreat "into the vastness of Russian territory." The operation was dubbed *Barbarossa* (Red Beard), after the nickname of Frederick I, a German emperor in the 12th Century who had died while leading a crusade to the Holy Land. The invasion was set for May 15, 1941.

"When they spread out a map of Russia before me I could scarcely believe my eyes," said Colonel General Heinz Guderian, the brilliant panzer commander who had won fame in the lightning invasion of France. "I made no attempt to conceal my disappointment and disgust." He believed Adolph Hitler's Germany even less capable of fighting a two-front war than had been the Germany of 1914. Other high-ranking officers, however, welcomed the directive. Colonel General Franz Halder, Chief of the Army General Staff, believed with the Führer that the campaign would take only eight to 10 weeks. So confident were the war planners that they ordered winter clothing for only one fifth of the invasion force. They were convinced that most of the Army would be back home long before the arrival of winter. "The surprising speed of our victory in the West had so befuddled the minds of our supreme commanders," Guderian wrote later, "that they had eliminated the word 'impossible' from their vocabulary."

The attacking forces were to plunge into the U.S.S.R. along three major axes (page 28). Army Group North would strike from East Prussia northeastward to Leningrad, thereby securing the Baltic Sea flank. Finland had agreed to assist on this front by throwing its army against the Russians from the north. Army Group South would move from southern Poland across the Ukraine to Kiev, to gain control of

A trigger-ready German antiaircraft crew guards fat storage tanks on the oil-rich fields of Ploeşti in southeastern Rumania near the Russian border. Military "instructors" dispatched by Hitler under the pretense of training Rumania's Army flooded into the German satellite country in the fall of 1940 to protect the oil supply vitally needed to fuel Germany's war machine. Shortly afterward, the instructors began converting Rumanian bases into launching pads for the attack on Russia.

the Soviet Union's breadbasket, and then southeastward to sieze the coal-rich, heavily industrialized basin of the Donets River. German-trained Rumanian troops would join in this part of the operation, invading with German units along the coastal areas of the Black Sea.

The main effort, or *Schwerpunkt* (heavy point), as the Germans called it, would be on the central front. From Poland and East Prussia, Army Group Center would smash through the Russian line in two wedges and drive toward Minsk and Smolensk with the aim of encircling and destroying large elements of the Red Army.

A disagreement arose between Hitler and some of his generals over what should be the main objective of Army Group Center. Only 700 miles from the frontier lay Moscow itself. Colonel General Halder and Field Marshal Walther von Brauchitsch, Commander in Chief of the Army, wanted Army Group Center to roll on to the Soviet capital as rapidly as possible. They were primarily interested not in the city's political value, but in its military importance; it was the communications hub of the Soviet Union, the center from which transportation lines radiated in all directions. Then too, they believed, a thrust toward Moscow would draw most of the Red Army's divisions into a concentrated defense of the city, giving the Germans the opportunity to surround and destroy them.

Hitler was more concerned about securing the Baltic states and conquering the agricultural and industrial areas of the south. He believed that the conquest of the south would wreck the Soviet economy and cause the people to turn against their Communist government. After that, he thought, the conquest of Moscow would be easy. He insisted that Army Group Center, when it had accomplished its initial aim of clearing the ground of Russian defenders as far as Smolensk, should be prepared to divert its forces to the north and south if necessary, and let Moscow wait. No clear-cut choice would be made, however, until Army Group Center reached Smolensk.

Planning of another kind was also under way. It concerned the fate of the Soviet lands and peoples once they came under the Nazi heel. Hitler was determined that not even a subservient phantom Soviet Union would remain west of the Urals. In his diary, Halder tersely summarized one of Hitler's many addresses to the German commanders concerning the matter: "Our goals in Russia: Crush armed forces, break up State."

Hitler appointed Alfred Rosenberg, who considered himself the party's leading philosopher and theoretician, to be head of a new Ministry of the East. Charged with the task of administering the conquered territory, Rosenberg began drawing up grandiose schemes for carving new, small states out of the U.S.S.R., to be governed, of course, by himself. But he was too ineffectual to stay on top long in the infighting of Nazi palace politics, and real power over the East's future soon devolved on Heinrich Himmler, who was overlord of the SS (*Schutzstaffel*, the state security police). The SS would follow the regular army into the Soviet Union, assuming control of territory and inhabitants as they were conquered.

The German planners intended that Russian agriculture would feed all of the German armed forces. That meant millions of Soviet citizens would have to starve. That suited the master plan. Racially unacceptable types—Jews, gypsies, many Slavs—were to be killed anyway. Himmler coolly estimated that 30 million Slavs alone would have to be exterminated. Peoples that the Nazis regarded as acceptable—Balts, some Ukrainians and Belorussians—were to be "salvaged" and Germanized. The newly depopulated lands would be colonized by Germanic peoples: Danes, Dutchmen, Swedes, Norwegians and even Englishmen, once the war in the West was over.

Hitler was determined that the waging of the war itself would be equally ruthless. "This enemy consists not of soldiers but to a large extent only of beasts," he said. "This is a war of extermination." Neither the Hague Convention on the rules of warfare nor the Geneva Convention on treatment of prisoners of war would have to be observed, he said, as the Soviet Union was not a signatory to either of the agreements.

In early May he issued two infamous orders. One was the so-called "Commissar Decree" that spelled out the fate of the Communist political officers who shared control with professional soldiers at every command level in the Red Army. "Commissars of the Red Army are not to be recognized as prisoners of war and are to be liquidated. . . . They will not be transferred to the rear." The other order forbade the prosecution of German soldiers who killed or mistreated Soviet civilians.

Many German officers were shocked by these directives and objected to them on moral grounds and because they felt that such orders would undermine military discipline. Guderian returned the order exempting soldiers from prosecution to Berlin and informed his superior that he would neither publish nor obey it. Another officer, a young man named Henning von Tresckow, urged Field Marshal Fedor von Bock, the commander of Army Group Center, who disliked the commissar order, to protest it in writing. Bock feared that to do so would cost him his job. "In that case," Tresckow told him, "you will at least have made an honourable exit in history." Bock filed the protest. He did not lose his job, but the order stayed in force. "I do not expect my generals to understand me," Hitler said, "but I expect them to obey my orders."

Throughout the early months of 1941, tanks, artillery and troops were pulled from the west and moved into East Prussia and Poland. Unexpected developments in southeastern Europe, however, soon stalled the build-up, and the invasion had to be put off from mid-May to June 22—a fateful setback.

Hitler's Italian ally Benito Mussolini had decided to enhance the glory of his renascent "Imperial Rome" through the conquest of Greece. On October 28, 1940, without informing Hitler, he launched an attack against Greece from Italian-occupied Albania. The Greeks, with British support, proved tougher and the Italian Army less valiant than the Duce expected, and in April 1941 an angry Hitler found it necessary to divert troops from the Russian frontier to help his Axis partner.

In the meantime, Germany was solidifying its control of the Balkans with diplomatic agreements that were negotiated under the threat of force. On the 25th of March a pact was signed that brought Yugoslavia into the German camp. Two days later anti-Nazi Yugoslavs threw out the pro-German government, revoked the pact and replaced it with a friendship treaty with the U.S.S.R. The enraged Hitler started more troops southward to use against the recalcitrant Yugoslavs. Suddenly the Russians realized that they were risking a military confrontation with the Germans.

Hastily the Russian government on April 5 explained to the Yugoslavs that, of course, their treaty did not imply any Soviet military commitment. The following day the Germans invaded Yugoslavia.

The German operations against Yugoslavia and Greece were well executed, swift, highly successful. By the end of April both countries had capitulated. Now Hitler could turn again to Operation *Barbarossa*.

German morale was at a high point. Three million soldiers in 148 divisions—about 80 per cent of the German Army—stood on the Russian frontier, poised for the strike. Nineteen of these were panzer divisions, which were ready to drive more than 3,000 tanks through and around the enemy with the same lightning tactics that had stunned the Poles and the French. Another 14 consisted of motorized infantry divisions that could advance as rapidly as the tanks and would support the panzer units in this new super-blitzkrieg. In addition, 14 Rumanian divisions took part in the invasion, and 20 Finnish divisions joined the battle three days after the attack was launched.

Along the border 6,000 big German guns were already zeroing in on their assigned targets and, in the rear, crews of more than 2,000 Luftwaffe warplanes were being briefed with the help of photos taken from reconnaissance aircraft that flew daily into Russian airspace.

And what of Stalin? How was he reacting to the fact that almost the entire German Army was on his doorstep? Incredibly, he appeared to ignore it. Was he the victim of some kind of hysteria that deprived him of the ability to act? Or were there other powerful reasons for not acting—reasons known only to him?

At the outset it may have seemed to Stalin that Hitler would not take on the Soviet Union while Germany was still locked in combat with Britain, or while the U.S.S.R. was faithfully supplying so much of what Germany needed for its war effort. Between February 1940 and June 1941 the U.S.S.R. sent Germany 1,500,000 tons of grain, 2,000,000 tons of petroleum products, and large shipments of chrome, manganese ore and other minerals. Russia was even buying copper from the United States and passing it on to the Germans. As the build-up of German troops on his border progressed, Stalin may have been genuinely convinced—as, in fact, were many Western observers—that it was a feint

Invited to Berlin in November of 1940 to discuss a proposal that the Soviet Union join the Axis as an ally of Germany, Japan and Italy, Soviet Foreign Minister Vyacheslav Molotov (third from left) cross-examines the Führer and his deputies. Over the fine crystal and coffee cups diplomatic relations were strained to the breaking point as Molotov brusquely jabbed home question after indelicate question about Hitler's incursions into Finland and Rumania. "No foreign visitor had ever spoken to him in this way in my presence," Hitler's interpreter later reported.

to cover the real Nazi plan: an invasion of Great Britain.

But Stalin could not have been deceived for long, and there is evidence that he did recognize the danger of attack. The Soviet newspaper *Pravda*, reporting a speech he made on May 5, 1941, to new graduates of Russian military academies, headlined the story: "We must be prepared to deal with any surprises." The article did not elaborate, but Alexander Werth, a Russian-born British journalist and historian who spent the war years in Moscow, interviewed Russian officers who heard the address. By Werth's account Stalin acknowledged that a war with Nazi Germany seemed inevitable—Bolshevism and fascism were, after all, natural enemies—and if it did not begin sooner, the Soviet Union itself might initiate it in 1942. But at the moment, Stalin said, the Red Army was poorly equipped and trained, and a delay would give him a chance to build up its strength. Stalling the Germans for a few months would allow winter to insulate Russia from attack until the spring of 1942. The most dangerous period, Stalin warned his listeners, was "from now till August."

If this was indeed Stalin's reasoning, then what later appeared to be foolishness and self-delusion can be at least partially understood. Stalin may have convinced himself that Hitler's first move, before an attack, would be to make new demands on the Soviet Union. After all, delivering an ultimatum was the Führer's usual practice before taking over a country. Thus it might have appeared to Russia's advantage to yield a little, to give up a piece of territory, to promise Germany more grain or raw materials in order to win more time to prepare for war.

What the Soviet Union could not afford, Stalin clearly thought, was to let itself be provoked in any way that might enable Hitler to justify an invasion. So it may be that Stalin deliberately appeared to ignore the men who brought him gloomy warnings, and staked Russia's future on the gamble that he could buy Hitler off with acts of appeasement.

Stalin adamantly insisted that German planes violating Soviet airspace were not to be fired upon. He urged his trade commissars to rush deliveries to Germany of oil and other supplies, even though the Germans had been withholding manufactured goods owed to the U.S.S.R. under their reciprocal agreement. Without even being asked to do so by Hitler, Stalin in May shut down the Moscow embassies of Yugoslavia and Greece, thus giving tacit approval to the German conquest of those nations. Most importantly, and most regrettably for his army and people, he continued to deny publicly the possibility of war and to forbid any defense preparations that Germany might construe as hostile.

The TASS communiqué of June 14 was the first official acknowledgment of the war rumors. It underlined Russia's

peaceful intentions, and Stalin probably had it issued to give Hitler an easy opportunity to confirm that Germany did not want war either. But the answer was silence. The communiqué was not even made public in Germany. Hitler's propaganda chief, Joseph Goebbels, one of the few Germans to read it, wrote in his diary: "Stalin is trembling."

The TASS communiqué may not have reduced the combativeness of the Germans, but it had precisely that effect on the Red Army. Colonel I. G. Starinov, visiting the frontier near Brest, was told by his old friend, Lieut. General N. A. Klich, artillery commander of the Western Military District, that the communiqué had "lowered the level of our battle readiness." Starinov noticed Russian soldiers with suitcases at a railway station near the border. Another officer complained to Starinov: "Until a few days ago they slept with their boots on; now they are allowed to go on leave. Why? Because of that TASS declaration." Their discussion occurred on Saturday, June 21, 1941, just one day before the invasion took place.

Practically nowhere on the front were the Russian troops ready for an attack. Trucks and tractors used to tow Klich's guns had been taken away to help in the construction of fortifications. Klich complained to his superior, but was told, "Don't panic. The Boss knows all about it." At bases along the border, the Red Air Force was just completing a routine schedule of night training exercises. By June 21 the pilots were short of sleep and the planes short of fuel. The soldiers who were meant to defend the important frontier city of Brest were scattered throughout the region on summer training maneuvers. In the Baltic Military District the commander, Colonel General Fyodor I. Kuznetsov, tried to move his big guns into defensive positions. But he lacked vehicles to tow them all and was short of ammunition for those that did reach their sites. Only in the Kiev Military District on the southern stretch of the border was there some semblance of preparedness.

A week earlier the Kiev district commander, Colonel General M. P. Kirponos, had informed Moscow that the German forces across the line were being strengthened. He suggested evacuating 300,000 civilians and manning certain fixed defense points. He was told, "There will be no war," but on June 19 Defense Commissar Semyon K. Timoshenko sent an order that cast doubt on the certainty of this state-ment. Kirponos was told to move his headquarters and to guard against surprise attack. Still, even then Timoshenko did not officially direct Kirponos to put his men on alert.

On the German side of the frontier everything was in readiness. At Army headquarters, Colonel General Halder made his first diary entry for June 21: "Code word Dortmund has come through." That single word, the name of a German city in the Ruhr River Valley, was the signal from Hitler that Operation *Barbarossa* was to proceed. The Führer himself left Berlin on a special train that was bound for a tree-hidden siding near Rastenburg, East Prussia, which would serve as his command post.

Guderian, waiting on the western bank of the River Bug, with his panzers, spent part of the day eyeing the formidable Brest fortress on the other side. He had already captured the fortress once—from the Poles two years before—and now would have to take it again, this time from the Russians, who had been allotted it as part of the spoils proceeding from the nonaggression pact of 1939. Guderian had been given an infantry corps to attack the fortress. His tanks would bypass it on either side. He was pleased to observe now that Russians in the fort were marching to the music of a military band and showed no signs of being aware of their predicament. Prospects of achieving surprise looked so good to Guderian that he momentarily pondered whether to cancel the artillery barrage scheduled to precede the attack in his sector. But he decided not to cancel it; the bombardment might save his units a few casualties.

Late that day German troops all along the frontier assembled by platoons to hear their commanders read a message from the Führer. The "greatest force in world history is now going into action," it said, "in order to save the whole of European civilization and culture." (Halder dismissed the message in his diary as "a longwinded manifesto.") Infantrymen began wrapping their weapons in blankets to prevent telltale rattles, and strict radio silence was enforced. But there was no way to muffle the noise of tanks, personnel carriers, mobile guns and supply vehicles moving to jumping-off positions. Anxious Russian officers across the frontier were soon reporting that the sounds of engines revving on the German side had mounted in intensity. And from Grodno, northwest of Brest, came news that the Ger-

On June 22, 1941, the meticulously planned super-blitzkrieg code-named Barbarossa sent the German Army advancing into Russia in four main drives along a front that stretched from the Arctic to the Black Sea. The attack's objective was a line running from Archangel down past Stalingrad to the Caspian Sea. The attacking force included Army Group North, which headed for Leningrad; Army Group Center, which attacked in two prongs toward Smolensk; and Army Group South, which was assigned the task of knocking out Kiev and taking the Ukraine.

mans were clearing away their own barbed wire, opening the roads that ran across the border.

In Moscow, as Stalin received the reports from the frontier on the final day before the attack, he apparently realized at last that he had lost his gamble, that his appeasement policy had not forestalled invasion. But he doggedly clung to the frail hope that Hitler was only trying to provoke a response from the Red Army that would give the Germans an excuse to attack. At 2 p.m. he ordered the manning of Moscow's antiaircraft defenses, but only at 75 per cent of combat readiness (General I. V. Tyulenev, commander of the Moscow Military District, risked Stalin's wrath by bringing his units to full combat readiness anyhow). At 5 p.m. Stalin conferred with Defense Commissar Timoshenko, who wanted to put the frontier troops on full alert and implement plans for an all-out defense. But Stalin refused; they must be very careful, he said, not to create "a panic for no reason."

Later in the evening, Stalin relented. He authorized a directive telling commanders in border regions to bring their troops to combat readiness and to occupy fixed defense emplacements—but secretly, so that the Germans could not use the preparations as an excuse to attack. The Red Army commanders were warned against responding to provocations "that could call forth serious complications." Finally, Stalin's Directive No. 1 warned that "no other measures are to be taken without special orders." It was sent out at 12:30 a.m., Sunday, June 22, less than three hours before the invasion was scheduled to begin.

Confused by the directive, Russian officers asked for clarification. A query from R. Ya. Malinovsky, then a corps commander in the southwest and later to be Defense Minister of the Soviet Union, was typical. "Could we open fire if the enemy invaded our territory?" he asked. The answer from Moscow: "Do not respond to provocation and do not open fire." Some Red Army officers, in districts with poor communications, never had a chance to question the directive. They were dead before it reached them.

The night of June 21-22 is the shortest of the year, the peak of the period that is known in the northern part of Russia as "white nights," because the sun never sets. Along the central section of the frontier that night there were only two or three hours of real darkness, and officers were up late celebrating the midsummer season. General Dmitry Pavlov, the commander of the Western Military District, was watching a comedy by Aleksandr E. Korneichuk, a popular Russian playwright, in the Officers' Club at Minsk. During the performance his intelligence chief arrived and whispered something in his ear. "That can't be," Pavlov replied. He turned to his deputy, General Ivan V. Boldin, and said the message was some "nonsense" about Germans firing at points along the border.

While Pavlov went on watching the play, saboteurs who had infiltrated his district during previous months slipped through the darkness, cutting telephone lines, quietly murdering isolated sentries and disabling unguarded Red Army vehicles. From the western shores of border rivers German soldiers pushed sections of pontoon bridges into the water. At Koden on the River Bug, German frontier guards at one end of a vital road bridge shouted to their Russian counterparts at the other end, asking them to come out and discuss "urgent business." As the Soviet guards emerged, the Germans gunned them down.

At approximately 3:00 a.m. "suddenly came a roar like thunder" as 6,000 German guns began bombarding Red Army defense posts, supply dumps and barracks all along the border. At the same time Luftwaffe aircraft swarmed out of the western sky, dropping their bombs on both military and civilian targets, but concentrating on airfields. By midday the Luftwaffe had knocked out 1,200 Russian warplanes—800 of them on the ground—while losing only 10 of its own.

On the River Bug, German assault parties darted across bridges on foot or on motorcycles, surprising Russian defenders before they could detonate demolition charges. Along the 500-mile length of the river the Germans successfully seized every bridge essential to their strategy. The tanks began rolling across to the east bank of the river, most meeting no immediate opposition. At places, especially in the southern sector, Russian border guards resisted valiantly, but nowhere did they manage to hold back the flood of German troops for long.

The sudden, massive blow shattered the Red Army. In the confusion, communications broke down, command centers vanished without trace and whole divisions could not be accounted for. German monitors gleefully plucked from the airways desperate Russian radio messages: "Staff third army wiped out. Send long range fighters," and, again and again, "We are fired upon. What do we do?" To one such plea the answer from Russian headquarters was: "You must be insane. And why isn't your message in code?"

In Moscow confusion was mixed with disbelief. At 3:15 a.m., Admiral Kuznetsov heard from the commander of the Black Sea fleet that German planes were bombing Sevastopol. Kuznetsov tried unsuccessfully to reach Stalin and finally conveyed the message to a skeptical Georgy Malenkov, one of Stalin's deputies. Kuznetsov later learned that Malenkov telephoned Sevastopol himself to check whether the report was true.

Timoshenko, upon learning of the attack, consulted with Stalin and then phoned the Western Military District headquarters in Minsk. "No actions must be taken against the Germans without our consent," he told Pavlov's deputy, General Boldin. "Comrade Stalin has forbidden our artillery to open fire."

"It's not possible!" Boldin shouted into the telephone. "Our troops are retreating. Whole towns are in flames. Everywhere people are being killed." The order stood, Timoshenko replied.

Meanwhile, in Berlin, Soviet Ambassador V. G. Dekanozov and First Secretary V. M. Berezhkov were called to the German Ministry of Foreign Affairs. They were blinded by the floodlights and flashbulbs of newsreel cameramen and photographers. Obviously, they were being used in a Nazi propaganda exercise. Inside they found Foreign Minister von Ribbentrop, eyes cloudy and inflamed, swaying slightly. Berezhkov wondered if Ribbentrop was drunk. Stumbling over his words, the Foreign Minister said that Russian soldiers had been violating the German border. Germany had been forced to take "defensive measures" against this Soviet "aggression."

"This is a lie," the Russian Ambassador replied. "You will regret you attacked the Soviet Union. You will pay dearly for this yet." The Russians turned to leave. At the door Ribbentrop stopped them and whispered, "Tell Moscow I was against the attack."

By this time the panzer wedges of all three German Army groups were several miles inside Soviet territory, cutting the Red Army into isolated pockets of troops to be mopped up by the columns of German infantry that were following close behind. The Luftwaffe continued making its bombing runs at the same punishing pace with which it had begun the day.

Colonel Starinov—who had seen soldiers going home on leave the day before the war began—was caught in a raid on Fourth Army headquarters at Kobrin, near Brest. "The bombs were falling with a piercing shriek," he recalled later. "The blasts rent the air and made our ears ring. Thick black pillars of smoke billowed up. Somewhere a high-pitched, hysterical female voice was crying out a desperate, inconsolable 'aaaaaa!'"

Shortly after the raid ended, the sound of the Moscow call signal resounded from a radio loudspeaker set up in Kobrin's main square, silencing the crowd of people that had gathered there. It was the 6 a.m. news. "With bated breath, Kobrin waited to hear what Moscow had to say," Starinov recalled. First came the usual catalogue of achievements that Soviet farmers and workers had made. The harvest was ripening and factory production was running ahead of schedule. Then came war news from Syria and the Atlantic. German air raids in Scotland were reported, and a weather forecast ended the newscast. But the people in the square did not disperse. They waited for what they thought would surely follow: a special announcement to explain what was happening, why they had been bombed, whether the Soviet Union was at war. But the next announcement concerned the daily setting-up exercises.

"Arms out," the Moscow radio announcer said. "Bend! That's it. Up, down, up, down. More! That's better." A man spat on the ground in disgust. The listeners walked away. They were even more shocked by the broadcast, according to Starinov, than they had been by the Stukas, the German dive bombers.

The bloodiest war in modern history—20 million Soviet citizens were to die in the conflict—had begun. But Stalin was still reluctant to admit it, even to the people under attack. And when, at 7:15 a.m., he issued a directive that at last authorized his soldiers to fight the invading enemy, he added strict instructions that the Red Army was not to cross the frontier into German territory. By then the Red Army was in no position to disobey.

RUSSIA'S WILY LEADER

Stalin, elbow to elbow with German Foreign Minister von Ribbentrop, watches contentedly as Molotov signs the German-Soviet nonaggression pact of 1939.

VENGEFUL KOBA'S PATH TO GLORY

In the summer of 1923, when Josef Stalin was locked in a struggle for control of the Communist Party, he revealed to a comrade, in a rare moment of candor, his preferred method of dealing with his foes: "To choose one's victim, to prepare one's plan minutely, to slake an implacable vengeance, and then to go to bed—there is nothing sweeter in the world."

If that was the case, life must have seemed truly sweet to the swarthy, saturnine man who became the most powerful and successful dictator of his times; in the three decades of his brutal rule, he chose his victims with stony ruthlessness, eliminating millions of enemies both real and imagined.

Born in 1879 to peasant parents in czarist Georgia, Josef Vissarionovich Djugashvili made up his mind to become a priest, but was expelled at age 20 from a theological seminary for reading radical literature. In 1901 he went underground and spent the next 16 years in the shadowy substrata of the revolutionary movement, agitating for strikes, organizing terrorist banditry, signing socialist broadsides with the by-line "Koba" (The Indomitable). He was jailed frequently and exiled six times to Siberia. During one stint of freedom, while organizing the oil-field workers of Baku on the Caspian seacoast, he chose the pseudonym Stalin, or Man of Steel.

Few of his revolutionary peers warmed to the enigmatic, sardonic Stalin. V. I. Lenin, outraged at his cruel suppression of a Georgian uprising in 1921, called him a "coarse, brutish bully." His archrival, Leon Trotsky, in a devastating misjudgment, thought him "the most eminent mediocrity in the Party." Through cunning and deceit Stalin manipulated his adversaries, and on the death of Lenin in 1924 he seized the helm of state. A reign of terror followed as Stalin liquidated peasants who resisted collectivization, crushed party contemporaries who displayed any vestige of independence and purged the Red Army of many of its most brilliant officers. "When are you going to stop killing people?" Lady Nancy Astor once asked him on a visit to Moscow. "When it is no longer necessary," Stalin replied.

The adolescent Stalin (back row center) stands with his classmates in his village school, where he made high marks but was regarded as a bully.

In his spacious Kremlin office, seated beneath a picture of Communist philosopher Karl Marx, the dictator looks up from his work for a benign portrait.

Police documents, such as this mug file dated March 1910 by czarist authorities, describe Stalin's physical peculiarities: a face that had been scarred by childhood smallpox, a shortened and stiffened left arm, and two toes on his left foot that were joined together.

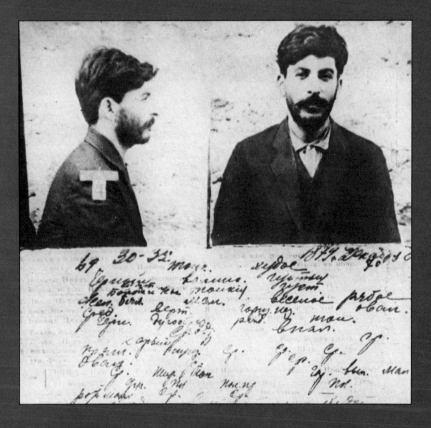

The "X" identifies Stalin among a group of political exiles who were living in the Siberian village of Kureika in 1903. Wrote Stalin from there: "In this forsaken spot nature is reduced to stark ugliness . . . and I am driven by a stupid longing for the sight of some landscape."

CZARIST JAILS AND SIBERIAN EXILE

In the decade that preceded the Bolshevik Revolution of 1917, Stalin's life gyrated among czarist jails, political exile and socialist agitation. In the austere vastness of Siberia he angled for sturgeon through the ice and argued socialist dogma endlessly with his fellow exiles. On the abdication of the Czar, the 38-year-old future dictator caught a train to Petrograd (soon to be renamed Leningrad) and joined his revolutionary comrades in waging three years of bloody civil war, from which the Bolsheviks emerged as Russia's rulers.

In 1912, the year in which he was elected to the Communist Central Committee, Stalin was shown in yet another police photo. In spite of the frequency of his arrests, his comrades suspected him of collaborating with the dreaded Okhrana, the czarist secret police.

A relaxed stroll to Petrograd revolutionary headquarters in the early 1920s gives no hint of the vengeance that was to come. Stalin's companions were tortured into making false confessions, later humiliated in mock trials and then executed on his own orders.

Lenin, recovering from the first of three strokes in August 1922, appears calm and rested as he receives Stalin on a bench at his home in Gorky, a Moscow suburb. The crafty Stalin thought to bring along a photographer for a picture later distributed by the millions.

RIDING TO POWER ON LENIN'S COATTAILS

In 1923, Lenin, chief architect of the Revolution, lay paralyzed and unable to speak, the victim of a stroke. Stalin took advantage of this vacuum in leadership to garner allies for his final thrust for control of the party. Displaying an impressive flair for treachery, he divided his rivals and picked them off one by one, deposing Trotsky and lesser enemies.

Lenin, suspicious of Stalin to the last, was helpless to interfere or to give voice to criticism that might have thwarted Stalin and spared Russia decades of misery. Ironically, it was Stalin's canonization of Lenin, his phony public allegiance to this venerated man—as illustrated in the drawings at right—that later helped to wither opposition and reinforce his image as the obvious successor to the father of the Revolution.

With a solemn handshake, Lenin and Stalin greet each other near Razliv, a coastal village in Finland, where Lenin spent the summer of 1917 in hiding from the Russian Provisional Government police. Stalin provided liaison between Lenin and the other Bolsheviks.

On October 25, 1917, the day of the Bolshevik take-over, Lenin proclaims the new Soviet government to an ecstatic throng gathered in the Smolny Institute in Petrograd. Stalin, whose role in these events was actually minor, stands behind him on the dais.

Stalin, backed up by a bust of Lenin, holds the podium at the 16th Communist Party Congress staged in the summer of 1930. His brutal farm collectivization program and the mass liquidation and starvation of resisting peasants had by this time already begun.

In a drawing contrived to evoke a Lenin-Stalin alliance, Stalin puffs his pipe thoughtfully as the two revolutionaries examine a teletype message bringing news of Bolshevik progress in the civil war that raged throughout the country after the Czar's abdication.

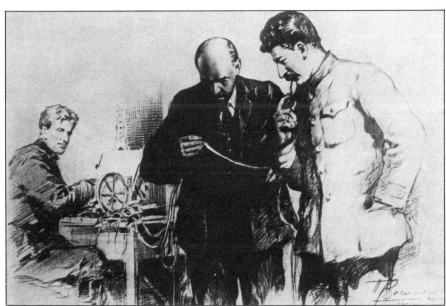

THE ADORATION OF AN AVUNCULAR DICTATOR

Before the outbreak of World War II, the notion of Stalin's infallibility was firmly entrenched in the minds of the Russian masses. His crudeness of manner, his veneer of simplicity, his lack of eloquence all combined, in the innocent eye of the common man, to make him a much more acceptable leader than the intellectual and sophisticated comrades with whom he had swept to power.

Eager hands strain to touch the smiling dictator, who receives accolades at a conference of wives of Red Army commanders in Moscow in the winter of 1937. A

few months later, Stalin, who suspected the military of plotting against him, triggered a purge of the Red Army in which thousands of officers were executed.

Once described by a revolutionary comrade as a "dry, heartless, soulless mechanism," the usually stern and forbidding dictator lets his guard down in a rare mood of playfulness and thumbs his nose at the camera for a photograph that was taken in the late 1930s.

On a family outing in 1933 at his country estate in Sochi, Stalin sweeps his eight-year-old daughter Svetlana into his arms and takes her for a ride. A favorite among his children, Svetlana would remember in later years the "tobacco-scented kisses" of her father.

A LOOK BEHIND THE MASK

Although the private life of Josef Stalin was embellished with amenities that were not available to his countrymen, it was also scarred with tragedy.

Stalin enjoyed wines brought from his native Georgia and eluded the rigors of work at his country retreats. But he encountered personal anguish as well. Stalin's first wife, Yekaterina, died in 1907 of pneumonia; his second wife, Nadezhda, distraught over his brutality, killed herself in 1932. When he heard that Yakov, the oldest of his sons, had botched his own suicide attempt at the age of 24, the dictator revealed his contempt for such human frailty. "Ha!" he exclaimed. "He couldn't even shoot straight."

A weary Stalin, his military tunic unbuttoned and his eyelids drooping with fatigue, relaxes by reading while stretched out on a wicker lounge in the early 1930s. This was one of the hard-working dictator's favorite pastimes, according to his daughter Svetlana.

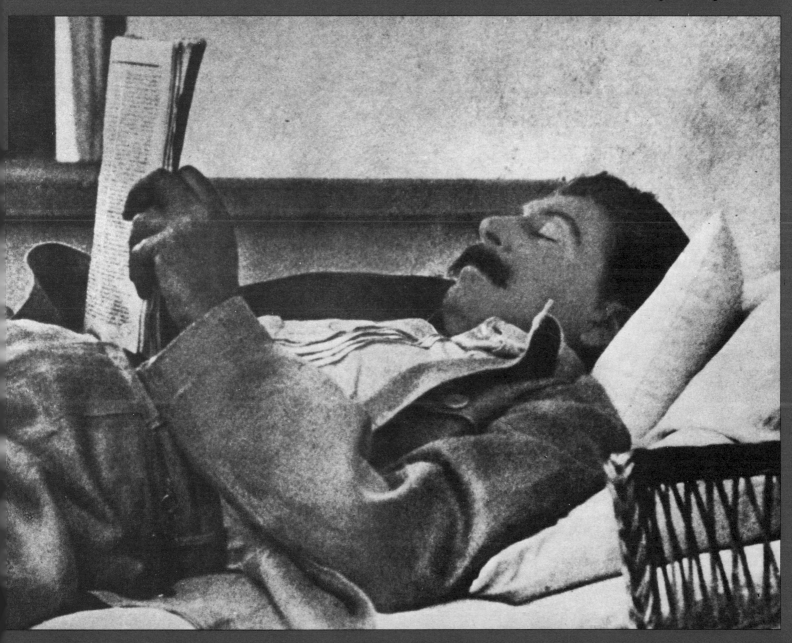

END OF THE LINE FOR STALIN'S ENEMIES

Before the Great Purge, an anguished comrade implored Stalin: "Surely you are not going to shed the blood of old Bolsheviks!" The dictator quoted the Bible in reply: " 'Remember, Abel. Who is not with me is against me.' "

In Stalin's mind, in the mid-1930s, those who were not firmly with him were legion. Determined to crush every trace of independence within the party, he launched the *Yezhovshchina*, or Great Purge. High party officials who incurred his displeasure faced arrest, torture, trial and execution. The NKVD, or secret police, reached everywhere and executed thousands of government officials, professionals, engineers and doctors. Stalin spared no one—not even his in-laws—and by 1938 some seven million Russians had become his victims.

A relaxed Stalin (top left) tours a collective farm in 1934 with his daughter Svetlana and his heir apparent, Sergei Kirov. Later that same year (bottom left), after engineering Kirov's assassination, the dictator marches solemnly behind the casket of his former friend.

A beaming Grigory Ordzhonikidze (top right, in fleece hat) stands pridefully with his old Georgian comrade, Stalin. Seven years later, the dictator gave him a choice of suicide or execution. He chose the former, and Stalin (bottom right) was one of the pallbearers.

Stalin, the heroic war leader, poised with binoculars, is depicted at the Moscow Front in December of 1941. The truth is, the Generalissimo seldom visited his soldiers in the field. He directed Russia's war effort from his offices deep inside the Kremlin.

MAN BEHIND THE PANZERS

Deep in enemy territory the panzer pioneer, Colonel General Heinz Guderian, watches his tanks fan out for an attack across the flat Russian countryside.

AN INNOVATOR WITH AN OBSESSION

The German invasion of Russia brought into action one of the war's boldest and most innovative commanders, Colonel General Heinz Guderian, creator of Germany's panzer forces and the leading exponent of its explosive blitzkrieg tactics. A soldier's son, Guderian served in World War I and was appalled by the loss of life in that conflict's static trench warfare. "Only movement brings victory," he said, and he gave the old military maxim new meaning by insisting that the modern combustion engine and the ancient concept of armor could be fused for maximum effect.

Obsessed with the tank's potential, Guderian grilled survivors of World War I tank battles, studied French tank manuals and pored over the writings of the British tank expert, General J. F. C. Fuller, at a time when Germany was specifically forbidden by terms of the Versailles Treaty to develop an effective army. Assigned as a tactical instructor for future staff officers, he used the lectern as a pulpit to expound his belief that the tank was the weapon of the future. Later, as a radical among conservative officers, he argued that the Army should be equipped not only with tanks, but with motorized artillery and infantry that together could deliver a quick knockout blow to the enemy. A relentless optimist, Guderian patiently put up with dummy tanks on maneuvers, using every opportunity to win over old-guard officers who did not believe that machines could be counted on to win a war.

Early in 1934, when Hitler watched experimental tanks go through their paces and exclaimed, "That's what I need! That's what I want to have!" Guderian's vision of lightning war appeared to be assured. But it was not until the Führer viewed a tank-shattered artillery outfit in Poland in 1939 that tank warfare received the German government's full blessing. ("Our dive bombers did that?" the Führer asked. "No, our panzers!" Guderian proudly replied.)

The panzer-led attack on Poland was topped by the shattering blitzkrieg in France eight months later. But the panzers' severest test—and initially their most spectacular success—was the campaign unfolding in Russia.

Second Lieutenant Guderian (left), with his family in Lorraine, thought himself lucky to be assigned to his father's infantry battalion in 1908.

As mobile as his troops, Guderian directs the assault in France from his special command vehicle, equipped with a coding machine and radio.

Mock tanks—tin plates mounted on small automobile chassis—skitter up a hill in Germany during a demonstration in 1932. Ridiculous as it was, the tin platoon was a marked improvement over the canvas tanks propelled by foot soldiers (right) that had preceded it. The dummies gave Guderian the opportunity to practice tank tactics while Germany secretly perfected a real tank, listed innocuously in inventories as a tractor.

A fleet of light tanks representing the earliest
model of Guderian's panzers rolls through
Nuremberg past a reviewing stand holding the
War Minister, the Commander in Chief of
the Army and the Commander in Chief of the
Navy, on Armed Forces Day in 1936. The
new tanks were equipped with two machine
guns, weighed 5.4 tons, carried a crew of
two and could travel 23 miles per hour on roads.

Guderian (second from right) and German officers huddle over a map of conquered Poland with a Soviet commissar (center) in Brest. At the time, the Soviet

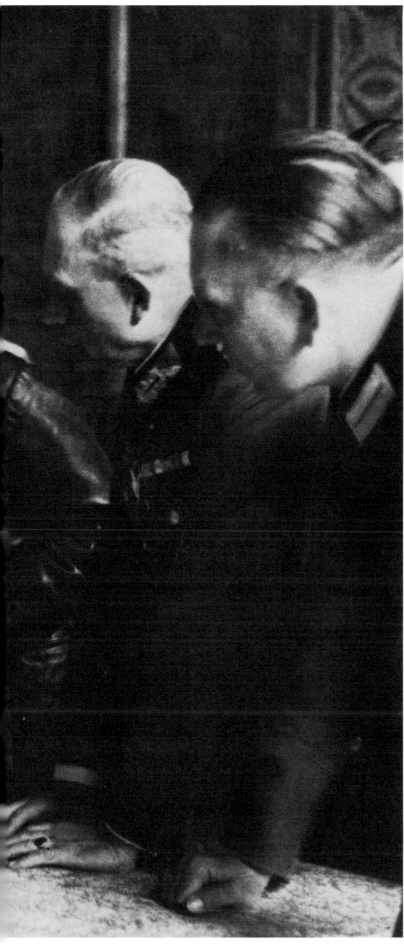

HURRYING HEINZ PUSHES ON

In Poland and France Guderian had his first opportunities to try out his theories under fire. In 1939, his panzers sliced through the Polish corridor to East Prussia, cutting off thousands of enemy troops in the process. In France, "Hurrying Heinz," as he was called, dashed through the Ardennes to the Channel coast in a 400-mile drive that took 17 days and 17 almost sleepless nights to complete. Later, he attacked east of Paris and then swept south. So fast did his tanks move that the French were stunned, and even the German High Command was incredulous when Guderian radioed Berlin that he was at the Swiss border.

Guderian stiffly greets two officers captured in his romp across France. By overrunning the French Army in a little over a month, the panzers accomplished what the entire German Army had not been able to do in four years of fighting during the First World War.

Union was bound to Germany by the nonaggression pact signed in August 1939.

THE FINAL PROVING GROUND

Guderian believed it would be a fatal mistake for Germany to fight a two-front war, and he was dumbfounded when he found out that Hitler was considering an attack on the U.S.S.R. In spite of his misgivings, he plunged ahead, preparing himself for the invasion by studying Napoleon's 1812 campaign. "I made it quite clear to my troops that the campaign ahead of them would be a far more difficult one than those they had fought in Poland and the West," he later wrote.

Russian tanks heavily outnumbered the German panzers, but most of the Soviet tanks were obsolete. Guderian counted on the superiority of the German models to make up the difference. With other panzer generals, he insisted that the initial assault be made by armored divisions rather than infantry so that deep penetrations could quickly be achieved.

The argument prevailed, leading to the Germans' spectacular early successes. But then the attack bogged down, with the tanks and men stalled only 10 miles from Moscow, the closest they would come before being driven back by the Russians.

Guderian (center) halts briefly in Roslavl in August of 1941 to discuss the next phase of his Russian push with one of his subordinate commanders, as motorized

Three days and 100 miles into Russian territory, Guderian clambers into a Panzer IV for a drive through no man's land southwest of Minsk to confer with the commander of his 18th Panzer Division. Because he believed "only leaders who drive in front of the troops will influence the outcome of the battle," Guderian repeatedly exposed himself to enemy fire while leading the attack in the Soviet Union.

artillery pieces move out in the background.

Armored troop carriers monogrammed with the proud white "G" of Panzer Group Guderian speed infantrymen down a Russian road in the summer of 1941.

During the first three weeks of the Russian campaign, Guderian's tanks and motorized troops advanced 413 miles, covering as much as 72 miles in a single day.

The state of unreadiness in which the Russians were caught on the morning of June 22, 1941, was much more serious than is suggested by references to unoccupied defensive positions and artillery stalled without motive power. Long before the Germans started shooting, the Red Army was a shambles. Although it was the world's largest army, with some five million men, it was also ill-equipped and dragged down by inefficiencies. And it had suffered two wrenching decades of violent change—mainly at the hands of Stalin—that left it debilitated, demoralized and deprived of its best leadership.

From its birth in 1918 the Red Army had developed as a hybrid creature, compelled to respond both to military realities and to the political exigencies of the struggles that shook and shaped the new Communist state. Leon Trotsky, selected by Lenin to create the new army, took some steps to achieve military excellence, but at the same time he approved other measures that almost guaranteed that excellence would not be attained.

Trotsky offended many Communists by decreeing that officers would be appointed, not elected as they had been during the Revolution. It had been all very well then, he said, for Bolsheviks to demand election of officers, because the aim had been to break up the old Imperial Army, but the same approach would not work now that they were trying to build an effective army of their own. It was a sensible decision.

But to ensure the officers' loyalty, and to mollify Communists who were alarmed because four fifths of the officers had served in the Army of the old regime, Trotsky instituted the commissar system, with a Communist political officer—a commissar—sharing power with every commander at every level. The professional soldier could not act without the consent of the party watchdog, whose signature was needed to make an order valid. This peculiar institution affronted a basic principle of warfare, unity of command, as Red Army officers would learn to their chagrin in 1941.

The new army made other concessions to the new politics. Traditional designations were abandoned and officers became known as "military specialists." In theory all ranks were equal, and officers and men addressed one another as "comrade." Saluting was abolished. But Trotsky balked at proposals that the Red Army adopt a whole new kind of

2

THE SHAM RED GIANT

"Marxist" military doctrine that would reject the strategic and tactical principles embraced by Western armies. When it came to making war, he said, the Communists needed proven techniques as much as the capitalists did.

For a while in the '30s, when Russia's safety seemed threatened by the growing strength of both Japan and Germany, the Red Army, with Stalin's blessing, gained new prestige and underwent changes for the better. Over a period of five years officers' pay tripled. In 1934 the authority of Army political commissars was severely curtailed; they were reduced to being advisors without veto power. In 1935 designations of rank and saluting were reintroduced and the secret police were forbidden to arrest Red Army officers without express consent from the Defense Commissar. In 1936 a new law made all Soviet citizens eligible for military service. Previously only peasants and workers had qualified. Army numbers swelled rapidly. At last the Red Army appeared likely to come into its own as an effective defender of the U.S.S.R. But then Stalin turned on it.

A hint of the dictator's displeasure with his Army came in May 1937, when he restored the commissar system at the higher levels of command. One probable reason for Stalin's change in attitude was growing opposition from Red Army officers to his forced collectivization of agriculture, which had already caused much pain and upheaval in the countryside. The officers objected because collectivization was seriously imperiling the morale of their troops, most of whom were peasants whose family lands were being taken away by the government. Stalin probably was also unhappy with the fact that almost all of the Army's top commanders were men who did not owe their positions to him. Some even dared to vote against him in the Central Committee (by 1937 most Red Army officers were Communists and some held high positions in the party).

Whatever his reasons, Stalin set about with a vengeance —literally—to remake the Army to his own satisfaction. On June 11, 1937, Marshal Mikhail N. Tukhachevsky, one of the master builders of the Red Army, and seven other leading officers were arrested and charged with treason. They were tried and convicted that same day and executed the next. Thus began the Great Purge of the Red Army. It was to last a year and a half, during which Stalin eliminated 35,000 of the Red Army's most talented commanders—in

all, half its senior officer corps. The victims included three out of five marshals, 13 of 15 commanders of armies and 220 of 406 brigade commanders. At the very top Stalin liquidated or imprisoned 75 members of the 80-man Supreme Military Council and all 11 Vice Commissars of Defense. Considered by ranks, the toll appears even more incredible: the Purge cost the country 54 per cent of the Red Army's generals and 80 per cent of its colonels. Few wars could have caused such high-level casualty figures.

Most of Stalin's victims, like Tukhachevsky, were accused of treason—spying for Germany. As the Purge began, their fellow officers, conditioned by xenophobic propaganda, accepted this explanation. But, as General Aleksandr V. Gorbatov, a divisional commander in the Ukraine, put it, "with each arrest it became more difficult to believe in the disloyalty, the sabotage, the treachery of these men."

When his corps commander, General Pyotr P. Grigoryev, was arrested, Gorbatov spoke up for him at a party meeting. "I have known Comrade Grigoryev for over fourteen years," he said. "Grigoryev never once vacillated on points of Party policy. He was one of the best commanders in the whole army." For his loyalty to his superior officer, Gorbatov soon found himself in prison, where he was repeatedly tortured. He was given pencil and paper to transcribe his "crimes", but kept telling his jailers he had nothing to confess. Fellow officers he met in the crowded cells told him he was crazy, that they had made up many stories of treason about themselves and colleagues to escape torture. He replied that he would rather die than give false testimony. Gorbatov was lucky; he was not shot, but was sent to Siberia.

The Great Purge broke the spirit of the Red Army. Most of those who escaped it felt that survival depended on servility. They eschewed initiative for timidity. "The Boss knows best" became the watchword of even the highest-ranking officers. Fear of misstepping stifled innovatory thought, and even some backward steps were taken. Seven mechanized corps that had been created according to the new concept of mass employment of armor were broken up and their tanks reorganized into smaller brigades, some of which were attached to infantry units.

Few of the new commanders emerging in the Army had any battle experience. In prison, Gorbatov worried about how Russia could be defended with yesterday's battalion commanders now heading divisions, and former divisional commanders in charge of whole armies. When a review of Gorbatov's case led to his release and reinstatement in early 1941, he did not find many familiar faces in the Army. He later wrote that when the Germans invaded, "my earlier fears still made my hair stand on end: how were we going to be able to fight when we had lost so many experienced commanders even before the war had started?"

The Red Army was as deficient in modern equipment as it was in leadership. Much of its transport for supplies and artillery depended on the same motive power the Imperial Russian Army had used in the 19th Century: horses. In an age of tank warfare, the U.S.S.R. was the only big nation that still had a large cavalry force, a full 30 divisions numbering some 210,000 horsemen. The Red Army possessed about 24,000 tanks, but all but 1,500 of them were small and obsolescent. Most had no radios and their crews lacked the training and skills of the panzer men. In any case, only 27 per cent of the Russian tanks were in full working order at the time of the invasion.

There were not enough trucks to go around, and no armored personnel carriers at all. When Soviet tanks advanced, they had to stop and wait for the infantry marching along behind to catch up. There were few staff cars or motorcycles. If a commander wanted to send a written message, he might have to detach a tank to carry it.

The Red Air Force was equally primitive and lacking in equipment. It had 12,000 planes, but of these 80 per cent were obsolete. The old fighters in general use, many of them biplanes, had top speeds of less than 300 miles an hour; some German Messerschmitts flew at more than 350 miles an hour. Because few planes had radios, Red pilots had to use wing-wagging and other flight maneuvers to convey signals. According to an American observer, maintenance of Russian planes amounted mainly to substituting new aircraft as the old ones broke down.

The decrepit condition of the Soviet forces had been clearly revealed in the winter of 1939-1940, when the Russians invaded Finland. To subdue the Finns, whose Army numbered only 200,000, the U.S.S.R. had to commit more than a million men. During the four-month war the Russians fired about eight million shells—three for every Finn. The

Red Army admitted to 200,000 casualties, although Western observers believed the true figure was much higher. At one point in the war, before Russian victory was finally assured, a Soviet general was said to have noted that "we have won enough ground to bury our dead."

After finally defeating the Finns in March 1940, Stalin belatedly tried to modernize his armed forces. New tanks and swifter planes were supplied as fast as factories could produce them. Noting panzer successes in Western Europe in 1940, the Russians realized their mistake in disbanding their mechanized corps, and 20 new tank corps were scheduled to be ready for action by October 1941.

Hamstrung as it was by a lack of proper equipment, the Red Army suffered from a further handicap. At the best of times it showed a lack of coordination. "Train timings are chaotic, motor transport is seldom available at the right time and place, petrol supplies break down and no one has any clear idea of what time anything is going to arrive," said a British intelligence report in early 1941.

When the Germans struck, the entire Russian military machine was in the throes of a reorganization process that would have made even an efficient army vulnerable.

One thing Russia did have, of course, was manpower. The Soviet Union's population, 190 million, was three times that of Germany, and the Red Army was much bigger than German intelligence assessed it to be. The Germans estimated that the Soviet Army in European Russia numbered the equivalent of 213 divisions, but by August 1941 they were to encounter at least 360 Russian divisions.

Another thing the Russians had plenty of, unfortunately, was misplaced confidence—at least before the war with Finland. Until then they saw their Red Army as invincible, the mighty force of world revolution. A pre-nonaggression pact novel by Nikolai N. Shpanov, called *The First Strike— The Story of the Future War,* described Soviet planes repulsing a German air attack on the U.S.S.R. within half an hour and proceeding to cripple German industry by bombing in less than a day. The book became part of a training-aid series for Soviet officers. Such cockiness continued to have official blessing even after the Finnish war. *Draft Field Regulations,* a manual issued to Red officers in 1939 and still in effect in 1941, spoke confidently of "the achievement of a decisive victory at a small cost in blood." It hardly men-

Russian fighters, damaged in strafing attacks by German planes, crowd an air base captured by the Germans. The fighters were caught on the ground because Stalin did not authorize the Red Air Force to take off until the Germans had been bombing airfields for four hours. Hundreds of Russian planes were destroyed. Even after Stalin ordered the Red Air Force into the air, many aircraft were shot down or failed to complete their missions because of the poor training of their crews.

tioned defense. Any defensive operation, it claimed, would be local and temporary; the Red Army, the manual said, was prepared to take the offense and defend the nation by carrying any war to the enemy's soil.

But on June 22, 1941, the Russians suddenly found themselves fighting a defensive war on their own territory, and all the shortcomings of the Soviet commanders and their forces were called to account. The result was disaster. Ordered that afternoon to bomb the enemy, Air Force Lieut. General I. I. Kopets did as he was told, although by then his fighters had been destroyed and the bombers would have no escorts. The pilots of the slow Russian Ilyushin and Tupolev bombers courageously flew off to be chewed up by the Messerschmitts. Luftwaffe Field Marshal Albert Kesselring said picking off the Russian planes was as easy as "infanticide." By the second day of the war, Kopets had lost all his undefended bombers, and subsequently killed himself.

Chaos was as great among the Russians on the ground. In the Baltic Military District, where Colonel General Fyodor I.

Kuznetsov, the district commander, had only two armies to defend the frontier, the panzers of German Field Marshal Wilhelm Ritter von Leeb's Army Group North sped along the forest tracks of Lithuania. Most of the Red Army units they met scattered in confusion into the woods. The thousands of Russians who had settled in Lithuania after the Soviet take-over of the Baltic states the year before quickly gathered up a few possessions and fled east, knowing they had little chance of survival if caught by Germans—or by Russian-hating Lithuanians. The refugees soon clogged the roads, thwarting Red Army attempts to bring up reserves.

South of Lithuania, most of the forces of General Dmitry Pavlov, commander of the Western Military District, were far forward in what was called the Bialystok salient—a piece of Soviet territory that jutted westward into German-held Poland south of East Prussia. Here three Russian armies were in danger of being encircled as the panzer wedges of Field Marshal Fedor von Bock's Army Group Center sliced into Soviet territory behind them, from the southern and northern sides of the salient. Pavlov, whose headquarters were in

Minsk, had heard nothing from his frontline armies since the attack, and late in the morning sent his deputy, General Ivan V. Boldin, to Bialystok by plane to investigate.

From the air Boldin saw railway stations, trains and warehouses burning and enemy bombers streaking through the sky unopposed. He landed at a small airfield near Bialystok and had walked only a few hundred yards from his aircraft when nine Junkers appeared and destroyed every plane on the field, including his.

He stopped a truck carrying Russian soldiers and told them to take him to Tenth Army headquarters. The route was very dangerous, they warned. Germans were strafing everything that moved and dropping parachutists all over the area. On the way to Bialystok, Boldin saw hundreds of refugees. He stopped a big ZIS-101 limousine in which a local official was fleeing with his wife, children and belongings, including a rubber plant. Boldin scolded the man for thinking of a house plant when his countrymen were dying. A few minutes later the ZIS was hit by machine-gun fire from a German plane and everyone in it was killed.

At about sundown, Boldin reached the Tenth Army's command post, which consisted of two tents, a wooden table and a few stools at the edge of a wood about eight miles from Bialystok. He asked the Army commander, Major General K. D. Golubev, why Western District headquarters had not heard from him. Golubev said that the telephone lines were down and he had been unable to establish a radio link. He began a long tale of woe. His trucks and tanks lacked gasoline because the Luftwaffe had set fire to his fuel dumps with incendiary bullets. Promised ammunition had not arrived. His tanks were old machines "only good for shooting sparrows." Movement was impossible because of the Luftwaffe's total control of the air. "My men are fighting like heroes," Golubev said, "but what can they do against tanks or aircraft?"

At this moment radio contact was reestablished with Minsk. Boldin heard the faint and distant voice of Pavlov. From Moscow, Defense Commissar Semyon K. Timoshenko, who obviously had no idea of what was happening at the front, had issued a directive for a general counterthrust. "Here is the order," Pavlov said. "Destroy the enemy with a counterattack. Tell Golubev to occupy Osovets, Visna, Belsk and Kleshchelye." These were all towns behind the German lines. "All this must be done tonight," Pavlov added. When Boldin objected that this was impossible, that there was no question of the shattered Russian forces taking the offensive, Pavlov cut him short: "That's all I have to say. Get started on the assignment."

Boldin thought "how far removed from reality" Pavlov was. In fact Pavlov probably understood the reality of the situation very well, but believed that if he so much as questioned the directive, the wrath of Stalin would descend upon him. He had witnessed the Purge. Most Soviet generals would rather issue an impossible order than risk any charge of hesitancy or disloyalty. They were more frightened of Stalin and of his Communist security forces, the NKVD, than they were of Hitler's armies.

Farther south, the Russians in the Kiev Military District under Colonel General M. P. Kirponos were putting up stronger resistance to the German onslaught. ("That's very good!" German Army Chief of Staff Franz Halder wrote in his diary. If the Russians did not retreat, he noted, there was more chance to surround them.) Most of the Red Army was concentrated in the Ukraine. Even so, the Army here as elsewhere on the front was crippled by lack of equipment. "Often our troops could not dig in, simply because they did not even have the simplest implements," wrote Colonel Ivan I. Fedyuninsky, commander of an infantry corps in the western Ukraine. "Occasionally trenches had to be dug with helmets since there were no spades." There seemed little hope of containing the panzer-led thrust of Field Marshal Gerd von Rundstedt's Army Group South, already pushing into the Ukraine just south of the vast Pripyat Marshes separating this area from the central front. Desperate fighting was needed just to slow the German advance.

Realizing this, Major General I. K. Bagramian, Kirponos' deputy chief of staff, was bewildered by a message from Timoshenko on the evening of June 22 ordering Kirponos to "surround and destroy the enemy group" and to capture Lublin, a Polish city on the German side of the frontier, within two days. Bagramian read the order aloud to the Chief of Staff of the Kiev Military District, Lieut. General M. A. Purkayev, who "reached for it in disbelief." Together they went to see Kirponos and told him frankly that his armies were hardly capable of defending the areas allotted them, let alone advancing and capturing Lublin the day after tomorrow. Kirponos reacted with the instincts of a well-cowed Red Army commander. He immediately sent for his political commissar, Nikolai N. Vashugin.

Vashugin was no friend of professional soldiers. He had won his present high position because he had played an enthusiastic role in the Purge, eagerly supplying names of "suspect" officers. When Purkayev tried to argue that the wisest course would be to withdraw until sufficient force for a counterattack could be massed, Vashugin questioned Purkayev's loyalty. "You've received the order," Vashugin insisted, "now you have to carry it out." Kirponos, heeding his commissar's threatening tone, meekly assented. In

fact, two days would pass before a counterattack could be mounted, and then it served only to slow the German advance at great expense in Russian lives. There was never the remotest chance of an advance toward Lublin.

Because commanders at the front were afraid to report the true extent of the debacle, it was assumed in Moscow on the night of the invasion that orders had already been carried out and a general counteroffensive was under way. At 10 p.m. the Chief of the Russian General Staff, Marshal Georgy K. Zhukov, assessed the situation after one day of war as favorable, "the enemy having been thrown back." On the German side of the front, Halder took a much different view. Things were going so well for the invaders

Triumphant SS troops in Russia celebrate with champagne Germany's stunning victories during the early days of Operation Barbarossa. When German panzers penetrated as deep as 273 miles into Russian territory in the first week of war, the invaders were confident that the campaign would come to a speedy end. Some soldiers looked forward to an early return home, others expected to remain in Russia and farm the rich land.

that on June 24 he could note in his diary that "the course of the entire battle evolves gratifyingly according to plan."

In the north, Leeb's Army Group made a sweep toward the Dvina River, the only major obstacle between it and its objective, Leningrad. General Georg-Hans Reinhardt's XLI Panzer Corps was briefly challenged by 300 Russian tanks near the Lithuanian village of Raseinyai on the night of June 23. But the Russians, part of the Red Army's newly organized mechanized corps, were unskilled in armored warfare. They wasted themselves in successive frontal assaults until the experienced German tankers finally drove them into a swamp with a flank attack. The Russians lost 185 tanks and the panzers continued toward the Dvina.

To Reinhardt's right, General Erich von Manstein relentlessly drove his LVI Panzer Corps toward Dvinsk as the Russians fled pell-mell before him. With both a road bridge and a rail bridge, Dvinsk was the most important crossing point over the 250-yard-wide Dvina. "Keep going!" Manstein shouted from the open turret of his command tank when divisional officers reported seizures of intermediate objectives. "Keep going!" By early morning on June 26 his leading tanks were 190 miles inside Russia and only four miles from bridges that led across the river to Dvinsk.

Fearing an attack would cause the Russians to blow up the bridges, the Germans stopped there and began the most daring and successful ruse of the invasion. An engineering platoon of 30 men piled into four captured Russian trucks, driven by Germans in Russian uniforms. Three of the trucks sped toward the Dvinsk road bridge. They passed a rear guard of about 50 Red Army soldiers who waved them by, apparently thinking the trucks carried Russian wounded.

As the leading truck neared the bridge, a Red Army sentry stepped out to challenge the driver. The German slowed as if to stop, then stomped on the accelerator, knocked down the Russian and raced to the far end of the bridge. The second truck followed. While men jumped from these vehicles and began dismantling the explosives fixed on the bridge, the Germans from the third truck leaped out and killed the remaining sentries. But more Russians, armed with machine guns, soon appeared at both ends of the bridge and the raiders sustained 20 minutes of intense fire that killed five of them before a heavier German force arrived to secure the bridge—intact. The fourth truck had

headed for a railroad bridge. But when it arrived there, the men in Russian uniforms were recognized as Germans and had to fight their way across. The Russians managed to set off an explosion, but it caused minimal damage.

Soon Manstein's panzers had crossed the river and were engaged in running battles through the streets of Dvinsk. Fighting was fierce, but by evening the city was captured. The war was only four days old and already the Germans were threatening Leningrad, about 300 miles away.

The successes of Army Group Center in Belorussia were even more dramatic. Two armored wedges—Colonel General Hermann Hoth's 3rd Panzer Group to the north of the Bialystok salient and Colonel General Guderian's 2nd Panzer Group to its south—rapidly penetrated weak Soviet

defenses and moved east like a giant pair of claws designed to close on Minsk, about 200 miles inside the U.S.S.R. If successful, this pincer movement would envelop the three hapless Russian armies under Pavlov's command that were in the Bialystok area. Hoth took Vilna on June 24, the same date on which Napoleon had captured it when the French invaded Russia in 1812, a fact that Halder described in his diary as an "interesting historical coincidence."

Guderian moved so fast that he often took the enemy—and even himself—by surprise. In a single day, June 24, he personally used the machine gun of his armored command vehicle to clear a Russian roadblock, was fired on by a Soviet tank at close range (a general with him was killed) and accidentally drove through a large group of Russian

infantrymen who were clambering out of their trucks for a counterattack. The Russians were too startled at the sight of a German general in their midst to fire. "They must have recognized me, because the Russian press later announced my death," Guderian recalled.

By June 26 his panzers were 175 miles inside Russia and 60 miles south of Minsk. Both he and Hoth, whose tanks were by now north of Minsk, wanted to push on about 200 more miles to the east and close the envelopment at Smolensk in order to bag more Red divisions. Hitler, worried that the Russians might break out if the German lines were drawn too thin, insisted they converge on Minsk.

Meanwhile, the infantry of two German armies advancing inside the panzer pincers were making a more modest pincer movement of their own to encircle the Russian armies near the frontier. They converged from north and south toward a spot roughly halfway between Bialystok and Minsk. General Boldin, inside this fast-closing ring with the armies Pavlov had sent him to visit the day the invasion began, mounted a counterattack to the northeast on June 24 to try to break out. He deployed both armored and cavalry forces in the attack, but they were beaten back by German infantry and antitank guns.

At this point, Pavlov made an ill-considered and fateful decision. Apparently unaware of the advance of the wider German panzer envelopment and perhaps hoping to impress Stalin with his energy and enterprise, he sent the remaining reserves of his command forward from the Minsk area to attack the German infantry. Moving his troops west, he left Minsk almost undefended. As the panzer jaws began to close, the few Red Army units left in the city, lacking artillery, were reduced to seizing a bottle factory and making Molotov cocktails to hurl at the oncoming tanks.

Minsk fell to Hoth on June 26 and the next day the trap snapped shut as Guderian's tanks moved in from the south. On June 28 the smaller infantry encirclement locked tight around the Russian armies to the west in the Bialystok area. The Soviets inside the two pockets fought frantically to escape, hurling themselves against their captors in costly, usually futile counterattacks. Some succeeded, and with a few battered remnants, Boldin managed to reach Russian-held territory 400 miles to the east in August. But most of the trapped Russians, pounded mercilessly by German air-

Some of the more than 100,000 Russian soldiers taken prisoner during the battle of Smolensk are corralled at a German collection center. At least a third of the captives eventually died of disease and starvation—partly because of a shortage of supplies in the prison camps and partly because the Germans, convinced by Hitler that the Russian people were subhuman, deliberately neglected them.

craft and artillery, surrendered within a few days. For the Germans the catch was magnificent: some 300,000 prisoners, 2,500 tanks and 1,500 guns. Five Soviet armies—22 infantry divisions and the equivalent of seven tank divisions and six mechanized brigades—had been knocked out of the war in little more than a week.

Pavlov himself escaped the Minsk encirclement by shifting his headquarters to Mogilev, some 100 miles to the east. Chief of Staff Zhukov learned of the disaster from jubilant German broadcasts and called Pavlov from Moscow on June 30. Was there "some measure of truth," Zhukov asked, in German claims that they had surrounded two armies east of Bialystok? "Yes," Pavlov answered ruefully, "a large measure of truth." He and several of his chief aides were immediately called to Moscow and shot.

That same day—June 30—was a festive one at the High Command of the German Army near Berlin. It was Halder's 57th birthday and the greetings were mixed with congratulations on the campaign. The Führer himself came to tea as a personal gesture of approval for the success of Operation *Barbarossa* to date. Hitler had reason to be pleased. Even in

the Ukraine, where a stubborn Russian defense made the German advance comparatively slow, progress was steady and the panzers had penetrated about 60 miles into Soviet territory within four days. Halder's confidence ran high. On July 3, 1941, he wrote in his diary: "It is probably no overstatement to say that the Russian Campaign has been won in the space of two weeks."

In spite of their rapid and stunning victories early in the war, the Germans faced a number of problems that were growing more serious day by day. Their intelligence was bad, and their maps were grossly inadequate. "The roads that were marked nice and red and thick on a map turned out to be tracks," complained Rundstedt. And sometimes there were no roads at all. The Germans designated the good roads as *Rollbahns*—runways—and carefully allotted them according to a strict system of priorities. Manstein was given only one *Rollbahn* for three divisions during his advance in the Baltic area. By contrast, in Western Europe during the blitzkrieg of 1940 the availability of good roads often made it possible to assign a whole road to one division. In Russia

traffic had to be closely controlled, rest and repair halts finely worked out. Once in Lithuania a convoy of 2,000 German trucks, many carrying telegraph poles, violated orders and got onto a high priority road, holding up the advance of a panzer division for hours.

Roads, climate and terrain combined to slow the German advance. When the weather was dry, dust stirred up by boots and tank treads hung over unpaved tracks in clouds as high as a house, clogging the engines of motorized vehicles, choking the infantry and reducing visibility. A German soldier in the Ukraine, Helmut Schreiber, told how his motorcycle company hastily took to the ditches as the shape of a Russian tank loomed out of the dust before them. They returned to their machines in embarrassment when the "tank" came close enough to be identified as a peasant's wagon piled high with manure. When it rained, foot soldiers rejoiced at the chance to wash off the dust, but tanks and trucks got mired in the mud.

The geographical shape of the Soviet Union, opening to the east like an enormous funnel, meant that the farther the Germans advanced, the wider the front became. The gaps between the German thrusts grew larger, allowing bypassed units of the Red Army and hastily recruited partisan groups to harass the flanks of the German columns.

Ironically, the Germans were also constantly harassed by their own leader, Adolf Hitler. Their strategy came to be less dependent on preagreed plans than on each day's new worried messages from the Führer. Halder referred to them in his diary as "anxieties of the Führer." Hitler meddled right down to corps level, demanding sudden redispositions of divisions and last-minute changes of objectives. The Führer and his generals argued constantly about what to do next. In the Baltic, the top military commanders wanted to make destruction of enemy forces their first priority—in the swift advance to the Dvina only 6,000 Russian prisoners had been taken—but Hitler, anxious to capture Leningrad, would allow no delays for mopping up. In Belorussia he had wanted Hoth and Guderian to close the armored envelopment far short of Minsk, just to be on the safe side, and had to be talked out of the idea.

But the biggest German problem was the stubbornness of the Russians who, despite their disorganization and unpreparedness, here and there along the front began to prove themselves tougher and more resistant than expected. Given the chance, Russian soldiers might abandon their defenses and flee, but when trapped they fought with desperation and often to the death, taking many Germans with them.

The Russian defense of the old border fortress at Brest, which had been bypassed by Guderian's tanks and left to the German infantry to eliminate, illustrated the stiffening resistance the Germans were beginning to meet. Through a week of artillery barrages and bombing, the Russians hung on, repelling every attempt by the Germans to root them out. It was only on June 29, after a rain of 4,000-pound blockbusters had blown much of the fortress to bits, that 7,000 Russians inside surrendered, among them wives and children of the garrison's defenders. Even then small groups and individuals barricaded themselves in the fort's labyrinthine dungeons and refused to surrender. As they awaited their fates, some of these last determined defenders scratched notes to posterity on the plaster walls of the chambers where they were holed up. One signed "Ivanov" tells the tale: "The Germans are inside. I have one hand grenade left. They shall not get me alive."

Hitler was to blame for some of this Russian determination. His infamous Commissar Decree, which called for the execution of all captured Red Army political officers, was often applied in practice to any Communist Party member or Jew. Thousands knew they had nothing to gain by surrendering. Political officers convinced their men that common soldiers, too, faced torture and death if captured.

Stories of German atrocities—many of them true—spread rapidly through the Red Army in the early days of the invasion. Special German SS police units called *Einsatzgruppen* —task groups—were working full time killing prisoners of war and Russian civilians in accordance with government policy. Otto Ohlendorf, commander of one *Einsatzgruppe*, testified at Nuremberg after the War that his group alone, some 500 men, killed 90,000 Russians in the first year. Even by Nazi standards the murders were indiscriminate. One day in Minsk, SS men pulled 280 prisoners from the jail, lined them up by a ditch and shot them. Because the ditch was not yet full, they took 30 more men from the jail and shot them too—including 23 skilled workers who had come from Poland to help the Germans and who just happened

On a jammed Russian highway, German couriers guide their motorcycles between columns of army vehicles moving bumper to bumper. Good roads were scarce, and for the drive on Smolensk Guderian could depend on only two. Yet he was able to move to their destination some 27,000 vehicles of his panzer group and another 60,000 carrying ammunition, fuel, supplies, headquarters personnel and communications troops.

to be living in the jail because of a housing shortage.

The Russians were also inspired to fanatical efforts by fear of their own masters. Stalin's execution of Pavlov was merely a reminder that brutality ruled in the Red Army. Kirponos' commissar, Vashugin, encouraged a corps commander with these alternatives: "If you occupy Dubno by this evening, we will give you a medal. If you don't, we'll shoot you." Of course such dire threats were demoralizing, but they also stimulated action against hopeless odds. Vashugin himself lived and died by the same demands he placed on others. On June 30, leading an armored unit, he blundered into a swamp and lost all his tanks. Knowing full well the game in which he played, Vashugin promptly killed himself.

Soviet soldiers taken prisoner by the Germans were declared traitors by the Russians; even if they escaped and made it back to their own lines they were liable to be imprisoned or shot. Families of Russian prisoners of war had their food rations taken away, which often meant starvation. When Stalin's eldest son, Yakov, was captured in 1941, the dictator imprisoned Yakov's wife, Yulia, apparently suspecting that his son had surrendered on purpose and that Yulia was part of the plot. Stalin released her in 1943 when reports of Yakov's honorable behavior in captivity convinced him that no treason was involved.

But not all of the Russian will to resist can be attributed to fear. Soldiers, partisans and noncombatants alike were also motivated by the love of Mother Russia. Stalin knew well the power of this patriotism, and he tapped it with a speech broadcast to the nation on July 3. It was his first public utterance since the invasion began. For 11 days his total silence had worried the people of the Soviet Union and puzzled the world. It had been rumored that he was in shock, immersed in severe depression, drunk. Then at last he reemerged as the Russian leader with his radio speech.

"Comrades, citizens, brothers and sisters, warriors of our Army and of our fleet," he began, "I am speaking to you, my friends." Never before had Stalin addressed his people in such warm terms—brothers, sisters, friends—and he never did so again. His speech was slow and halting, but it touched the hearts of his listeners. Many of them retained vivid memories of the talk long after the war.

The enemy, he continued "is out to seize our lands watered by the sweat of our brows, to seize our grain and oil, secured by the labor of our hands." Russia was fighting a "national patriotic war," he declared, a "war for the freedom of our Motherland." Recalling how Russia had defeated Napoleon, he urged his countrymen to "scorch the earth" before yielding any territory to the Germans.

"The enemy," he said, "must not be left a single engine, a single railway car, a single pound of grain, a single gallon of fuel. All valuable property that cannot be withdrawn must be destroyed. Sabotage groups must be organized to foment guerrilla warfare everywhere, blow up bridges and roads, set fire to forests, stores and transport."

Whether from patriotism or fear, Soviet soldiers soon acquired a reputation for courage; even Hitler, with all his contempt for "sub-human" Slavs, grudgingly acknowledged their determination. He wrote Mussolini in the first weeks of war that "the Russians fight with a truly stupid fanaticism. Pillbox crews blow themselves up rather than surrender." The Russians counterattacked, he said, "with the primitive brutality of an animal that sees itself trapped and then in wild rage beats against the walls of its cage."

Stories of Russian fanaticism circulated widely among the Germans: how a single Soviet tank, punctured by antitank missiles and ablaze, charged on against a German position, firing wildly, until its crew burned to death; how the pilot of a damaged Soviet fighter, instead of bailing out, plunged his machine into a convoy of German fuel trucks. It was said that Russian women and children were fighting in the front line and stories abounded of pretty teenaged girls found dead on the battlefield, still clutching automatic weapons.

Germans soon began complaining that the Red Army was breaking the rules, not fighting fairly, using "Asiatic tricks" unworthy of true soldiers. Russians, they said, would lie on the ground pretending to be dead, then leap up and shoot Germans who passed over them. Or they would wave white flags of surrender, then fire at those coming to capture them. Such incidents became battlefield horror stories and raised the war's already high level of hatred and barbarity. Having heard tales of false surrenders, many Germans killed any Russians trying to give themselves up.

But even where they fought most vigorously and effectively —in the Ukraine—the Russians could not halt for long the invading juggernaut. The main effort of German Army

Captured near Smolensk, Yakov Djugashvili, Stalin's son by his first wife, waits at an airfield to be led away for interrogation. The Germans considered him a prize, but Stalin did not. When Yakov lived in Moscow before the war, Stalin bullied him mercilessly. And later when the Germans proposed to trade him for a German POW, Stalin refused.

Group South was a drive by Colonel General Ewald von Kleist's 1st Panzer Group across the Ukraine from northwest to southeast. The aim was to get behind the main Soviet forces, cut them off from retreat to the east, then crush them. A smaller force of Germans and Rumanians invading from Rumania would help herd the Russians into the trap.

The Russians made the Germans fight all the way. The Soviet Fifth Army under Major General M. I. Potapov, which had been pushed northeast into the Pripyat Marshes by the initial German breakthrough, took advantage of its hiding place and emerged from the wooded swamps again and again to slash at the enemy's north flank with brutal counterattacks. One German regiment lost a quarter of its men to Potapov's raiders in two days.

Retreating Russians dug in, fought until almost overrun, then fell back and dug in again. The Red Army had no qualms about leaving behind a rear guard that knew it would have to die to the last man to cover the main body's withdrawal. In the Ukraine, the Germans paid with lives for every mile they advanced. "Our ranks got thinner every day," said Colonel Dietrich von Choltitz, commander of an infantry regiment in the southwest Ukraine. "Numberless cemeteries full of our dead appeared along our route."

In spite of Russian resistance, the panzer thrust in the northwestern Ukraine threatened to cut off three Russian armies near Lvov as early as June 30. Apparently Stalin and the Red Army bosses had at last decided that it was wiser to save armies than territory, because Kirponos—whose old Kiev Military District had now been designated the Southwest Front in a hurried reorganization of the Soviet command structure—was authorized to pull his forces back 150 miles to the east and establish a new defense line. But by July 8 this line, too, had been penetrated and German tanks were only 100 miles from Kiev, the ancient capital of the Ukraine and the Soviet Union's third largest city. Some German generals urged a lightning panzer raid to take the city, but Hitler said no, ordering that the advance be continued to the southeast.

Russian efforts were to no avail against the force of the German onslaught. In early August in the region of Uman the Germans trapped some 20 Russian divisions between Kleist's panzers and the infantry closing in from Rumania. The Uman pocket yielded 103,000 prisoners, 300 tanks and 800 guns. Except for Kiev itself and an isolated garrison that was to try to hold the Black Sea port of Odessa, the Red Army withdrew its remaining forces from the Ukraine west of the Dnieper by the end of August. *Barbarossa* had scored another big success.

It was almost a footnote, however, to the victory that Army Group Center achieved during the same period in the

area that the Russians were now calling the Western Front. Guderian had fretted for more than a week in the Minsk area, waiting for the order to advance across the Dnieper River to Smolensk. On the 7th of July, fearing that if he waited any longer Soviet defenses along the Dnieper would grow too strong, he issued the order himself, telling his panzer group to make the necessary preparations for crossing the Dnieper.

Two days later Field Marshal Günther von Kluge, who had been given command over both Guderian and Hoth in a newly designated Fourth Panzer Army, arrived at Guderian's headquarters and insisted that the operation be canceled. The panzers had to wait for German infantry to catch up

with them. "I told him my preparation had already gone too far to be canceled," Guderian wrote later. He had massed his tanks for the jump-off, he said, and if they did not move quickly, what was left of the Red Air Force would locate and attack them. At that Kluge gave his approval, but reluctantly. "Your operations," he told Guderian, "always hang by a thread!"

The operation paid off. Halder's diary records the story: July 11: "Guderian has crossed to the eastern bank of the Dnieper." July 12: "In Guderian's sector, good progress." July 13: "Guderian's attack is developing surprisingly well." July 14: "Guderian's attack has made astonishing progress." July 15: "Guderian has been amazingly successful;

A PRECEDENT FOR DISASTER

Exactly 129 years before Hitler attacked Russia, Napoleon Bonaparte began a similar venture with much the same brazen confidence. Like Hitler, Napoleon was certain that he could subdue Russia in a matter of weeks. All summer the Russian Army fed his confidence, retreating as Napoleon pushed east to Moscow. When, in mid-September, the Emperor finally glimpsed the dazzling city, victory seemed assured.

This tantalizing moment, as captured in the painting at right, by Russian artist Vereshchagin, proved all too fleeting. When Napoleon entered Moscow, he found the city almost deserted. Fires, some accidental, some set by the Russians, soon reduced most of it to rubble. His offers of peace made no impression on Czar Alexander I. Baffled, Napoleon abandoned Moscow—and the tide of the war began to turn. The Russians harassed his troops, his system of supply failed him, and a bitter winter began to close in.

Discipline forgotten, the French made a desperate scramble for home. Nothing had prepared them for the horrors they encountered on the way. French soldiers by the thousands died of frostbite and typhus; they drowned in icy rivers, froze in great snowbanks. Less than one third of Napoleon's half million men survived.

Later, he confessed that he had not realized Russia's might. "She overflows unrestrainedly on you," he wrote. "If she loses, she retires into the middle of the ice, to her allies, desolation and death, and then she can suddenly come out again. Does she not resemble the mythical Hydra who could only be vanquished through close combat? . . . We tried, but we made a clumsy job of it, that I must admit."

Smolensk was reached as early as 10 o'clock this morning."

The Smolensk operation was another double envelopment, with Hoth's panzer group advancing toward the city along a northerly route through Vitebsk. The Russians in the area were still staggering from the blows of the Minsk encirclement two weeks earlier. Gorbatov, the Purge victim who had been released from prison to take command of an infantry corps, was dumbfounded by the shattered morale of his troops, who were supposed to defend Vitebsk. As soon as German artillery began firing, his leading regiment of 1,500 men fled from the field en masse. Gorbatov personally rounded them up and ordered them to dig in, but when he returned a few hours later he found that they had deserted again. Tracking them by the broad path they had trampled through the grass, he managed to catch up with many of them in small groups. "I shamed them, I cursed them, I ordered them to return and I watched as they unwillingly set off, and went on to catch the next lot. To me, newly back in the army, this all seemed an evil dream. I could not believe my eyes."

But Gorbatov also witnessed displays of great bravery by his soldiers. Touring his sector's hard-pressed front line, he saw a wounded Russian being tended by a medical corpsman. "When I went up to them the wounded man was clenching his teeth," Gorbatov said. "His eyes were closed and his cheeks wet with tears. When he heard us talking he opened his big grey eyes and said as though justifying himself: 'I am not crying from pain. I am crying because I promised myself not to die until I had killed five Fascists.' The medical orderly said quickly, afraid of being too late, 'Five! You killed fifty with that machine gun. I saw them falling under your bursts.' " Gorbatov said he did not know whether the corpsman was telling the truth or just calming a dying man, but on hearing the words the wounded soldier stopped crying and died peacefully.

Hoth's tanks closed the envelopment at Smolensk on July 16, trapping two Russian armies and hundreds of stray units that had escaped the net at Minsk. Timoshenko, who in a Soviet command shuffle had given up his job as Defense Commissar to take charge of this vital front, launched a series of desperate counterattacks from the south and east against the outside of the encirclement. But the panzer ring held until German infantry caught up to finish the job in early August. From the Smolensk pocket the Germans took 100,000 prisoners, 2,000 tanks and 1,900 guns. During August they trapped some of the counterattacking Russian forces as well, bringing the total of prisoners from the Smolensk operation to 138,000.

In only two months of fighting Russia and the Red Army had paid a monumental price for unpreparedness. Almost one million soldiers had been taken prisoner and another 700,000 had been killed or wounded. The enemy controlled, roughly speaking, the westernmost 500 miles of the Soviet Union. In the Baltic area the Germans had advanced from the Dvina and were pushing against a hastily thrown-together Russian defense line that ran through Luga, only 100 miles from Leningrad. In the south they had seized half of the Ukrainian breadbasket and were on the Dnieper, ready to pounce on the industrialized region on the other side of that river. And in the center, they were little more than 200 miles along a concrete highway from Russia's heart: Moscow. Convinced that Moscow had to be the next German target, the Red Army hurriedly collected raw recruits from all over the Soviet Union, handed them guns and dumped them on the Smolensk-Moscow road, along which German tanks were expected to move at any moment.

Most German generals certainly wanted to fulfill this Russian expectation. Guderian was amused to see his troops erect dozens of hand-painted signs east of Smolensk reading "To Moscow." He, along with Hoth, Halder and many other German commanders, believed that total victory was within their reach if they would only grasp it immediately. By an advance on Moscow they thought they could wipe out what was left of the Red Army.

But Hitler had other ideas. Although in late July he authorized the infantry to advance toward Moscow, he ordered Hoth to turn his tanks north to assist in the seizure of Leningrad, and Guderian to head toward the Ukraine. "This meant that my Panzer Group would be advancing in a southwesterly direction," Guderian noted with disgust, "that is to say toward Germany." Halder tried to talk Hitler out of his chosen objective but the Führer had made up his mind, "enemy or no enemy, or any other considerations. The Führer right now is not interested in Moscow; all he cares about is Leningrad."

THE FALSE LIBERATION

Women in the Ukraine, convinced that the German Army has come to free them from atheistic Communism, greet approaching soldiers with religious fervor.

RIDING IN ON A WAVE OF WELCOME

"In every village we're showered with bouquets of flowers, even more beautiful ones than we got when we entered Vienna." So wrote a German soldier when his regiment moved into the western Ukraine in June 1941. Flowers were only part of the welcome. Villagers brought the newcomers food and drink, serenaded them with balalaika music and erected arches bearing the slogan, "The Ukrainian peoples thank their liberators, the brave German Army. Heil Adolf Hitler!"

The western Ukrainians felt they had reason to rejoice. They had been encouraged by German radio propaganda to believe that Hitler would reestablish an independent Ukrainian state. Moreover, the western Ukraine had been part of the Soviet Union only since 1939, when Stalin grabbed it from Poland. The inhabitants detested the Communist regime, which had closed down their churches and wiped out the upper class.

Many of their fellow Ukrainians in the Soviet-dominated eastern Ukraine shared this hatred. There, over the years, Stalin had purged local officials, persecuted intellectuals and brutally enforced collectivization, at one point confiscating so much of the harvest that famine swept the area. Thus the eastern Ukrainians, too, turned hopeful eyes toward the conquerors.

Initially the invaders lived up to the population's expectations. German troops reopened churches, released Ukrainian soldiers they had taken prisoner and allowed villagers to relax collective farm rules. When separatists formed a national government shortly after the attack, the Germans gave no immediate sign of opposing it.

But the truth was that Hitler did not view the Ukrainians as allies in his war on Russia. He knew that the Ukraine, the Soviet Union's breadbasket and major industrial center, could feed and supply Germany while providing *Lebensraum*—living space—for Aryan settlers. And as his troops took more and more of the Ukraine, he worked out plans to cut "this big cake in a handy way" so that he could "1) occupy it, 2) administer it, 3) exploit it."

Two Ukrainians give vent to their anti-Communist feelings by smashing a statue of Lenin with a sledge hammer before toppling it with a noose.

Dressed for the occasion in traditional Ukrainian costume, peasants toss bunches of flowers at smiling German troops riding triumphantly into a village.

Alfred Rosenberg, Reich Minister for the Occupied Eastern Territories and ideologist behind Nazi racist policies, receives flowers from friendly Ukrainians.

Local women and children mingle with German soldiers in a Ukrainian village square as the invaders' band strikes up a tune.

An Orthodox priest and Ukrainian sympathizers stand by approvingly while a German officer makes a public announcement. The Army took advantage of the Ukrainians' respect for the church by using the pulpit for the transmission of directives and propaganda.

A BRUTAL TURN IN EVENTS

Ukrainian disenchantment with the Germans came all too soon. Five days after the Ukrainians formed a separatist government the SS dissolved it and arrested its supporters. In its stead, Hitler sliced the Ukraine into four pieces. He gave a southern section to his Rumanian ally, added the west to Occupied Poland, turned the central portion into a civil administrative unit —known as *Reichskommissariat Ukraine*— and placed the rest under Army control.

But far worse than a division of their land lay in store for the Ukrainians. If they were to provide *Lebensraum* for Aryans, their numbers had to be reduced. And no one was more suited to this task than the Nazi bureaucrat Erich Koch.

"Gentlemen," Koch boasted to his aides, "I am known as a brutal dog. For this reason I was appointed *Reichskommissar* of the Ukraine. I am expecting from you the utmost severity toward the native population." Koch's approach was methodical. His subordinates and the SS exterminated first Jews, then other Ukrainians—often on the slightest pretext. One official memo matter-of-factly stated: "A transmitter has been damaged in Kiev with evil intent. Since the culprit could not be detained, 400 men from Kiev were shot."

Koch's men used other brutal methods to depopulate the Ukraine as well. They deliberately neglected sanitation measures to encourage the spread of disease and prohibited the transportation of food to needy areas. They also deported inhabitants for slave labor in Germany; in Kiev 38,000 people were sent off in cattle cars.

"There is no Ukraine," said Koch. "We must remember we are the master race."

A woman searches for her husband among the corpses of hostages slain by the Germans. They were not the only killers of Ukrainians. After the invasion Communists slaughtered thousands of nationalists in the western Ukraine, and a few days later the nationalists reacted by murdering many Communists.

Ukrainians dangle from a gallows in the city of Nikolayev, a center of underground activity.

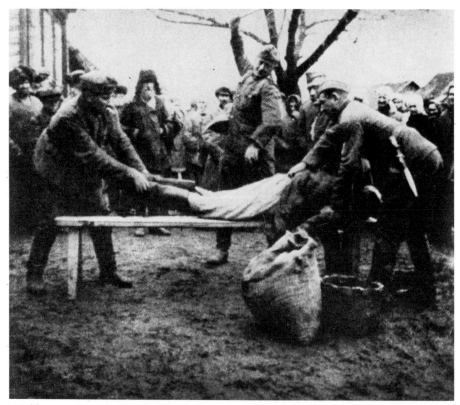

Neighbors are forced to watch while German soldiers whip a peasant accused of shirking work.

A despairing woman watches her house burn.
Though the Germans often set fire to the
homes of those who fought deportation, fleeing
villagers sometimes burned their own houses
in compliance with Stalin's orders to
leave nothing behind the enemy could use.

Disillusioned civilians join Red Army troops in retreat as the Germans advance. Though mounting evidence of Nazi barbarism spurred some Ukrainians to take flight, others did so because of a belief in Russia's cause.

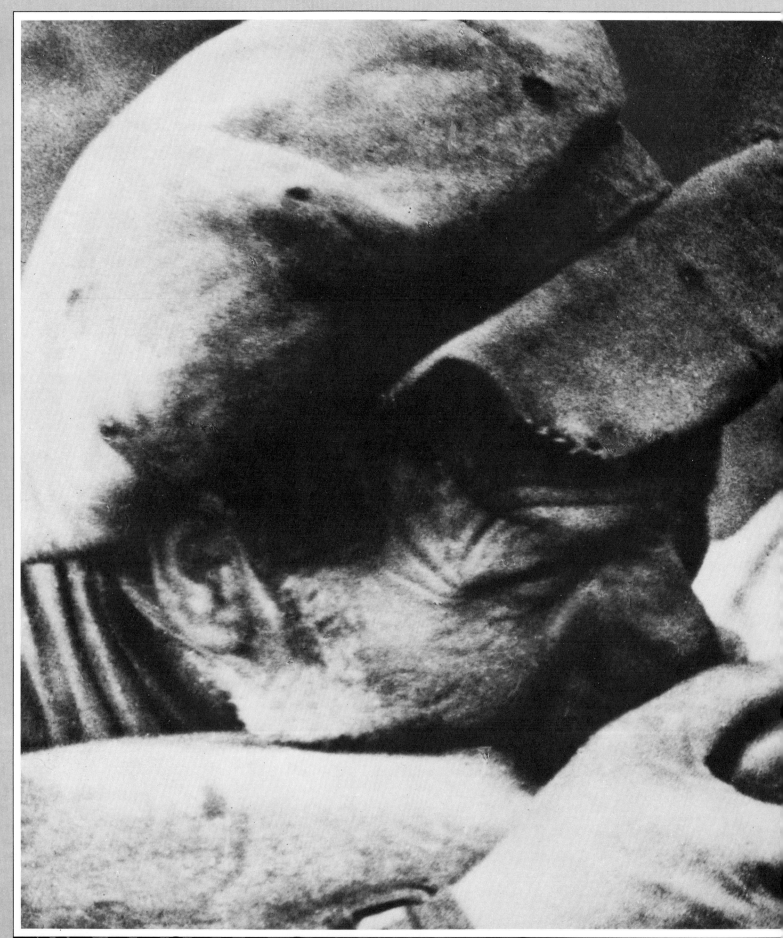

THE PEOPLE STRIKE BACK

Between raids, a partisan soldier practices shooting at a target with a Moisin 7.62mm, the basic Russian rifle, while a kerchiefed comrade-in-arms looks on.

THE IMPLACABLE WAR BEHIND ENEMY LINES

On July 3, 1941, Stalin addressed the nation by radio. "In the occupied regions," he said, "the enemy and all his accomplices . . . must be hounded and annihilated at every step and all their measures frustrated." At the end of the year there were 30,000 partisans; by the following summer their number had grown to 150,000. Although some Russians joined partisan units in order to escape the German labor draft, most did so out of patriotism or hatred for the invaders. Said one partisan of the members of his detachment, "There was not one person in whose family blood had not been shed. These people were fired with one desire—to kill Germans."

The partisans were concentrated mainly in the forests of Belorussia, bordering on Poland and the Ukraine. From their hideouts, they made forays against the German rear lines, gathering intelligence of troop movements, blowing up bridges, derailing trains, slashing telephone and telegraph lines, pouncing upon small enemy forces and setting fire to supply depots. At first their activities were limited by the lack of arms and radios, and by hostile villagers who betrayed them. But their operations soon expanded, as the Soviet High Command started airlifting supplies to them and peasants began giving them food and concealing them from the invaders.

Lacking the strength to engage major units in battle, the partisans nevertheless proved to be an ever-present threat to the Wehrmacht. A warning had to be issued to the troops: "We Germans make the mistake of thinking that if neither offensive nor defensive operations are in progress then there is no war at all. But the war is going on . . . when we are cooking potatoes, when we lie down to sleep. A soldier must carry his weapons always and everywhere."

The majority of the pictures on these pages come from Russian sources. It is impossible to tell whether all are legitimate action shots: Russian war photographers were not above setting up photographs to suit their purposes, and it may be that a few of those that follow were staged. Most, however, are clearly authentic.

One of the most famous partisan leaders was Sidor A. Kovpak, a minor Soviet official who led a regiment near the Ukraine's northern border.

With their rifles stacked carefully off to one side, partisan soldiers receive their instructions prior to splitting up into demolition and reserve groups for a raid.

Two peasants deliver mammoth loaves of brown bread to a pair of hungry partisans, after paddling to a secret meeting place in a marshy forest in Belorussia.

A DESPERATE LIFE AMONG THE SHADOWS

Partisans holed up in camps in the forests, where they spent nights in camouflaged dugouts—often in rain water up to their knees. On the march they rested in concealed locations—in bristly thickets and the drier areas of swamps.

The partisans were dependent upon the countryside for almost all of their food. They gathered potatoes from storage bins in burned-out villages, ate the carcasses of horses killed in the fighting, and foraged in the woods for mushrooms and bitter rowanberries. For many partisans, malnutrition led to scurvy and pellagra. Adding to their problems was a critical shortage of medical supplies. Festering battle wounds were often bound with reused bandages and disinfected with vodka.

A determined woman stands guard over fellow partisans resting in a clearing in the woods after a foray. Always in combat readiness, the men sleep with grenades and rifles nearby.

The partisan on the right holds out a clay jar in one hand to be filled with lard.

93

With guns slung over their shoulders and fragmentation grenades dangling from their belts, partisan troops tramp through a forest on their way to battle.

HIT-AND-RUN TACTICS TO CRIPPLE THE ENEMY

The partisans fought with whatever weapons they could lay hands on. They hurled handmade Molotov cocktails—bottles of gasoline—at trucks. They raided German convoys and supply dumps and scavenged weapons from battlefields.

Stealth, deception and surprise were the hallmarks of their operations. Many an enemy motorcyclist was toppled by a wire strung across the road. German tanks hiding in the woods sometimes found themselves ringed with flames when partisans set fire to the trees. And on at least one occasion, as enemy vehicles rumbled over a bridge, it collapsed; the partisans had sawed through its beams.

While comrades stand guard, partisans mine a railroad track located near Moscow. One uses a knife to hollow out a space underneath a rail, where a companion will place the packet of explosives that he is holding.

A partisan adds a fuse to explosives fastened under the supports of a bridge, while a friend keeps a lookout for Germans. Blowing up bridges to disrupt supply lines was one of the partisans' most effective tactics.

A partisan raiding party flees after setting fire to a freight train and smashing a railroad switch at a German Army supply station. The railroad switch (foreground) was a high-priority target because it was difficult to repair.

Always on the lookout for weapons, a partisan on the attack grabs a machine gun from a dead German while advancing with other members of his detachment.

An elderly Russian partisan who was captured by German soldiers and bound to poles attracts sympathetic looks from people passing by on a busy street.

THE GRIM FATE OF CAPTURED PARTISANS

The Germans reserved a special hatred for the partisans. They built gallows in each village, a gaunt reminder of the fate awaiting those who resisted them. But public hanging was merciful compared to the tortures accorded some captives. The Germans broke their fingers, burned the soles of their feet, and even amputated women's breasts, before finishing off the maimed and dying with a bullet or noose.

Anybody under suspicion of even giving help to the partisans stood in danger of a horrible death. In one pro-partisan town the Germans set every house on fire and kept every window and door under gunfire to guarantee that none of the inhabitants would come out alive. Often the Germans accused innocent civilians of being partisans or partisan-supporters and ruthlessly slaughtered them. Hitler approved. "This partisan war has its advantages," he told his associates. "It gives us a chance to exterminate whoever opposes us."

Germans parade three Belorussians through the streets (top), forcing one to carry a sign that declares in German and Russian, "We are partisans who have shot at German soldiers." Led to the scaffold, the condemned are hanged while their executioners coldly look on.

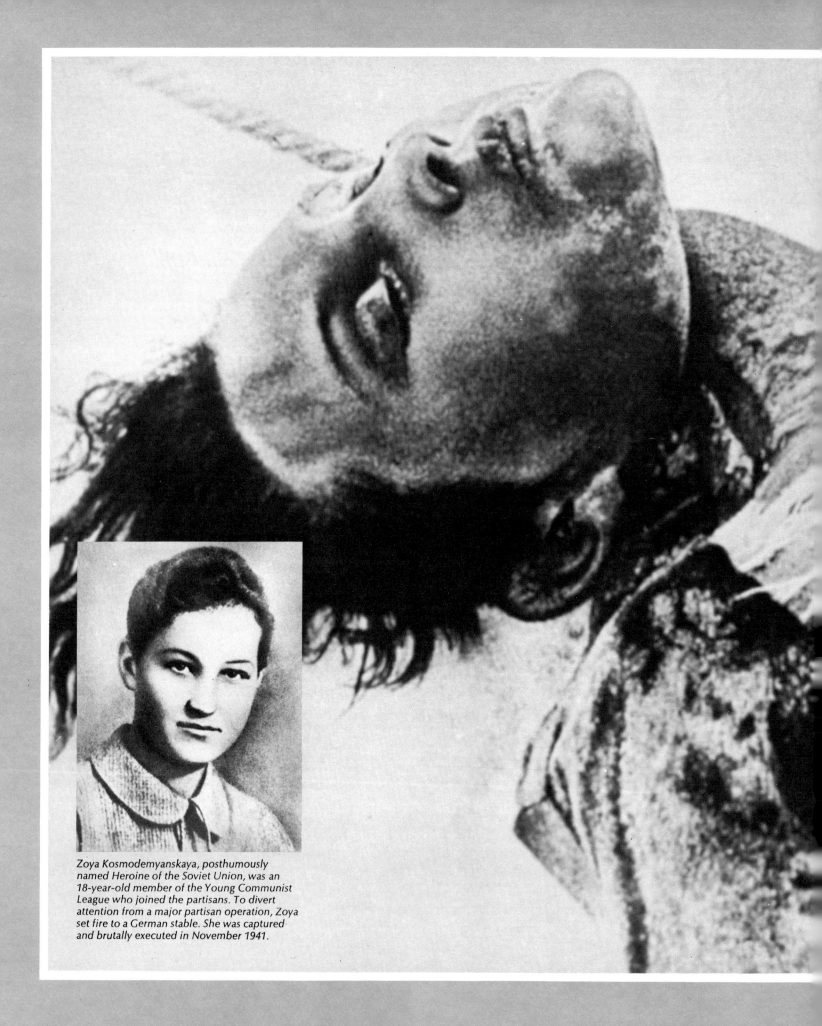

Zoya Kosmodemyanskaya, posthumously named Heroine of the Soviet Union, was an 18-year-old member of the Young Communist League who joined the partisans. To divert attention from a major partisan operation, Zoya set fire to a German stable. She was captured and brutally executed in November 1941.

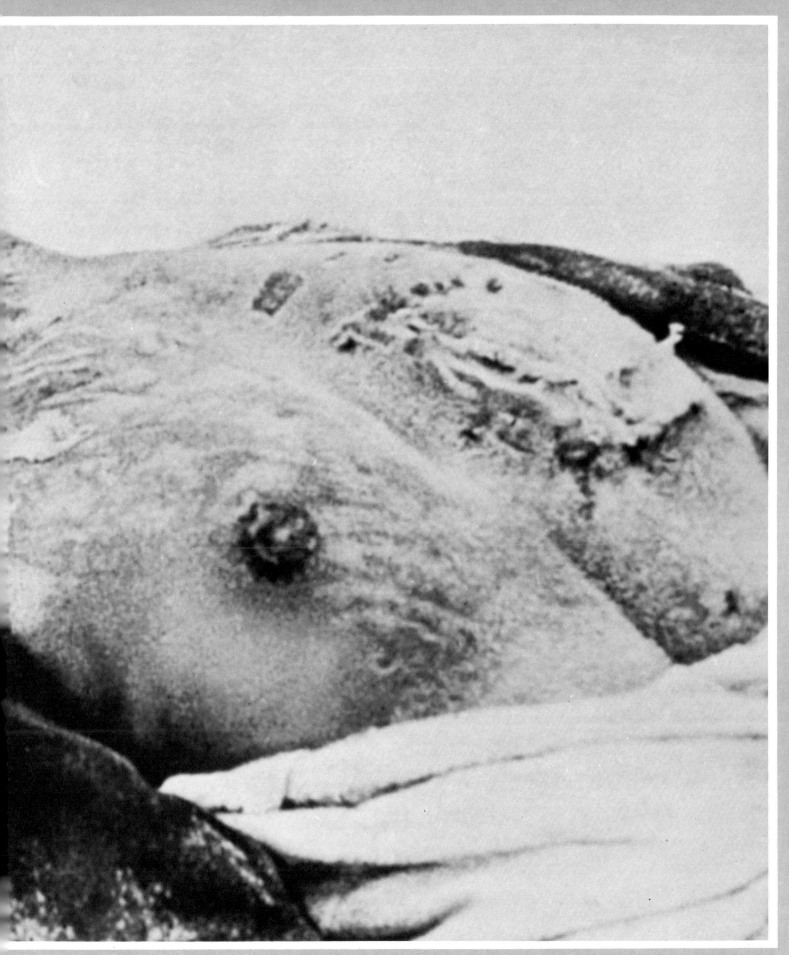

The corpse of partisan Zoya Kosmodemyanskaya, who was tortured, mutilated and hanged, lies frozen in the snow in the village of Petrishchevo near Moscow.

3

On September 4, 1941, Stalin sent a message to Churchill: the enemy was at the gates of Leningrad. Stalin did not tell the British leader that five days earlier the Germans had captured the railway junction of Mga, 25 miles southeast of the city, and that there was now no rail communication between Leningrad and Moscow. Nor did Stalin tell Churchill that he was actually contemplating the city's surrender.

Leningrad, the old imperial capital (formerly called St. Petersburg) and Russia's most beautiful city, was a victim of geography and pragmatic military strategy. As the Russians retreated in a giant, contracting semicircle toward Moscow, Leningrad lay exposed to German attack. It was especially vulnerable because of its location on the narrow Karelian Isthmus, with the Baltic on one side and Lake Ladoga on the other. Finns coming from the northeast and Germans closing from the west could easily block its land approaches.

On July 21, Hitler had visited the headquarters of Field Marshal Wilhelm Ritter von Leeb, commander of Army Group North, in Latvia, and demanded that Leningrad be finished off quickly. At the end of July, reinforced by the VIII Air Corps, Leeb set out to surround the city. His plan was to outflank the Luga line, a system of fortifications along the Luga River southwest of the city, and connect with the Finns. He had 29 divisions; the Red Army, 15.

The offensive began on August 8. On August 13, the German Army captured the ancient city of Novgorod, on the main Leningrad-Moscow highway. The Luga line was outflanked, and the Russian defenders were forced to retreat in confusion. "One last push," Leeb proclaimed to his troops, "and Army Group North will celebrate victory."

On August 25, the Germans captured Chudovo, on the main-line railway between Moscow and Leningrad. Five days later they seized Mga, and on September 8, four days after Stalin sent his message to Churchill, they entered Schlusselberg, on the southwest corner of Lake Ladoga, 25 miles east of the city.

Leningrad and its strip of land between the sea and Lake Ladoga were now cut off on all sides, surrounded either by enemy forces or by water. After September 8, the city had no access to the outside except by air or across the lake.

The scene within the city was one of frenzied activity. Preparations for stubborn resistance had been going on for two months. With most of the city's able-bodied men al-

THE SIEGE OF LENINGRAD

ready mobilized and at the front, hundreds of thousands of women of all ages were pressed into working on defense lines; they spent the summer building bunkers, digging antitank ditches and felling trees across the roads leading into town. One woman who was 57 at the time later told of digging rock-hard soil 12 hours a day for 18 uninterrupted days. Every park and square bristled with antiaircraft emplacements, and guns were mounted on the roofs of the tallest buildings. More guns were stationed on the islands in Leningrad's Neva River, and warships in the harbor were armed for defense against the expected air raids. By August the Leningraders had prepared air-raid shelters for 918,000 people and had dug enough slit trenches to hold 672,000 more. But that amounted to only about half the population.

When Soviet troops captured some gas shells from the Germans' Army Group North, Leningrad's leaders warned the populace of the "vile means" that might be employed by "the Hitlerite bandits" when the attack came. Somehow, in response to this threat, the city managed to issue gas masks to most of the inhabitants.

The mobilization was not without the expected bureaucratic foul-ups. At one point even the production of Molotov cocktails was hampered while the Leningrad authorities waited for Moscow's State Defense Committee to issue a permit for a Leningrad bottling plant to convert to a different type of bottle. But the worst snarl involved the city's children. Trainloads of them had been evacuated from Leningrad in June and July—to such cities as Pskov and Novgorod, in the southwest, in the path of the advancing Germans. Even while enemy attacks on the rail lines were killing some of the youngsters, the authorities continued mindlessly to transport more of them in the same direction. Finally most were brought back to Leningrad, and eventually trains were found to take the children east to Kirov and Sverdlovsk. Even then, they were often delayed on sidings for days, while their parents worried about where their children were and what their destination was. When the Germans reached the outskirts of Leningrad in late summer, there were still nearly half a million children in the city.

There had also been an attempt to evacuate the older citizens of Leningrad, the "useless mouths" who could not be counted on to help defend the city. This project, too, was a near disaster. A Soviet official later described the mess: "They are assembled, loaded into railway cars, and sent ten to twelve kilometers to Sortirovachnaya or Rybatskaya, or somewhere else, where the trains remain standing on the track, eight to ten trains at once. They stand three days, five, a week, waiting to be sent on at any moment; the people cannot get in touch with their relatives, who imagine that they have departed long since."

Even in the face of imminent attack, many Leningraders did not want to leave; they considered it bad form. The official History of the Great Patriotic War of the Soviet Union admits that such misplaced patriotism was actually encouraged by the authorities. "You often heard officials saying, 'Our people are ready to dig trenches right up to the front line, but they don't want to leave Leningrad.' " Many Leningraders referred to evacuees as "rats." When one Jewish family, concerned over accounts of the Germans' anti-Semitic atrocities, appealed to the Leningrad authorities for evacuation permits, all of the members were arrested on the ground that they were "spreading defeatist rumors by saying that the city would be captured by the Germans."

What evacuation there was did little to ameliorate Leningrad's plight; as fast as people departed they were replaced by refugees flooding into the city ahead of the advancing Germans in the west and the Finnish Army in the north.

Leningrad's leaders were concerned about a possible fifth column within the city. Indeed, Leningrad, like Moscow, did have its German sympathizers—or, more accurately, enemies of Communism. A woman wrote in her diary: "Is our liberation truly approaching? No matter what the Germans are like—it cannot be worse. . . . Forgive me, God!" Under the circumstances it was no surprise that many Leningraders developed an obsession with "traitors." Among other things it was widely believed that the city was full of enemy agents firing flares into the night sky to guide the Luftwaffe. In fact, what the people were seeing was Soviet antiaircraft fire.

As the Germans drew closer, Leningrad's Chief of Staff, General D. N. Nikishev, complained to the Red Army Chief of the General Staff, Boris M. Shaposhnikov, that he had no reserves and that even the smallest German breakthrough could be dealt with only haphazardly. On August 20, Andrei A. Zhdanov, Leningrad's Communist Party leader, announced that the whole population would be given elementary training in grenade throwing and street fighting. "Either the workers of Leningrad will be turned into slaves, with the best of them exterminated," he declared, "or we shall turn the city into the fascists' graveyard." Plans were made to defend the city street by street, house by house.

There was only one contingency the Leningraders had not provided for—and that was the very one that Hitler had decided on: a siege.

In early July, as the German blitzkrieg stormed across Russia, Colonel General Halder had recorded in his diary that "it is the Führer's firm decision to level Moscow and Leningrad and make them uninhabitable, so as to relieve us of the necessity of having to feed the populations through the winter." Accordingly, as the Germans closed in on the city Hitler decided that he would not follow the normal practice of accepting its surrender and occupying it militarily.

He and his generals considered various other possibilities: perhaps sealing off Leningrad with an electric fence and machine-gun posts, evacuating the children and old people and allowing the rest to starve, then destroying the city and turning over the area to the Finns.

Finally, on August 12, Hitler issued a directive to Army Group North to encircle Leningrad and link up with the Finns coming down from the north. Cut off from all supplies, the city would be bombed, shelled and left to die through the winter.

The reasoning was coldly logical. A winter siege would mean at least one million deaths by starvation—and that would damage Soviet morale even more than the city's surrender. The German Army would be spared the casualties that a direct attack would entail and the epidemics that might be expected to follow the city's collapse. Nor would the Germans suffer the inconvenience of having to feed a

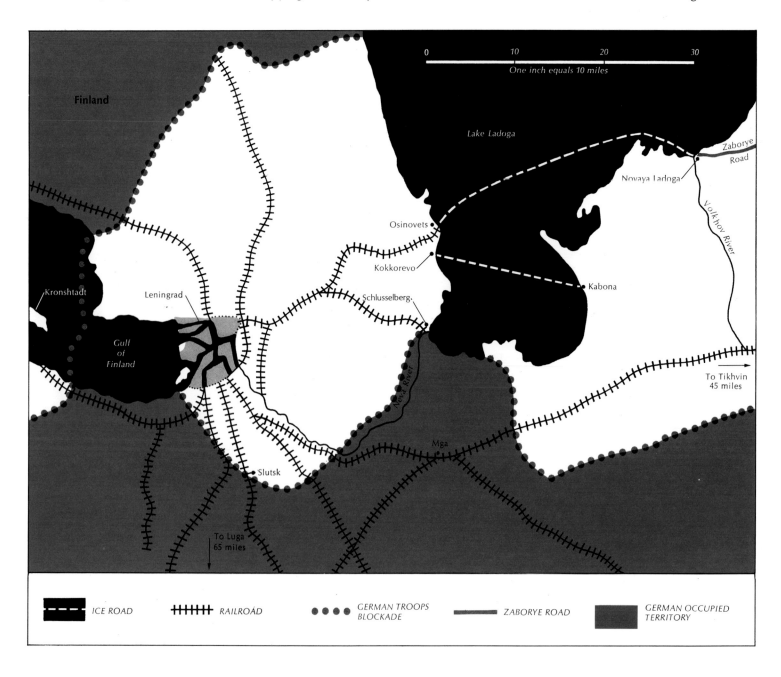

population of 3,000,000. Moreover, the release of large numbers of half-starved civilians into the interior of Russia in the spring would cause chaos on the Soviet side and help the German Army. It all seemed to make very good sense.

Leningrad, though girded for last-ditch defense, was totally unprepared for a siege. Only at the end of August did the Leningrad authorities become alarmed about the city's diminishing food supplies. In July, when rationing was begun in all the large Soviet cities, Leningrad's allowances had been no worse than those elsewhere. Workers received 800 grams of bread a day and 2,200 grams of meat a month, with plenty of cereals, sugar and fats. Restaurants were still open and offering such delicacies as crab meat and caviar.

But by the end of August, Leningrad's defenders discovered that, on the basis of current rations, they had less than a month's supplies left. On August 29, a telegram was sent to Moscow asking for emergency rations to be dispatched by rail to the eastern shore of Lake Ladoga, to be shipped to the city down the River Neva flowing out of the lake. But within a few days German troops were lining the south bank of the Neva, and the food could not be sent. The Russians still held Osinovets, a railhead on the western shore of the lake. Some supplies could therefore be delivered by rail and boat, but the piers and port facilities were inadequate to handle shipping on a large scale, especially with German bombers only a few minutes' flying time away.

Leningrad's Army leaders still hoped to recapture Mga and reestablish the all-land rail link. But their foe had realized the value of this prize, and quickly reinforced the vital junction. By September the Germans were moving eastward toward Volkhov and Tikhvin, both on the rail line between Lake Ladoga and the east. If either fell, there would be no way to send supplies at all, even across the lake.

On September 4, German artillery shells started landing on the city. After that the artillery assault became a regular affair designed to interfere as much as possible with the routine of daily living. By the end of November, the city had been subjected to 272 artillery bombardments, over a total of 430 hours. Before the year was out the number of shells fired would reach 30,154.

On the 6th September, German bombers attacked for the first time, and two days afterward the citizens of Leningrad endured a massive bombing assault, as wave after wave of Junkers dropped thousands of incendiaries. In the process they dealt Leningrad a crippling blow. The bombing attack set fire to the Badayev warehouses, where much of the city's food was stored. The warehouses were wooden buildings, separated from one another by gaps of no more than a few feet—exactly the wrong sort of place in which to store the city's sustenance. The flames spread from building to building until they covered the entire four acres of the depot. The flour and fats burned furiously, throwing a deep red light over the sky and attracting more incendiaries from successive waves of Junker bombers.

The city's fire brigade, totaling 168 units, was sent to Badayev, ignoring thousands of other serious fires; but the fire fighters did not accomplish much. Leningrad's entire sugar supply, 2,500 tons of it, melted and flowed into the cellars, then solidified into a hard candy-like substance; it was later sold to the population in that form. Almost every other foodstuff was gone. On September 2, six days before the air raid, the bread ration for workers had already been reduced to 600 grams per day; on September 12 it was reduced once more to 500 grams.

After the war, Leningraders would complain that they had received little help from Moscow during the early days of the siege. In part, this was the fault of Marshal Kliment E. Voroshilov, commander of the Leningrad Front. Voroshilov was extremely reluctant to send bad news to Moscow, for fear of Stalin's reaction. Instead of reporting reverses to the High Command, he preferred to wait and hope that somehow the situation could be restored.

Voroshilov had good reason to fear Stalin's wrath. It was he who had lost Schlusselberg and the all-important railway junction of Mga. To make things worse, he had failed to report either loss. When Stalin discovered what had happened, he demanded an explanation, and shortly afterward Voroshilov was relieved of the Leningrad command. Stalin was determined to make one last effort to save the city.

On the 8th of September, General Georgy K. Zhukov, who had been credited with slowing down the advance of the Wehrmacht in the central sector of the Soviet Union, was summoned from the Central Front at Yelnya to the apartment in the Kremlin that was the nerve center of Russia's defense. Waiting for him there was a reception

The 900-day siege of Leningrad began after German and Finnish troops fought their way to the city's outskirts and occupied the shaded areas on the map by autumn 1941. The Germans cut rail lines south to Luga and east to Tikhvin and Moscow. During the siege, most of Leningrad's meager supplies were brought to the city via the Zaborye Road to Novaya Ladoga and across frozen Lake Ladoga to Osinovets. Another route ran from Kabona to Kokkorevo on the Leningrad side of the lake.

committee that included Foreign Minister Vyacheslav Molotov, Stalin's aide Georgy Malenkov and several other members of the Politburo.

Stalin congratulated him and asked:

"Where will you be off to now?"

"Back to the front," Zhukov replied.

"Which front?" Stalin asked.

Taken aback, and now realizing why he had been summoned, Zhukov said, "The one you consider necessary."

"Then go to Leningrad," Stalin told him. "It is in an almost hopeless situation."

Zhukov asked only to be permitted to take along a couple of generals to, as he diplomatically put it, "replace our over-exhausted commanders."

"Take whomever you want," Stalin said.

On September 9, Zhukov flew from Moscow to Leningrad. Stalin bade him goodbye and said, "Take this note and give it to Voroshilov." The note bluntly ordered: "Hand over the command of the Front to Zhukov and fly to Moscow immediately."

The plane carrying Zhukov and his contingent came skimming across Lake Ladoga pursued by two Messerschmitts, and landed at the Leningrad airport. Chafing over the absence of air cover, Zhukov presented himself at Smolny, the headquarters of the Leningrad Front—and was stopped at the gate by guards who demanded to see his passes.

"I identified myself," Zhukov later wrote in his memoirs, "but even that did not help. Orders are orders after all." The new commander waited outside the gate for 15 minutes before word came that he could be permitted to enter.

Zhukov phoned Moscow in Voroshilov's presence and said, "I propose to proceed more actively than my predecessor." Voroshilov left the room in silence. But before leaving the city he said a few words of farewell to his officers: "I'm old and this is the way it has to be. This isn't the Civil War. It has to be fought in another way." He went to the airport and flew to Moscow. He expected to be shot. In fact, Stalin spared his old crony of civil war days, and Voroshilov became President of the Soviet Union in 1953.

Trying to assess the situation in Leningrad, a Zhukov aide asked Major General F. S. Ivanov, Commander of the Forty-second Army, where the front line was. "I don't know where it is. I don't know anything," Ivanov replied. Zhukov dismissed him. Other generals were bombarded with questions and threatened with court martial. Zhukov was a hard man, in the Stalinist mold. But that was what Leningrad needed: he bullied many of his more docile colleagues out of their despair, and tightened the city's resistance.

Leningrad's situation, as Stalin had said, was desperate. German planes were bombing the city, German shells were

DIARY OF DEATH

The poignant story of one family's tragic experience during the two-and-a-half-year siege of Leningrad is carefully recorded in the school notebook of Tanya Savicheva, an 11-year-old who lived with her family in an apartment in the heart of the city. As food supplies dwindled and German shelling intensified, death overtook members of Tanya's family one by one. "Zhenya died 28 December, 12:30 in the morning, 1941. Babushka died 25 January, 3 o'clock, 1942. Leka died 17 March, 5 o'clock in the morning, 1942. Dedya Vasya died 13 April, 2 o'clock at night, 1942. Dedya Lesha, 10 May, 4 o'clock in the afternoon, 1942. Mama, 13 May, 7:30 a.m., 1942. All died. Only Tanya remains."

Tanya Savicheva herself was presumed for years to have perished after making the last entry in her notebook. But later it was discovered that, like many other Leningraders, she was evacuated from the city in mid-1942. Sent to a children's home, she died in the summer of 1943 as the result of chronic dysentery that she had contracted during the siege.

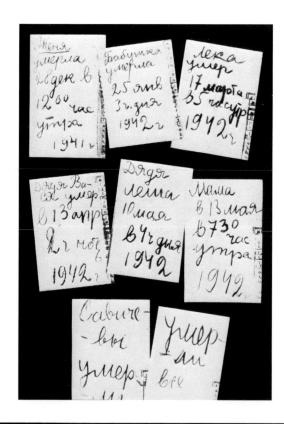

Tanya Savicheva, whose notebook (left) recorded the deaths of six members of her family, was survived by an older brother and sister who were not in Leningrad during the siege. In 1944 the sister returned to the family's apartment and found Tanya's notebook lying in a box with their mother's wedding dress.

falling on it and the panzers were within 10 miles of the center. One Leningrader later said, "It was horrible to think of it, but at that time one had to consider the possibility of seeing the Germans in the Winter Palace, and of shelling them from the fortress on the other side of the Neva." Leningraders would form up in one of the many queues for bread, only to run for shelter when shells came whistling over the city or planes appeared in the sky. On the way to or from work, one survivor reported, "one has to get off the trolley car three or four times to take cover in the trenches, hallways or shelters. . . . We waited, we prepared—but did anyone think that it would be like *this?*"

Leningraders grimly resolved that if the city fell nothing would remain that could help the German war effort. Explosive charges were placed under all bridges, factories, institutions and in ships of the Baltic Fleet. Whole areas were prepared for destruction, with the detonators connected to a single electrical circuit. On September 16, an article in *Leningrad Pravda* asked the question on everyone's mind: "Leningrad—To Be Or Not To Be?"

Every factory had its battalion of volunteer guards, though some had to make do with spades as weapons, for there was a shortage of rifles. Streets in southern Leningrad through which the Germans were expected to come were blocked with concrete obstructions, barbed wire and steel pillboxes known as "Voroshilov hotels." There was a 10 p.m. curfew every night. Police patrols were stepped up in the search for enemy agents, who were almost nonexistent, and black marketeers, who were numerous. The police also were on the lookout for forged ration cards and forged money, which were supposed to have been showered on Leningrad by the Luftwaffe to throw the city into confusion. The Luftwaffe did drop leaflets promising to spare the lives of those who killed their leaders and surrendered. But few Leningraders picked up these leaflets, because anyone found with one was liable to be shot by the patrols.

On September 17, Zhukov issued an order to the leaders of the armies defending Leningrad: from now on, any retreat would be viewed a crime against the Motherland. The penalty: death. Zhukov's methods were crude but effective (there is no evidence he ever carried out his threat).

Meanwhile, on the German side, the 4th Panzer Group had been ordered to leave the Leningrad Front; its new mission was to attack Moscow from the north. Now that Leningrad was surrounded, the city would be left to die, as planned. Halder predicted that after the departure of the panzers, there would be a stalemate on the Leningrad Front "until hunger begins to take effect as our ally."

Soon afterward, Soviet intelligence officers reported that German panzer units were moving south; tanks were being loaded onto railway flatcars and moved toward Moscow. Zhukov did not believe the reports. The maneuvers seemed to him an attempt to lull Leningrad into a sense of false security. But within a few days the tanks of the 4th Panzer Group were seen by the defenders of Moscow, and the rumor was confirmed.

To Stalin as much as Zhukov this was a surprising development, and it presented a new challenge. In the short term it meant that the pressure was off Leningrad. Moscow, on the other hand, would now feel the full force of the German offensive. Stalin had to choose between priorities. To divert forces to lift the siege of Leningrad would mean exposing Moscow. Leningrad was the birthplace of the Revolution; but Moscow was the heart of Soviet Russia.

On October 5, the message center in Leningrad's Army headquarters alerted Zhukov: "Stalin wants to speak with Front Commander over direct line." Zhukov went to the communications room and stood by the teletype operator. Stalin's message came over the wires: "I have only one question: can you get on a plane and come to Moscow?"

Zhukov delegated his command to his aide Ivan Fedyuninsky, and flew to Moscow on October 7. Stalin's chief bodyguard met him, explained that the Supreme Commander had the flu, and whisked him to the Kremlin apartment. Stalin's greeting was an abrupt nod. He was studying a map of the battlefront before Moscow. German panzers had broken through the Russian defenses around Vyazma, west of Moscow. They were closing in toward the Russian capital from all directions.

"Look at this," Stalin said, pointing to the map. "A very grave situation has developed." He ordered Zhukov to the front to assess the situation. "Phone me from there at any hour, day or night," he said. "I'll be waiting for your call."

Exhausted by his flight from Leningrad, and fortified only by a cup of tea, Zhukov rode through the night to the headquarters at the front outside Moscow, studying maps and reports by flashlight. Every time he nodded off, he ordered the driver to stop the car, and got out and ran along the road until he was awake again. By 2:30 the next morning he was ready to report, and called the Kremlin. Stalin was up and waiting. Zhukov told him that German troops were rapidly advancing toward the weakly held Mozhaisk defense line and were threatening to break through to Moscow. Zhukov recommended that every possible force must be brought up to the Mozhaisk line. Two days later Stalin put Zhukov in charge of the defense of Moscow. Leningrad would have to do without him.

In the short term Leningrad was saved by Hitler's decision not to attack; but in fact its sufferings were just beginning. Hunger and cold, not the German Army, would now be the killers. Leningrad's only lifeline was across Lake Ladoga to the east. On the opposite shore, at Novaya Ladoga, a railroad line still linked the city to the rest of Russia and was its sole source of supply. But it was a thin, vulnerable lifeline. In the few weeks from mid-September to mid-November, barges on the lake managed to deliver 25,000 tons of food. This was a rate of 450 tons a day, and to survive, the city needed over 1,000 tons a day. Still, it all helped. Dmitry V. Pavlov, the officer in charge of Leningrad's food supply, wrote: "The 25,000 tons were only a fraction of what was needed, but they enabled Leningrad to last out for an extra 20 days, and in a fortress under siege every day counts."

Unless more food could be brought in, however, the people of Leningrad would slowly die, all three million of them. Pavlov took drastic measures. On October 12, he had 3,000 party workers check every ration card: citizens had to appear personally with their identity papers and prove that they were the rightful holders. As Pavlov had suspected, some people were using cards belonging to friends or relatives who had left Leningrad and joined the Army or had died. His men were also on the lookout for cards that had been forged by Leningrad black marketeers, or printed without authority.

The Leningrad Military Council made virtually any offense involving a ration card a capital crime. A woman who worked in a ration-card printing shop was found in possession of 100 cards and was immediately shot. After October 18, ration cards that did not bear the stamp of the party checkers became invalid. The process revealed that nearly 300,000 unauthorized cards had been in use. Their elimination meant a significantly fairer distribution of food.

But by now the food shortage was so desperate that there were some incidents of violence. Older Leningraders were robbed of their bread rations after leaving the bakery. Some youngsters were so crazed by starvation that they would snatch the bread from others' mouths. A witness recalled a confrontation outside a bakery: "A young boy tore the bread from the hands of a woman and ate it up before her eyes. She beat him with her fists, but she was too weak to take it back and had to watch as her bread disappeared. She cried like a child."

A desperate woman described in her diary the deadly effect of hunger: "Suddenly I sat down in a snowdrift. I sit and I don't understand why I have sat down. And suddenly I understood . . . it was so horrible and—above all—disgusting: to die, but from what? Not from a shell fragment, not from a bomb, but from hunger. This idea made me so sick, so miserable that I jumped up—I don't know where I got the strength—and even ran a few steps."

Yet incidents like these were isolated. Leningrad had no food riots. This was partly because such actions would have been punished by death. But it could also be credited to the stubborn loyalty of the Leningraders, who understood why supplies were short, and were determined to hold out.

On November 20, rations were reduced to their all-time low: 250 grams of bread a day for manual workers—only about a third of the amount normally needed by adults—and half this amount for office workers, dependents and children. The Leningrad authorities tried to find food substitutes. Anything was considered, however unpleasant, provided only that it could be made digestible and that it contained calories, the fuel of life that the people of Leningrad were rapidly depleting. Several barges of grain had been sunk by German bombing near the western shore of the lake. Divers were sent down and the grain was brought to the surface. It was moldy and vile tasting, but it was nutritious, and it was used as part of the dough mixture in city bakeries.

Even weirder ingredients were employed, including sawdust. Cattle and horse feed was issued to humans; the

Pulling a cart loaded with corpses, three Leningraders arrive at the Volkovo Cemetery, littered with unburied dead. In the winter of 1941, while the city was under siege, the ground was frozen so hard that only dynamite could loosen it for graves, and wood was so scarce that every bit had to be used for fuel and there was none left for coffins.

horses ate only what humans could not digest—leaves and grass. Botanists pointed out that certain common plants were edible. The countryside was scoured for stinging nettles, which make a nourishing soup. Valuable bulbs disappeared from the city's Botanical Gardens.

All over the city, storerooms were searched and little caches of food discovered. In one warehouse 2,000 tons of sheep guts that had been stored away were found; they were processed into jelly, flavored with aromatic herbs to disguise the revolting smell and sold as part of the meat ration. People laid traps for dogs and cats, crows and sparrows, even rats and mice, and made soup out of them, often adding hair oil, vaseline or glue—anything for extra nourishment. The diary of a Leningrad woman recorded that she was existing on bread, salt water and cooked glue.

One man described a soup made from "gray cabbage"—a hard, wooden-like leaf that was cooked in salt water without any fat, and gave off an overpowering odor. Served to the employees at his power station, it filled the room with its stench. "One has to eat it without breathing."

Leningrad's death toll began to rise. People were dying of starvation in rapidly growing numbers—11,000 in November, 53,000 in December, according to official figures that were certainly lower than the true count. Even the workers with the larger rations were dying by the thousands. A factory supervisor said, "How many workers came to this office saying: 'Chief, I shall be dead today or tomorrow.' We would send them to the factory hospital, but they always died." The city's dirge was recorded by one resident in his diary: "Death . . . death. . . . Everywhere death. . . . In Leningrad only one thing happens—dying. . . . Leningrad is dying. Slowly and painfully. . . . The city is perishing."

Nobody had the energy to bury the dead. Gravediggers were too weak to hack holes in the frozen ground. When someone died, the corpse was wrapped in a sheet and taken on a child's sled to the gates of the cemetery. Army engineers, summoned from the front, dynamited pits for mass burials. And sometimes the authorities discovered

that the bodies had pieces of flesh carved from them.

This is the one aspect of the siege not described in Soviet histories or memoirs. But there were numerous reports from Russian sources indicating that hunger finally drove some Leningraders to cannibalism. According to the reports, it was practiced on the dead at first. Then there were cases of murder for food by starvation-crazed people. Finally, there were reports of human flesh being sold. Soldiers, the best-fed people in the city, reportedly were killed on their way home from the front. They started going about armed and in groups. One rumor had it that children were beginning to disappear, and parents kept their youngsters off the streets. Other stories spread that gangs of well-fed cannibals roamed the city; the stories added terror to all the other anxieties. Anyone who looked healthy was under suspicion—as were the little meat cakes that could still be bought for enormous prices in the black market.

As the year wore on, cold weather intensified the suffering of the people of Leningrad. The city's oil and coal supplies were disappearing, and by the end of September there was no central heating. Without it, the pipes froze and the water supply was cut off. The people were forced to take buckets and draw water from the muddy River Neva.

Parties of women and young girls were sent into the forests to cut timber, which they loaded onto trucks on a narrow-gauge railway track that they had built themselves. On the outskirts of the city unoccupied wooden houses, whose owners had been evacuated, were hacked to pieces and used as fuel for the city's stoves, which were now the only means of combating the cold. Soon Leningraders kept their overcoats on permanently, when they went to sleep as well as at work or in the streets.

But no matter what they did, they suffered terribly, and there was no relief from the bitter weather. A student described the "feeling of being cold" that plagued them: "One gets up with it, one walks with it, one goes to bed with it. It seems to wander around somewhere under the skin; it penetrates the bones and sometimes it seems as if it even enters the brain. One can't escape from it." Many people froze to death before they could starve to death.

Yet as the temperature fell during November and Leningraders huddled together in their frigid apartments, there were some who realized that the cold could be their ally as well as their enemy: the only thing that could save them now was ice—ice over Lake Ladoga, providing a solid highway to the rest of Russia.

The weathermen could not predict how soon this would happen. In some years the lake did not freeze over until January. That would be too late this year. By January nearly everyone would be dead. Four inches of ice would be needed to support a man or an unladen horse; eight inches would support a truck with a one-ton load. One day of 5°F. (—15°C.) temperature would make four inches of ice; eight days at the same temperature would make 12 inches, or enough to support a whole convoy.

Leningrad's leaders not only knew this, but had been making plans to use the frozen lake. The situation was growing more urgent every day. During the early autumn a few supplies had trickled into the city. They had come by train to Tikhvin, east of Leningrad, been transferred to a point on Lake Ladoga and then carried across the water on barges. But in October, a German force under General Rudolf Schmidt had moved to cut this supply line, and on November 9, Tikhvin fell. With Tikhvin in the enemy's control, there was no existing overland route. A few tons of dehydrated food were being flown into the city each day, but nowhere near enough for everyone; even this puny amount was reduced when the airfield at Novaya Ladoga, on the east shore of the lake, was bombed. And when the lake finally did freeze solid, what use would it be if there were no rail link to the other Russian cities?

Soviet forces, military and civilian, were mobilized for a great effort in the area east of Leningrad. There were two objectives: the recapture of Tikhvin, and the construction of a new road from Zaborye, a railhead for trains from Moscow, to Novaya Ladoga.

If the first aim was obvious, the second bordered on the fantastic. The "road" would be a 200-mile-long circle along forest tracks, through uninhabited bogs and occasional tiny villages. Yet, amazingly, it was completed on December 6. It hardly deserved to be called a road, but at least a path had been cleared. Several hundred laden trucks were immediately dispatched along it to Novaya Ladoga.

The trucks could cover no more than 25 miles a day. One convoy took 14 days to reach Novaya Ladoga and return to

Zaborye. In some places there was no room for two trucks to pass each other. There were steep hills and a slippery snow surface. On one stretch, 350 trucks became stuck. This obstacle course could never have done much to save Leningrad. Luckily, it did not have to, because on December 9, the first aim was also accomplished: Soviet forces under General Kirill Meretskov recaptured Tikhvin.

By mid-November the ice had begun to form on Lake Ladoga. On November 17 two parties set off on foot across the ice, roped together and wearing life belts, planting markers every few yards to indicate a route across the lake. The ice was thick enough to support them, but there were occasional unfrozen areas that had to be circled. It took the parties 16 hours to reach Kabona, 20 miles across the lake from Osinovets. A few hours later an officer set out alone on a horse. He followed the marked route and reached Kabona in four hours. Two days afterward a Soviet general crossed by the same route in a light car.

By November 20, with Leningrad's food rations cut to their lowest point, the ice was thickening; and that day a column of horse-drawn sleds set out for Kabona. They returned, loaded with dehydrated food. It was a start, but not the answer to Leningrad's problem. The sleds could transport only goods that were already stored in Novaya Ladoga and brought down by sled to Kabona. A sled could carry from 200 to 250 pounds. Even with a thousand sleds crossing the lake every day, only 100 tons would be delivered. The normal prewar daily consumption of flour alone had been 2,000 tons. This had been cut to the starvation level of 500 tons. Leningrad needed not only 1,000 tons of flour and other foods but also oil, guns and ammunition.

On November 22, motor vehicles were used for the first time on the lake. Sixty trucks crossed it that night, bringing 33 tons of flour to Leningrad. But the tonnage brought across the lake fell far short of the city's needs, and an unexpected thaw slowed deliveries at the end of November.

The Russians' recapture of Tikhvin on December 9 was the turning point, opening rail connections to Novaya Ladoga and other east-bank ports. But the Germans had blown up all the railway bridges, and it took the Russians almost a month to repair them. Rations were increased slightly on December 23, but the people were still starving. In January, however, the ice road began to fulfill its true function. A branch line was built to take goods by rail straight to Kabona; several more roads were cleared on the frozen lake.

At the height of its activity as many as 400 three-ton trucks chugged across the ice road every day. Not only did they bring vital supplies, they also helped by evacuating some of the city's residents—11,000 in January, 117,000 in February, 221,000 in March, 163,000 in April. Because of these evacuations—and because so many Leningraders had died—life improved for the others; there were fewer mouths to be fed and more food. On January 24, the daily bread ration for workers was increased to 400 grams; on February 11, it was increased again.

During the spring and summer another half million people were evacuated by boat across the lake. An oil pipeline was laid on the lake bed, as well as a cable to supply electricity. By March food was no longer a major problem, and thanks to the Lake Ladoga lifeline, rations could actually be set at a higher level than in the rest of the country. Some Leningraders still died from the delayed effects of starvation; but food and medical treatment were now available, and the death rate slowly returned to normal.

Nobody knows how many people perished that winter in Leningrad. The official total is 264,000. But this figure was laid down during the Stalinist years, when Leningrad's sufferings were minimized. Most Western scholars believe that the number of deaths from starvation during the entire siege exceeded one million, and that several hundred thousand more were killed by bombs, shells or gunfire. By contrast, the United States and Britain together suffered fewer than 800,000 deaths during all of World War II.

Leningrad was to remain besieged. But its supply corridor was now open for good. Life returned to something approaching normalcy. Newspapers resumed publication. Theaters and movie houses reopened. And the Leningrad Philharmonic performed Dmitry D. Shostakovich's *Seventh (Leningrad) Symphony* to a packed house on April 9, 1942.

The focus of war shifted to other cities—Moscow, Stalingrad. Only when the Soviet Army launched its massive counterattack would the Germans retreat from their siege lines around Leningrad. But not until January 27, 1944, would fireworks arc over the city, to mark the end of Leningrad's 900-day agony.

A CITY THAT REFUSED TO DIE

Before the Germans' 900-day siege, Leningraders build a wooden shelter to protect the Bronze Horseman, a statue of the city's founder, Czar Peter the Great.

THE STRUGGLE FOR SURVIVAL

When Hitler's armies drew a noose around Leningrad in September 1941, cutting it off from all supply routes except one across nearby Lake Ladoga, the inhabitants were almost immediately threatened with starvation. By early November the daily bread ration had declined to 200 grams for children and 400 grams for workers. Nutritionists estimate that a manual worker requires a minimum of 3,000 calories a day; the 400 grams of bread provided only 500 calories. Other energy-producing foods—sugar, fats, meat and cereals— were available only intermittently or not at all. To control scurvy, the city authorities had vitamins extracted from 40 carloads of pine needles gathered by the Komsomol, the Young Communist League, and distributed the resulting infusion to the population.

Some Leningraders dissolved cattle-horn clothes buttons to make soup; some chewed boiled leather, or made pancakes of sawdust and powdered wallpaper paste; others ate tree bark. A Soviet admiral gave his pigskin briefcase to a friend's wife. "In a few days," he recalled, "I received a box containing a small piece of fairly eatable 'pork aspic.'" The woman sent along the metal parts of the briefcase to reassure him that they had not gone into the aspic—and that she had not lost her sense of humor.

Hunger drove some citizens to terrible extremes. One girl pulled out her dead father's gold teeth to barter for food. Two children told an adult, "Papa and Mama died, and we and Grandmother hid their bodies in the attic, and now we have five ration cards for three persons." Yet there were also incidents of people sharing their meager rations. One man, who gave his day's food allowance to his wife, telling her he had received an extra ration as a reward for making grenades, admitted in his diary, "It was the first time I ever have told Elizaveta a lie about anything."

When the siege ended, thousands had died of starvation. The fact that still more had not perished is a tribute to the tenacity of the Leningraders. "If you make nails of these people," one proud Leningrader wrote during the siege, "there will be no harder nails in the world."

Tanks bearing the slogan "We will defend the gains of the October Revolution!" rumble through Leningrad's streets on their way to battle.

Bundled up against the cold, a girl drags firewood—the only available fuel in the city—past a large poster proclaiming "Death to the killers of children."

PREPARING FOR THE ATTACK

In the summer preceding the siege, the government of Leningrad mobilized every able-bodied citizen to prepare for the expected German attack. Over a million people were drafted to dig trenches, put up barbed-wire fences and build tank traps. Government papers were destroyed, and at the Hermitage Museum, the city's greatest cultural landmark, priceless art objects were packed up and shipped off to Sverdlovsk, some 1,000 miles away.

In the meantime, three People's Volunteer divisions, or *opolchenia*, as they were called, were hastily organized and sent to the front to help the Red Army stem the German tide. Most of the 30,000 volunteers were factory workers with little or no military training. There were not enough rifles to go around, and only a few machine guns and light artillery pieces. Despite scant preparation and equipment, the men were sent to the front. One division, drawn largely from the Kirov tank factory, was sent out four days after its formation. "It is no secret," the factory director said later, "that a large portion of the workers' division never came back."

A female construction brigade sets up concrete antitank obstacles around the outskirts of the city.

Volunteer soldiers from the Kirov Works march past an arch honoring Russia's victory over Napoleon.

Russian and Classical Roman vases, tables and statues clutter the basement of the Hermitage while awaiting shipment. The museum sustained 34 air attacks, but its most valued treasures—including Da Vinci's Madonna Litta and Rembrandt's Holy Family—were saved by the evacuation.

THE LIVING AND THE DEAD

During the winter of 1941-1942 the city of Leningrad was littered with corpses. Decaying bodies lay in the streets, in cellars and in courtyards. Hospitals were jammed with cadavers and cemeteries were filled to the point of overflowing.

German shelling caused a large percentage of the casualties. But an even more deadly enemy was hunger. Bread became so scarce that Leningraders became fasci-nated by it. "Bread can be eaten in different ways," one wrote. "One can eat it by biting off a piece, or by breaking off crumbs. Others cut it: some into thin, transparent slices, some into thick squares. All agree the crust is the most filling. The thoughtless ones eat the bread before they have even left the bakery, the others—they are in the minority—divide the ration into three parts: for breakfast, lunch and dinner. To know that one can eat one's own piece of bread right away, and stop one-self from doing it, is an act of heroism."

Corpses lie sprawled on Leningrad's main street, Nevsky Prospekt, as shells explode nearby. The Germans employed some of their heaviest artillery, including 420mm railroad guns whose range was 17 miles. Factories, utilities, and warehouses sustained the most damage.

One of the siege's countless casualties is dragged off to an overcrowded cemetery on a child's sled.

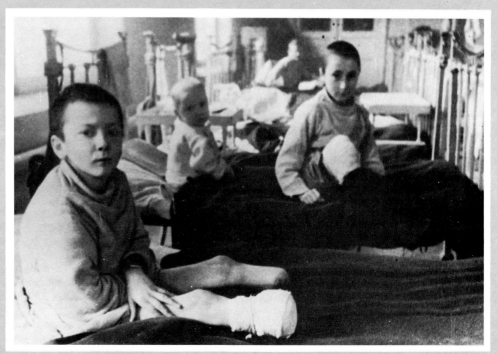

Maimed children—among 33,000 Leningraders wounded during the fighting—await hospital care.

121

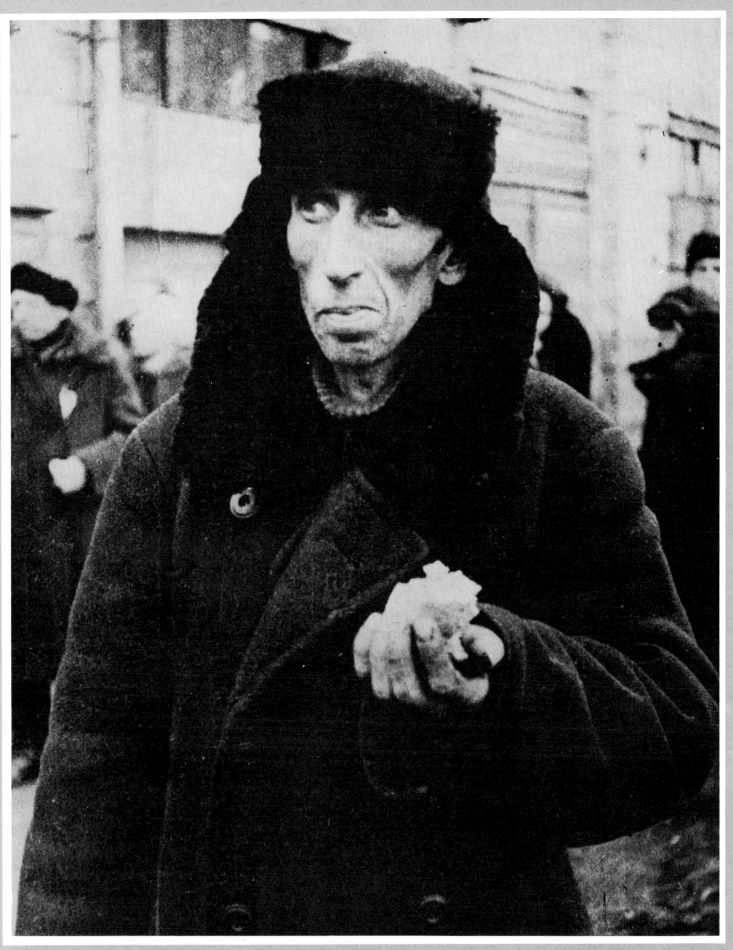

A starving citizen clutches his daily ration of bread. Leningrad bread was often made of odd ingredients, such as moldy flour, cellulose and cottonseed.

Anxious Leningraders eagerly study public notices offering clothing, furniture, jewelry and other valuables in exchange for food. In barter markets like this one, a grand piano might go for a few slices of coarse black bread. But by the end of 1941 food was so scarce that almost no trade offers found takers.

Too weak to walk, a starving and dejected citizen of Leningrad travels through the city streets huddled on a sled that is hauled by a female companion.

A PRECARIOUS LIFELINE ACROSS A FROZEN LAKE

The treacherous supply route over Lake Ladoga was the Leningraders' only hope for survival. Supply barges took 16 hours to cross from Novaya Ladoga on the lake's eastern shore to Osinovets, a port on the western side linked by a railroad to Leningrad. The slow-moving vessels were inviting targets for German planes, and dive bombers sank 24 of the barges in the first two months of the siege. On average, the boats delivered less than one thousandth of the food the city needed each day.

After the lake froze in November, so that trucks could be driven across it, supplies to Leningrad increased. But truck convoys too were bombed and machine-gunned by German planes; furthermore, the vehicles sometimes fell through the ice, drowning their drivers. The route changed constantly as fissures opened in the ice and nearly 150 makeshift bridges had to be constructed over them. In blinding blizzards drivers frequently wandered off course and froze to death. More than 1,000 vehicles were lost in crossing the lake, yet the supply line was maintained and in the final analysis was the city's salvation.

A column of horse-drawn sleds hauls sacks of food to Leningrad along icebound Lake Ladoga.

Workers at a port on the Leningrad side of Lake Ladoga stack supplies on flatcars bound for the city.

AN ARTFUL CALL TO ARMS

Under the banner of the hammer and sickle, a sailor and his soldier father in this dynamic poster exhort Russian warriors to fight with the old revolutionary fervor

USING WALLS TO STIR RESISTANCE

Four days after Germany invaded Russia, Moscow artist Mikhail Cheremnykh arrived at the Telegraph Agency of the Soviet Union (TASS) carrying a savage caricature of a German soldier, done in poster form. His work, which was promptly put on display, was the first of a series of Russian war posters that were notable for their visual power if not for their imaginative messages.

Only two days before Cheremnykh went to TASS, the decision to revive poster propaganda had been made at a joint meeting of Moscow's government-sponsored artists' and writers' unions. About 80 writers and poets and 125 artists, many of them well known to the public, were quick to respond. Their posters were soon being called "TASS windows," the name used during the Revolution for political posters hung in the windows of the telegraph agency. But as the months passed they were hung everywhere—on walls, on fences, even in homes. Within two months after the war's outbreak there were more than 100,000 in print.

At first the artists worked in Moscow. But soon they were joining frontline Red Army units to observe the struggle, living with the soldiers to give their posters authenticity. As time passed their work developed sophistication. The early ones were simple caricatures in primary colors, duplicated by stencils; later posters (by the war's end some 1,500 different ones had been created) were often multicolored paintings. The subjects varied from mocking views of the enemy to highly idealized portraits of embattled Soviet soldiers, sailors and partisans, as well as workers in factories and on farms.

Perhaps the most surprising development occurred after a November 1941 speech by Stalin; in it he appealed to Russian patriotism by evoking the historic past—making it possible, for the first time since the Revolution, for artists and writers to include great prerevolutionary figures in their work. Heroes of the czar's Imperial Army loomed in the background of posters for the Red Army, and soon the heritage of Mother Russia was being linked with the defense of Communist Russia.

Members of Moscow's artists' and writers' unions brush colors onto hand-stenciled posters. Opaque watercolors and oils were used to vivid effect.

БЕЙ НЕМЕЦКИХ ЗВЕРЕЙ!
УНИЧТОЖИТЬ ГИТЛЕРОВСКУЮ АРМИЮ — МОЖНО И ДОЛЖНО.

A brutally impaled tiger adorned with a Nazi swastika appears over the caption "Kill the German beast. Destroy Hitler's Army."

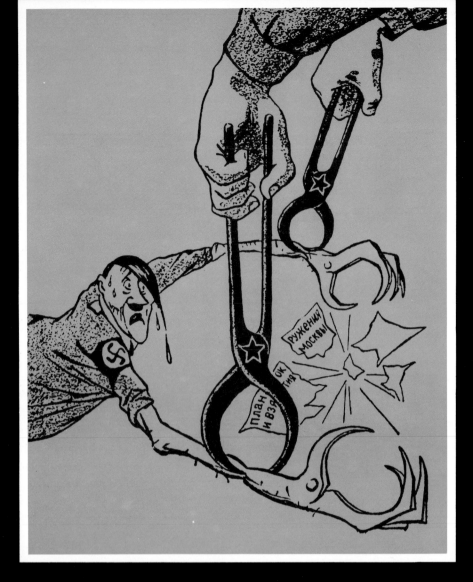

SATIRICAL SALVOS FOR HERR HITLER

The most popular war posters in Russia were the savage satires signed "Kukryniksy." The name was not that of any one individual but an acronym derived from the first few letters of the names of three artists—Kuprianov, Krylov and Nikolai Sokolov—whose collaboration won the Josef Stalin Prize in 1942 for best political cartoons. Hitler was their favorite target, and in their cartoons the Führer appeared not so much a dangerous and brutal enemy as a brainless fool. There was little subtlety in their humor: Nazi soldiers were depicted as looting hyenas and lice-ridden louts; Hitler's generals built careers on the skeletons of their own men; and the Russians outsmarted the enemy at every turn.

The strong hands of a Red Army soldier apply pincers to Hitler's own grasping claws. The German failure to complete the pincer movement that was to crush Moscow in 1941 inspired this Kukryniksy cartoon.

A Russian beats back a Napoleonic Hitler with a rifle butt while his historical counterpart repels Russia's would-be conqueror of 1812. The caption reads: "Napoleon suffered defeat. So it will be with the conceited Hitler."

"What shall we do?" asks a general back from Russia (right). Using his head, Hitler answers, *"Give me a chance to collect my thoughts."*

TAKING COURAGE FROM RUSSIA'S PAST

The poster artists often combined themes and figures from Russia's czarist past with those of the Communist era. At times the attempts produced some strange combinations, as in the poster below. Its message evokes not only the memory of V. I. Chapayev, a World War I partisan general who led Communist soldiers against the forces of the Czar, but also that of Aleksandr Suvorov, an 18th Century general, field marshal and prince. Suvorov routed Napoleon's army in Italy, and served Catherine the Great and her son, Czar Paul I.

"Forward! Westward!" to meet the invaders, this poster urges. Sailors figured importantly in poster art because mutinies on czarist ships in 1917 had sparked the Bolshevik Revolution.

The red star of Communism on these soldiers' helmets is joined with an appeal to "the grandsons of Suvorov, the children of Chapayev," Russian heroes

ПОД ЗНАМЕНЕМ ЛЕНИНА
— ВПЕРЕД К ПОБЕДЕ!

HEROIC WOMEN ON THE HOME FRONT

Posters gave full recognition to women for their contribution to the wartime struggle. In 1940, before Hitler invaded Russia, the Soviet work force numbered more than 31 million. By November 1941, as men were drafted from farm and factory, it had fallen to 19.8 million. Women were called on to fill the gaps. By the end of the war, they held 51 per cent of Russia's industrial jobs.

A stern-faced peasant woman holds a sheaf of grain in one hand and a submachine gun in the other in a poster that was directed at the fighting men. The caption reads: "Soldier, answer the motherland with victory."

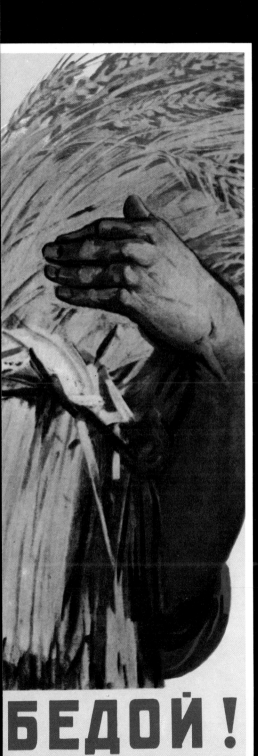

БЕДОЙ !

БОЛЬШЕ ХЛЕБА
ДЛЯ ФРОНТА И ТЫЛА

УБРАТЬ УРОЖАЙ ПОЛНОСТЬЮ!

4

As they lost battle after battle, Russians began to wonder what Britain and the United States could do to help them in their agony. Needed—and needed at once—were basic weapons and supplies that would enable the beleaguered Red Army to fight on. But so far, while indicating concern for their plight, Britain and the U.S. had done little more than to treat the Russians to flowery words and promises.

Prime Minister Winston Churchill, from the beginning, had seen the need to help the Soviet Union. Even before the invasion, he had recognized that a German attack on the U.S.S.R. would be to Britain's advantage. He knew that if Russia could manage to resist for more than a few weeks, the pressure on Great Britain would be considerably eased. And if Russia were to last, it would have to have help. This was an opportunity that could not be missed.

But what form should that aid take, how much could be given and how could it be delivered? And what would the public attitude be? On the eve of the invasion, he had announced to his dinner guests at Chequers, his country estate, that the attack was certain, and that Britain and the United States should do everything in their power to help Russia resist the Germans. Later, John Colville, his private secretary, asked Churchill how he, an arch anti-Communist, could bring himself to assist the U.S.S.R.

It was a reasonable question: As Secretary of State for War at the time of the Russian Revolution, Churchill had been unflagging in his support for the White Russian armies and passionately opposed to Bolshevism, which he described as "foul baboonery" and a "plague-bearing infection." The Russian attack on Finland in the winter of 1939-1940 had done nothing to moderate his repugnance for the Communists.

The Prime Minister's reply to Colville was unequivocal. "I have only one purpose," he said, "the destruction of Hitler, and my life is much simplified thereby. If Hitler invaded Hell I would make at least a favourable reference to the Devil in the House of Commons."

When news of the German attack on Russia came to Chequers the following morning, Churchill made immediate preparations for a response to be broadcast over the BBC. "I had not the slightest doubt," he later recalled, "where our duty and our policy lay." Millions of people in Britain and the United States heard the speech he gave

REACTION IN THE WEST

that night, translating his views into official British policy.

"No one has been a more consistent opponent of Communism than I have for the last 25 years," he declared. "I will unsay no word that I have spoken about it. But all this fades away before the spectacle now unfolding." The attack on Russia, he declared, was no more than a prelude to an attempted invasion of the British Isles and the subjugation of the Western Hemisphere. "The Russian danger is therefore our danger, and the danger of the United States."

Great Britain, Churchill said, had only one aim. "From this nothing will turn us—nothing. We will never parley, we will never negotiate with Hitler or any of his gang. We shall fight him by land, we shall fight him by sea, we shall fight him in the air, until, with God's help, we have rid the earth of his shadow and liberated its peoples from his yoke. Any man or state who fights against Nazidom will have our aid."

President Roosevelt's reaction to the attack was, though less eloquent, equally positive. The day after Churchill's speech, Acting Secretary of State Sumner Welles met with the President, and out of their meeting came a statement echoing Churchill's own: "Any defense against Hitlerism, any rallying of the forces opposing Hitlerism, from whatever source these may spring, will hasten the eventual downfall of the present German leaders, and will therefore redound to the benefit of our own defense and security."

But announcements of a policy favorable to Russia and implementation of such a policy were two different things. As much as the leaders of Great Britain and the United States might welcome the entry of Russia into the War, the sudden transformation of Stalin into an ally was not an unmixed blessing.

Of primary concern was the question of how long Russia would be able to resist. Leading military authorities in both Britain and the United States were convinced that Russia would be knocked out of the War within six to eight weeks, leaving Hitler free to turn his full force against the West. Was it wise to send matériel to Russia if it was only going to fall into Nazi hands? And where would the supplies come from? Much of the matériel that Stalin would require simply did not exist. Hitler's campaign in the West, the retreat at Dunkirk, the Battle of Britain—all these were recent events, and together they had depleted British resources. Only now were the British beginning to replace their losses with

weapons from their own munitions factories and aid from the United States. To divert supplies to Russia the British would have to make severe sacrifices at a time when they could not help wondering how soon they would again be Hitler's primary target.

Added to this was the problem of shipping. While the German forces in Russia could supply themselves by air, by rail and even by road from European bases, supplies from Britain and America could reach Russia only via the long Pacific route to Vladivostok and the North Atlantic route to Murmansk and Archangel. Moreover, shipping was in critically short supply as the Battle of the Atlantic exacted a mounting toll of British merchantmen and warships.

Direct military intervention on the Continent to relieve some of the pressure on the Red Army would pose even greater difficulties. British manpower was heavily engaged on the home front, in the western desert and the Middle East, in the Atlantic sea war and in preparations for the defense of the Malay Peninsula. A landing on the French coast would mean an encounter with at least four times as many divisions as the British could hope to muster. It also would require not only superiority on the sea and in the air but, according to Churchill, "a vast armada of specially constructed landing-craft," which were only then abuilding.

Even if the troops and supplies for such a military undertaking had been readily available, public sentiment in Britain and the United States was not yet fully committed to helping Russia. Stalin's ruthless purges and the Nazi-Soviet nonaggression pact of 1939 had left a legacy of suspicion and mistrust that was to plague relations between the Western democracies and the Soviet Union throughout the War. Beneath the pragmatic attitudes of Roosevelt and Churchill lay sharp divisions among the people of both countries.

In the United States, conservatives and isolationists regarded the war between Russia and Germany as a conflict between two equally evil and detestable forces. Senator Bennett Champ Clark, Democrat of Missouri, gave vehement expression to this view. "It's a case of dog eat dog," he said. "Stalin is as bloody-handed as Hitler. I don't think we should help either one." Senator Burton K. Wheeler, Democrat of Montana and a leading Senate isolationist, said: "Now we can just let Joe Stalin and the other dictators fight it out." Ohio's Republican Senator Robert A. Taft went even further. "The victory of Communism in the world," he declared, "would be far more dangerous to the United States than a victory of Fascism."

The pro-German stance taken by Communists in the United States and Britain right up to the moment of the attack had done little to encourage sympathy for the Russian cause. Ever since the signing of the nonaggression pact, the Moscow-dominated Communist organizations in both countries had done everything in their power to impede the war effort against the Germans, from disrupting production in factories to inviting soldiers to desert.

Now, caught off guard by the sudden turn of events, they did a swift about-face. Robert Sherwood, playwright and speechwriter for Roosevelt, attended a Fight for Freedom rally held in New York's Harlem on the day of the invasion. On the way into the rally he passed through a picket line of Communists who were waving placards condemning him and his friends as tools of Britain and Wall Street. When he left 90 minutes later the protesters were gone: the Communists had digested the news of the German attack, withdrawn their pickets and canceled a proposed peace march on Washington. The next day the *Daily Worker*, the anti-British, anti-Lend-Lease and anti-interventionist Communist newspaper, turned pro-British, pro-Lend-Lease, pro-interventionist—and pro-Roosevelt.

In Britain the Communists were not as quick to do a turnabout. They were still issuing pamphlets that attacked Churchill and his "imperialist war" when the invasion occurred. But soon they were darkly linking the invasion with the parachute landing of Nazi Deputy Führer Rudolph Hess in Scotland a month earlier and with Hess's futile effort to arrange a separate peace with Britain. They saw the German attack as "the sequel of the secret moves which have been taking place behind the curtain of the Hess mission," and warned "the people against upper-class reactionaries who will seek by every means to reach an understanding with Hitler." Not until June 25, three days after the invasion, did the British Communists catch up with reality and formally announce that they would support the government in its efforts to fight the War. Party activists stopped disrupting production in the factories and started calling for a second front—that is, for a British attack on the European mainland to relieve the pressure on Russia. It was a cry Stalin would repeat incessantly for months to come, along with increasingly strident demands for more and more matériel.

Understandably, official Britain was resentful of the Soviet attitude both before and after the invasion. Up to the moment of Hitler's attack, the Soviet government and Communist machine had, in Churchill's words, "shown a total indifference to the fate of the Western Powers, although this meant the destruction of the 'Second Front' for which they were soon to clamour." Up to the moment of Hitler's attack they had watched the plight of the Allies "with stony composure." Indeed, while the German armies were advancing in the West, the Soviet government was sending economic aid to Germany and attacking Britain and America through its massive propaganda machine. It would take a rare kind of courage and statesmanship—based on a healthy self-interest—for the democracies to come to the aid of their enemy of yesterday.

Stalin's willful, inscrutable, suspicious nature would further complicate dealings between Russia and the West. While Churchill was acutely aware that no substantial flow of matériel could possibly reach Russia before the middle of 1942, he tried, at least, "to fill the void by civilities." Stalin, on the other hand, seldom bothered with even a show of courtesy as he escalated his demands.

It was against this background of conflicting pressures, mutual mistrust, and doubts about the Red Army's ability to survive that Britain and the United States tried to determine how they might best help Russia. As early as June 23, a day after the invasion, Churchill had asked his service chiefs to consider the feasibility of a diversionary raid on the French coast, which might aid the Russians by compelling the Germans to shift some of their massive fighting forces from the Eastern Front. But the British military and intelligence chiefs were dead set against it. Churchill himself was reluctant to appear to be acting too precipitously. He could ill afford to launch a venture that might cost British lives without achieving anything.

While the debate dragged on, German panzers sliced ever deeper into Russian territory. Toward the end of June the Soviet Union's Ambassador to Great Britain, Ivan M. Maisky, approached both Lord Beaverbrook, the Minister of Supply, and British Foreign Secretary Anthony Eden to re-

Harry Hopkins (left), standing half a head taller than his host, visits Stalin in July of 1941 as President Roosevelt's special representative to assess the plight of the Russians. Hopkins, who spent eight hours conferring with the Soviet leader, reported to Roosevelt that as Stalin "shot rapid Russian at me he ignored the interpreter, looking straight into my eyes as though I understood every word that he uttered."

quest the opening of a second front to force the Germans to split their Army into two separate fighting units. His requests were rejected.

Churchill, moved by the plight of the Russians and anxious to find some way to help them, proposed that the British send a military mission to Moscow to survey the situation and coordinate British and Russian war efforts. The Russians, in turn, were invited to send their own mission to London. The Soviet leaders agreed to the exchange.

General Noel Mason-MacFarlane, a leading expert on German tactics, was chosen to head the British mission. Accompanied by British Ambassador Sir Stafford Cripps, he reached Moscow on June 27. Foreign Minister Vyacheslav Molotov immediately summoned Cripps and demanded to know just how much help the British were prepared to give. Would the British, for example, consider signing a political as well as a military agreement? Cripps, thinking it premature to discuss a political agreement, pointed out that the only bond uniting the two countries at the present time was their mutual hatred of Hitler and that the new relationship

between Russia and Great Britain was only five days old. It would be better, he said, to wait until they had learned to trust each other before attempting "to put our political relations in the form of a written agreement."

Then what about military help? Molotov persisted.

That, Cripps replied, was a matter to be discussed with the military mission.

The next day Cripps and Mason-MacFarlane called on Marshal Semyon K. Timoshenko, the Commissar of Defense, and General Georgy K. Zhukov, the Red Army's Chief of Staff. Mason-MacFarlane asked for information about the Russian military situation in order to give the British Chiefs of Staff some basis for deciding how to aid the Russians. But the Russians seemed suspicious of British motives, and were reluctant to reveal anything about activity on the front. It was Cripps's impression that Zhukov—who expressed no interest in Britain's own plight—"was out for all he could get, and without something with which to barter we shall achieve nothing."

On June 30, Molotov made a direct appeal to Cripps for a second front. Cripps politely turned down the plea. But an attempt was made to please the Soviets. On July 12, Cripps and Mason-MacFarlane signed an Anglo-Soviet pact that, among other things, committed the two countries "to render each other assistance and support of all kinds in the present war against Hitlerite Germany."

From the British viewpoint, the pact was proof enough of Britain's good intentions. But the Russians were still suspicious and mistrustful. In meetings to discuss military matters, senior Soviet officers treated Mason-MacFarlane courteously but coldly. They gave him little information about the progress of the war that was worth reporting to London, and complained continually that Britain was doing nothing to help them.

On July 19, Churchill received his first direct communication from Stalin in belated response to several messages of his own. It was a demand for a second front. The next day, Churchill telegraphed the Soviet leader to tell him that a British landing in France had indeed been considered carefully, but rejected as impracticable. The Germans still had 40 divisions in France, and the whole French coast, having been fortified diligently over the course of more than one year, "bristles with cannon, wire, pillboxes and beach-

mines. . . . To attempt a landing would be to encounter a bloody repulse," Churchill said. "It would be all over . . . before they could move a single unit from your front."

The truth was that Churchill could do little to satisfy Stalin or help the Russians. He had already increased the number of planes flying missions over Germany from 200 a night to 250 as a diversionary tactic. When he proposed sending a small mixed squadron of British ships to the Arctic to operate with the Russian naval forces there, his military chiefs were slow to accept even this modest proposal.

Still, Britain could not abandon a people who, in Churchill's words, "had shown themselves worth backing." In the last week of July, after Russia had been fighting for more than a month, Churchill informed Stalin that he had arranged to send the Soviet Union such essentials as tin, rubber, wool, lead and 200 American Tomahawk fighters, "in spite of the fact"—as he took pains to point out to the Russian leader—"that this will seriously deplete our fighter aircraft resources." Also to be included were two to three million pairs of ankle boots for the Red Army.

The inadequacy of Britain's aid was as embarrassing to Churchill as it was disappointing to Stalin; but it was all that could be made available at the time.

On the other side of the Atlantic the United States was coming to the realization that it must do something too. On July 8, the Soviet Ambassador in Washington, Konstantin A. Oumansky, had submitted to Acting Secretary of State Welles a shopping list of nearly two billion dollars' worth of weapons and equipment desperately needed by Russia, including 3,000 fighters, 3,000 bombers, 20,000 antiaircraft guns, plus large quantities of industrial equipment, aviation fuel, lubricants and raw materials.

American war production had not yet swung into high gear; the request was clearly unrealistic. Oumansky was assured that his list would be "treated on its merits" and would get high priority, but in private Welles conceded that industrial output would only allow "very modest deliveries to Russia over the next year."

The deliveries were modest indeed; shortages, slow bureaucratic consideration and interagency snarls caused delays that contrasted sharply with the speed of events on the Russian front. By the end of July less than seven mil-

lion dollars' worth of goods had been shipped, and it was estimated that no more than $29 million worth could be sent by October.

By July the situation had grown so desperate that Harry Hopkins, who was visiting London as Roosevelt's personal representative, decided something had to be done—and done quickly—to persuade the Russians "that we mean business on a long term supply job." Also, since all British and American aid decisions depended on an estimate of how long Russia was likely to hold out, it was imperative to obtain an accurate picture of conditions and prospects on the front. Mason-MacFarlane had been given little information; perhaps an informal, personal approach to Stalin might have better results. Hopkins asked Roosevelt to let him go to Moscow.

The President approved his request, and Hopkins, a frail and ailing man, set out for Moscow on July 27. With him he carried two personal messages for Stalin. One, from Roosevelt, expressed "the great admiration all of us in the United States feel for the superb bravery displayed by the Russian people" and stressed the need for clarification of Russia's most urgent requirements. The other was from Churchill. "Tell him," Churchill had said, "that Britain has but one ambition today, but one desire—to crush Hitler. Tell him that he can depend on us."

Hopkins had two long talks with Stalin; each of them lasting four hours. Like many other Western leaders, he was impressed by Stalin's powerful personality as well as his physical appearance. "No man could forget the picture of the dictator of Russia," Hopkins wrote later, "—an austere, rugged, determined figure in boots that shone like mirrors, stout baggy trousers and snug-fitting blouse. He wore no ornament, military or civilian. He's built close to the ground, like a football coach's dream of a tackle. His hands are huge, as hard as his mind."

With unprecedented candor, Stalin reviewed the military situation for Hopkins. He felt, he said, that the Germans had underestimated the strength of the Russians and lacked sufficient troops to both carry out a successful offensive and protect their lengthening supply lines. He revealed that even though the war had been going on for only six weeks, the Red Army was already encountering new German divisions at the front. To him this meant that the fighting was

The alliance of Britain, Russia and the United States prompted an outpouring of cartoons in the four countries that were directly affected. In the assortment at right, a British cartoon celebrates the alignment with a friendly handshake; a German commentary picturing Stalin as the Russian bear and Churchill as the British lion is sardonically inscribed, "I wouldn't want anything to come between us, or we might have a falling out"; a Russian cartoon, portraying Europe in chains about to be freed by the swords of the United States, Britain and Russia, proclaims "Europe will be free," while the American entry shows Britain and the United States unceremoniously being joined by a new bedfellow.

Great Britain

„Ich möchte dir keine Hindernisse in den Weg legen – wir könnten uns sonst entzweien . . ."

Germany

ЕВРОПА

БУДЕТ СВОБОДНОЙ!

Russia

Our New Bedfellow

DOWN WITH HITLER

United States

taking a heavy toll of German soldiers and that replacements were required. He added wryly that the Germans had already found out that "moving mechanized forces through Russia was very different than moving them over the boulevards of Belgium and France."

Stalin did not minimize the threat to Russia: the German Army was well organized and well equipped, with large reserves of food, men, supplies and fuel. However, he was confident that, while the Russians might have to yield more ground, they would be able to hold Moscow, Leningrad and Kiev until winter, when the weather would halt the German advance.

The Russian leader was frank in his assessment of the future. He felt that the outcome of the war in Russia probably would depend on how well supplied the Red Army was in the spring of 1942, when the fighting was bound to intensify. Repeatedly, he outlined for Hopkins the critical shortages that were plaguing the Army—even scribbling on a scrap of paper a list of armaments for Hopkins to show Roosevelt, and expanding on it as he talked. He needed antiaircraft guns of light and medium caliber, machine guns, rifles, aluminum for building airplanes, and high octane aviation gasoline.

The American Ambassador in Moscow, Laurence A. Steinhardt, cabled Washington with a preliminary report on Hopkins' talks. On August 1, Roosevelt brought up the whole question of aid at a lengthy Cabinet meeting. Fuming over the administrative confusion and bureaucratic dawdling that had delayed shipments to Russia, he pointed out that as yet the United States had done almost nothing to provide the required weapons and supplies. Secretary of the Treasury Henry Morgenthau noted that the President "went to town in a way I never heard him go to town before. He was terrific. He said he didn't want to hear what was on order; he said he wanted to hear what was on the water." Wayne Coy, a management expert, was appointed to coordinate the Russian aid program. "Act as a burr under the saddle and get things moving," the President told him.

On August 2 the Administration officially notified the Soviet government, through Oumansky, "that the Govern-

ment of the United States has decided to give all economic assistance practicable for the purpose of strengthening the Soviet Union in its struggle against armed aggression."

Meanwhile, Hopkins had left Moscow, taking with him 90 pages of notes on Russia's needs and prospects, and a conviction that the U.S.S.R. would not soon collapse. His destination was the British battleship *Prince of Wales,* then anchored at the British naval base at Scapa Flow, preparatory to heading for Newfoundland waters and a momentous meeting between the President of the United States and the Prime Minister of Britain.

On the flight between Archangel and Scapa Flow, Hopkins' plane bucked heavy head winds for 24 hours and was fired on by an unidentified destroyer off the arctic coast of Russia. Hopkins, who had suffered from cancer at an early age, forcing the removal of a large part of his stomach, usually carried with him a satchel of life-sustaining medicines. But somehow the bag had been left behind in Moscow, and by the time he reached the British naval base he was desperately ill. Put aboard the *Prince of Wales* by a wallowing launch, he had dinner and then collapsed into a drugged sleep in the admiral's cabin.

Three days later, with Churchill on board, the ship sailed for the Atlantic Charter meeting at Placentia Bay in Newfoundland, where the Prime Minister and the President were to come face to face for the first time during the War.

Shortly after the four-day meeting began, the ailing Hopkins gave Roosevelt a first-hand account of his talks with Stalin. Later he reviewed the grave but far from hopeless military situation in Russia for the benefit of the assembled British and American staffs. Prompted by what he told them, the leaders agreed to set up a conference with the Russians as soon as possible, to review Russia's needs thoroughly and find the most practical way to meet them.

Ironically, the Atlantic Charter meeting contributed to a worsening of relations with Russia. Publicly the Soviet Union welcomed the declaration issued at the end of the session, which underscored the undying commitment of Britain and the U.S. to the "destruction of Nazi tyranny" and "the rights of all peoples to choose the form of government under which they will live." But privately the Russians were angry that it contained no reference to their country. They were also miffed that Roosevelt and Churchill, without consulting them, had seen fit to set out in the Charter ideas on how the postwar world should be run. Moreover, it seemed strange to the Russians that the American and the Englishman could find time for long ocean voyages while the Red Army was being battered. Active military cooperation from both the United States and Britain would be far more to the point.

In fact, Britain had already taken the first steps to provide such cooperation in what was to become an important but little-remembered episode in the War: a joint British-Soviet invasion of Russia's southern neighbor, Iran.

There appeared to be sound reason to bring the country under Allied control. Reza Shah Pahlavi Kabir, ruler of Iran and founder of the Pahlavi dynasty, was suspected of sympathizing with the Germans. The pro-German government of neighboring Iraq had recently been forced out of power and a number of anti-British Arab notables had taken refuge in Iran. Several hundred German agents were also alleged to be active in Iran, working among the powerful tribes and stirring them up against Britain, whose strong influence in the country had long been a cause of resentment.

Churchill was worried that an increase of German influence might threaten the important oil fields and the refinery of Abadan on the Persian Gulf, then under British management. He was also concerned about protecting the trans-Iranian rail link between the port of Abadan and the town of Julfa on the Soviet border. It could provide a fast route for supplies to Russia and one without the dangers of the northern supply line that cut through U-boat infested waters. Strong messages were sent to the Shah inviting him to oust the German agents. He replied on August 21 regretting that such an act was inconsistent with his neutrality.

Britain and the Soviet Union now concluded that they had no choice but to invade the country. The manpower to carry out the operation was readily at hand. A British-Indian division was stationed near Abadan itself, and other British forces, including a few tanks, lay across Iran's western frontier in Iraq. Russian soldiers stood poised on the border of Soviet Azerbaidzhan to the north.

Early on August 25 the British and Soviet Ambassadors in Tehran met with the Iranian Premier, Ali Khan Mansur, and told him that their forces were about to occupy his coun-

Royal Air Force pilots—members of a squadron sent to Arctic Russia to help the Russians forestall a German attack from Norway and Finland— are filmed by appreciative Russians. The British airmen taught the Russian pilots how to fly their Hurricane fighters, and when the mission was completed, they turned the planes over to the Russians for their own use.

try. Iranian security was threatened, they said, by the presence of the German agents. That morning a British infantry brigade landed at Abadan and seized the vital refinery there. The British then advanced toward Tehran. Along the way they encountered some opposition, especially near the easily defendable mountain passes, but barely enough to delay them. The Soviets came down from the north and linked up with the British; within three days the Iranian forces had surrendered.

Churchill rationalized the take-over with the argument that "Britain and Russia were fighting for their lives." And he cited the Latin proverb: *"Inter arma silent leges"*—In time of war the law is silent. The refinery and oil fields were secure; the German agents were under arrest; and the rail link was now available to transport supplies to Russia. Before the end of the war, some four million tons of equipment would move over its tracks.

In the light of the success of this joint British-Soviet operation, Churchill appears to have been taken by surprise when Maisky called on Eden again at the end of August to discuss "the danger of growing mistrust between our two countries." He pointed out that in the past two months his country had suffered 700,000 casualties and that—the joint Anglo-Soviet Iranian venture notwithstanding—Russia still had not received the kind of support it most urgently needed from Britain, a landing in France. Eden reminded Maisky that for a year Britain had fought the War alone, had been forced to concentrate on its own survival, and was now in no position to launch further ventures.

On September 4, Maisky went directly to Churchill with an urgent message from Stalin. Ignoring Eden's reply to Maisky, the Soviet leader called once again for a second front. Stalin was glad, the note said, about the success in Iran. "But Persia is but an episode. The issue of the war will not of course be decided in Persia." The Red Army had suffered severe reverses during the preceding week, and the only solution to the grave situation on the Russian battlefields was a second front capable of drawing some 30 to 40 German divisions away from the East—plus "a monthly minimum of aid amounting to four hundred aircraft and five hundred tanks." Stalin realized, he said, that his message would cause Churchill dismay, but what was he to do under the circumstances? Russia faced "a mortal menace" and might even suffer defeat without the requested aid.

Maisky reminded Churchill that for 11 weeks Russia had stood virtually alone against the German onslaught. The battle now in progress, he said, represented a turning point; how could Britain win the War if Russia was defeated?

Churchill, angered by what he considered a menacing undertone in Maisky's appeal, addressed the Soviet Ambassador—whom he had known for many years—with unaccustomed bluntness. "Remember," he said, "that only four months ago we in this Island did not know whether you were coming in against us on the German side. Indeed we thought it quite likely that you would. Even then we felt sure we should win in the end. We never thought our survival was dependent on your action either way. Whatever happens, and whatever you do, you of all people have no right to make reproaches to us."

As the Prime Minister warmed to his theme the abashed Ambassador exclaimed: "More calm, please, my dear Mr. Churchill!" Thereafter, the Russian moderated his tone, but he did not abandon his plea for an immediate second front.

Churchill wired Stalin that night, promising regular shipments of aircraft, tanks, rubber, aluminum and cloth, but re-emphasizing that "action, however well-meant, leading only to costly fiascos would be no help to anyone but Hitler."

From Moscow, Cripps wired Churchill that he believed Stalin's message to be "a perfectly frank statement of the situation," and confessed that he was appalled that Britain had not yet opened a second front. "Unless we now at the last minute make a superhuman effort," he said emphatically, "we shall lose the whole value of any Russian front, at any rate for a long period and possibly for good."

In reply to Cripps, Churchill dealt summarily with the Ambassador's call for a superhuman effort: "You mean, I presume, an effort rising superior to space, time, and geography. Unfortunately these attributes are denied us." He made it clear that he was sympathetic to Soviet demands and to Cripps's efforts to help Russia, but reiterated that "nothing that we could do or could have done can affect the terrible battle proceeding on the Russian front."

The pressure on Churchill to act on Russia's behalf was mounting. Newspapers suggested that it was only laziness or lack of resolution on the part of Whitehall "Brass Hats" that prevented an immediate British invasion against the "token forces" of the enemy in France.

But Britain's military experts still would have none of it. Churchill continued to press his Chiefs of Staff to explore every possible avenue of attack, and found them not only united but convincing in their opposition to any full-scale diversionary action. On September 6 a brief intelligence report stated: "We have examined major operations in great detail from Murmansk to Bordeaux. Nothing seems practicable without incurring a major disaster." The most the experts could suggest was a dummy invasion of the Cherbourg peninsula, and the spreading of rumors of another possible invasion of northern Norway.

The three-power conference that had been set up at the Atlantic Charter meeting, so crucial to the survival of the Soviet Union, convened in Moscow at the end of September. Hopkins' health had deteriorated and Averell Harriman, who was Roosevelt's special representative in Britain, was selected to take Hopkins' place at the meetings. Lord Beaverbrook represented Britain.

The two men met three times with Stalin. They found him moody and unpredictable. That was not surprising: Churchill, in his long telegraphic correspondence with the Soviet leader, had received "many rebuffs and only rarely a kind word." It seemed to him that "the Soviet Government had the impression that they were conferring a great favour on us by fighting in their own country for their own lives." This attitude permeated the Moscow conference.

At the opening session, Beaverbrook and Harriman were greeted cordially enough by the Soviet Premier and given a rundown of the military situation. But when they reconvened the following day, Beaverbrook noted that Stalin "was very restless, walking about and smoking continuously, and appeared to be under an intense strain." The British delegate gave Stalin an important letter from Churchill, and waited for him to read it—but the letter remained unread. During the dialogue, the Russian leader doodled constantly, "drawing numberless pictures of wolves on paper and filling in the backgrounds with red pencil." He interrupted the session three times to make unexplained telephone calls, even dialing the numbers himself. The Germans were attacking toward Moscow at this point, and Beaverbrook

surmised from Stalin's edginess that he had heard bad news.

That evening, Harriman reported later, "was very rough going. Stalin gave the impression that he was much dissatisfied with what we were offering. . . . He seemed to suggest that we wanted to see the Soviet regime destroyed by Hitler; otherwise we would offer more help." Once he turned to Harriman and said: "Why is it that the United States can only give me 1,000 tons a month of armor-plate steel for tanks—a country with a production of over 50,000 tons?" When Harriman tried to explain how long it took to increase the capacity of that particular type of steel, Stalin replied brusquely, "One only has to add alloys."

The Russian Premier was less obdurate and suspicious at the final session the next evening. Point by point the participants went over the list of Russia's military needs. By the end of the conference the Western representatives had guaranteed to send Russia about one billion dollars' worth of supplies between September 30, 1941, and June 30, 1942: 400 planes and 500 tanks every month; 1,256 antitank guns; 5,000 jeeps; destroyers and trucks, scout cars and barbed wire, medical supplies and shellac, food and raw materials; 400,000 pairs of army boots per month. The final arrangement had the mercurial Stalin, as Beaverbrook put it, beaming like "sunshine after rain."

Within the next two months 130,000 tons of supplies were sent to Russia, only a small part of what had been promised. Unwieldy bureaucratic machinery and the long, uncertain supply routes continued to delay deliveries. After the Japanese attack on Pearl Harbor plunged the United States into the War in December 1941, aid to Russia diminished for a time, but shipments picked up dramatically in the spring. By the end of the War the United States would have dispatched more than $11 billion worth of supplies to the Soviet Union, some via the northern Atlantic route to the Russian ports of Murmansk and Archangel and some through Iran, and some also through Alaska.

But in the winter of 1941-1942, the first flow of vital goods came too late to help the Red Army as it fought to save Leningrad, Moscow and the Soviet Union itself. In those critical days the answer to the German attack was decided by the Russians alone: on their own battlefields, using their own resources, and with scant support from the Western democracies.

TO RUSSIA WITH LOVE

Their fists raised in a solidarity salute, enthusiastic workers at a London tank factory hoist the Union Jack and the Russian flag over tanks they made for the U.S.S.R.

ALL HELP — FOR — RUSSIA NOW

A SUDDEN CHANGE OF HEART

In a poster published in Britain shortly after the German attack, a British convoy is escorted into the port of Murmansk by Russian fighter planes.

"Surly, snarly, grasping, and so lately indifferent to our survival," is how Winston Churchill described Britain's new ally in the War, the Soviet Union. Until the German attack, the U.S.S.R. had been, of course, an ally of Germany. But Churchill was willing to let bygones be bygones and to help Russia by offering all "we could spare and dare." Still, trust came slowly. After a joint British-American mission flew to Moscow in late September, 1941, to negotiate Allied aid for the beleaguered Russians, a story went the rounds about the Royal Marine who was shown the sights of Moscow by a Russian. "This," exclaimed his guide, "is the Eden Hotel, formerly Ribbentrop Hotel. Here is Churchill Street, formerly Hitler Street. Here is Beaverbrook Railway Station, formerly Goering Railway Station. Will you have a cigarette, comrade?" The Marine replied, "Thank you, comrade, formerly bastard."

As Russian defeats mounted, the attitude of Britons toward the Soviet Union became increasingly compassionate. "There is no one in this country," noted Mrs. Churchill, "whose heart has not been deeply stirred by the appalling drama going on in Russia." Recognizing that the Russian effort was giving them "quiet nights" by deflecting German bombers from Britain, the British demonstrated their appreciation in many ways. Workers enthusiastically got behind the government's call for a "Tanks for Russia" week, during which every tank and tank part made was set aside for the Red Army. A voluntary Aid to Russia Fund was established and people everywhere contributed whatever they could to buy surgical supplies.

In America—where a Gallup Poll published in July 1941, showed that 72 per cent of the people wanted Russia to defeat Germany—ordinary citizens and luminaries alike did what they could to relieve the Russians' plight. The members of a dressmakers' union pooled their money to buy X-ray units. Other people took up street collections. Thousands more flocked to pro-Russian rallies in New York and other major cities, and contributed funds for food, clothing and medical supplies.

An American official inventories sacks of supplies destined for Moscow. During the war, the U.S. shipped four million tons of food to the Soviet Union.

A sign on the tower of the stately Coliseum in London announces the opening of a new musical show, which featured the Russian ballerina Dela Lipinskaya.

Soviet Ambassador Ivan Maisky (at microphone) inaugurates an aid-to-Russia drive at the dedication of Lenin's former London residence as a city landmark.

A smiling Londoner models a fashion quirk—a hammer-and-sickle scarf.

The fad for things Russian stimulates a Briton to learn the language.

A dapper Andrei Gromyko, Chargé d'Affaires of the Soviet Embassy in Washington, addresses a Russian war relief rally that was held in New York's Madison Square Garden on October 27, 1941. Gromyko was one of 11 prominent speakers who pleaded that medical aid and supplies be sent to help the Soviet Army.

A gigantic "V" for victory dwarfs the speakers' platform at the rally at Madison Square Garden on behalf of Russia. Twenty thousand people were there.

Movie stars Cary Grant, Jean Arthur and Ronald Colman converse with a Russian military attaché visiting the studios of Columbia Pictures in April of 1942.

AMERICA SHOWS ITS SUPPORT

As Americans wakened to the plight of the Russians, a wave of sympathy swept the country. Rousing war relief benefits were staged to show support and raise money. A rally in Boston attracted 10,000 cheering people; another in New York packed Madison Square Garden *(left)*.

In Hollywood, writers turned out scripts about Russia, dressmakers stitched up Russian flags for movie sets, actors wore fake Russian beards, people gave Russian costume parties. Clothiers sold Russian-style apparel, a Chinese eatery became a Russian tearoom and the Ritz cocktail bar was renamed "The Volga."

Author Erskine Caldwell works on his script for a movie based on former U.S. Ambassador Joseph E. Davies' book, Mission to Moscow. Caldwell, who had been to Russia as a war correspondent, was one of many quick experts hired for films about the Soviet Union.

American stevedores load light bombers aboard a merchant ship bound for Russia via the North Atlantic route. The planes were among 15,000 shipped from the U.S. to bolster the Red Air Force. Also sent were 5,700 spare engines and more than 4,100 extra propellers.

A column of British Mark IIA tanks forms part of the force that invaded Iran in August 1941 and seized a rail line over which aid could be shipped safely to Russia. By V-E Day, more than four million tons of supplies were delivered to the Russian Army over this line.

The aid arrives: Russian tank crewmen, clad in winter camouflage, eagerly accept a wartime delicacy—chocolate—being passed out by a woman first-aid worker

on the Soviet Union's snowy western front. The candy, sent as a gift to the U.S.S.R. from the West, was distributed on the 24th anniversary of the Red Army.

On August 23, 1941, Colonel General Heinz Guderian of the 2nd Panzer Group left the Russian front and flew back to Germany on a singular mission. The panzer leader intended to confront the Führer and try to persuade him to change his battle plan.

Hitler's latest directive ordered the conquest of no less than the entire Ukraine. The troops of Army Group Center—the forces that had taken Smolensk on July 15 and been there ever since, waiting for the command to advance on Moscow—were to be redeployed. A few would go north to join in the siege of Leningrad, but a vital 14 divisions were to peel off for the south.

Almost to a man, the German generals in the field believed the Führer's orders to be a mistake. They wanted to move on and take Moscow, the focus of Russia's military, political and industrial might, and the hub of its road and railway networks.

This conflict between Hitler and his generals over objectives was not a new one; it had waxed and waned ever since the inception of the Russian campaign. In July, Hitler had restrained Army Group South from marching on Kiev—the capital of the very region he was now throwing so many of his forces against. In early August he had given Leningrad top priority. Now he was reversing himself again.

After so encouraging a beginning, the war was proving tougher and more costly in German lives and equipment than anyone had expected. By late August, German casualties numbered 440,000, with 94,000 dead. But victory still seemed possible. The Russian armies were reeling from the blow to Smolensk. The best way to exploit this situation, the German generals believed, would be to head straight for Moscow. A detour to the south was something they could ill afford while the finest months of the year were slipping away. What was more, such a detour would hardly give them the time that they would need to regroup and attack Moscow before the cold weather set in—and the Russian winter was known to be fierce.

The generals had some strong support in high quarters. Colonel General Franz Halder, Chief of the Army General Staff, and Field Marshal Walther von Brauchitsch, Commander in Chief of the Army, had—in Halder's words—"spent five weeks wrangling for the drive to Moscow." On August 18 the two submitted a plan of attack to Hitler. The

5

A CONFLICT OVER GOALS

Führer turned it down. But Halder would not give up. He went to Novy Borisov, headquarters of Army Group Center on the outskirts of Minsk, and there held a meeting in a last-ditch effort to save the Moscow scheme. To the meeting he summoned Field Marshal Fedor von Bock, Commander in Chief of Army Group Center, and the Army and panzer commanders who answered to Bock—Field Marshal Günther von Kluge, Colonel General Adolf Strauss, Colonel General Maximilian Freiherr von Weichs, and of course Guderian. Wearily, Halder asked the officers present what could be done to alter the Führer's "unalterable resolve." In Halder's view, one of the assembled should go to Hitler and, speaking as a general from the front, lay the relevant facts immediately before him. The lot fell to Guderian.

He was just the man for the mission. A Prussian, he came of a tradition that held that even the King could be argued with when a strong issue was involved. He already had an acquaintance with Hitler, having attended the opera in the Führer's company in prewar days. As a brilliant tactician in the field, he was well known to the Armed Forces High Command—and was considered by some of his Army colleagues to be in line for promotion to the High Command himself. To his further advantage, he was very articulate. If anyone could succeed in getting the Führer to change his mind, Guderian seemed the likely one to do it.

Guderian had no sooner reached his destination than he encountered his first obstacle. At the compound of gray concrete huts in the oak forest where Hitler presided over the war, Guderian was met by Brauchitsch who, with Halder, had worked out the Moscow plan. Now Brauchitsch seemed to have lost his nerve—a common experience of those surrounding Hitler. He greeted Guderian with discouraging words. "I forbid you to mention the question of Moscow to the Führer," he said. "The operation to the south has been ordered. The problem now is simply how it is to be carried out."

Guderian was shown into Hitler's quarters—a plain room furnished in spartan fashion, with not much more than an oak table and chairs, and a few maps on the wall. Flanking the Führer was an array of military brass. Taking his cue from Brauchitsch, Guderian began with some diplomatic temporizing. He told Hitler about the conditions at the front, where his troops had not had a day of rest since June, and where losses were mounting. In the face of Guderian's sobering report, Hitler asked him, "Do you consider that your troops are capable of making another great effort?" Guderian was ready with a challenging answer. "If the troops are given a major objective, the importance of which is apparent to every soldier, yes."

"You mean, of course, Moscow," Hitler rejoined, and then bade Guderian say what was on his mind.

"I described to him the geographical significance of Moscow," Guderian later recalled. "I tried to show how a victory in this decisive direction, and the consequent destruction of the enemy's main forces, would make the capture of the Ukrainian industrial area an easier undertaking." He insisted that once the Germans had reached the communications hub of Moscow, "everything else would be ours for the taking."

Finally with an impassioned plea "that all other considerations, no matter how important they might seem, be subordinated to the one vital necessity"—seizing Moscow—Guderian rested his case.

Hitler, who had listened in silence, was ready with a passionate reply of his own. He sprang to a wall map, gestured toward the Ukraine, and spoke up in his high-pitched, earnest voice. He said that the region's raw materials and agriculture were vitally necessary for the prosecution of the war, as was the industrial area of the Donets River basin; that the Soviet Union must be denied the oil supplies of the Caucasus; and that Germany required control of the Crimea, which the U.S.S.R. was using as an "aircraft carrier" against the all-important oil fields in Rumania. "My generals know nothing about the economic aspects of war," he exclaimed.

Bread, industry, oil and a gateway farther into the east—these were the fruits of conquest that Hitler lusted after. In the view of the officers in the field—who would have to execute the conquest for him—the Führer was putting the cart before the horse; economic considerations were academic until the enemy's nerve center was disabled, and that meant seizing Moscow first.

When the meeting finally came to an end at midnight, Hitler's view prevailed. The only one surprised was Halder, who had been absent from the meeting; when he heard its outcome, he complained bitterly to Bock on the telephone that Guderian had let them all down.

Guderian took the disappointment more realistically. To his senior staff officers Kurt von Liebenstein and Fritz Bayerlein, he said: "There was nothing I could do, gentlemen. I was faced by a solid front of the High Command. All those present nodded at every sentence the Führer said, and I had no support for my views." Then, making the best of it, he added: "Now we can't go into mourning over our plans. We must tackle our new task."

With that he threw himself, and his panzer group, wholeheartedly into the drive for the Ukraine. The first objective was to be Kiev, and the tactic would be the now highly developed pincer movement. From the positions the Germans already held to the north and the west, the pincers would sweep around to close east of the city. The northern claw would consist of Guderian's 2nd Panzer Group—to be temporarily detached from Army Group Center and moved south—acting in concert with the Second Army led by Colonel General von Weichs. Weichs's force, like Guderian's, was to be borrowed from Army Group Center and lent to Field Marshal Gerd von Rundstedt's Army Group South. The southern claw would comprise the Sixth and Seventeenth Armies under the command of Field Marshal Walther von Reichenau and Colonel General Karl Heinrich von Stülpnagel respectively, and the 1st Panzer Group under Colonel General Ewald von Kleist.

All together the forces assigned to the operation totaled six tank, five motorized and 35 infantry divisions, or about 360,000 men. Against them, the Germans estimated, the Russians had five armies of about 35 divisions—about the same strength. These were under the command of Marshal Semyon Budenny, now Commander in Chief of the Southwest Theater, a hero of the Russian Revolution and for many years a particular favorite of Stalin's.

The drive on Kiev got under way on August 25, a blistering summer day. Tanks, trucks, wagons and boots threw up clouds of dust as thick and soft as flour, coating machinery and weapons, and choking the men. Nevertheless, Guderian's panzers in the vanguard made spectacular progress, capturing in quick succession the Russian strongholds of Pochep and Novgorod-Seversky, roughly halfway between

Smolensk and the objective. In two weeks' time they covered a distance of 250 miles, getting as far as Romny, east of Kiev. Meanwhile, Guderian's counterpart on the southern flank, Kleist, leading the 1st Panzer Group, crossed the Dnieper, breaking through a stiff line held by the Russians' Thirty-eighth Army at Kremenchug, 170 miles southeast of Kiev, and pushed on northward.

Once again, the Russians misjudged the Germans' intentions. They were expecting a drive on Moscow. "From the enemy's operation I concluded that with his powerful advanced units, supported by strong armored formations, he was engaged in an active reconnaissance," wrote Colonel General A. I. Yeremenko, who was commander of the newly formed Bryansk Front southwest of Moscow. The High Command had even informed Yeremenko "that Guderian's blow was aimed at the right wing of the Bryansk Front—in other words, against Moscow."

On September 11, Budenny, perceiving at last that the Germans were coming his way—and from at least two directions—asked Stalin for permission to withdraw from Kiev. Stalin angrily refused. "Not a step back," he ordered. "Hold out and, if necessary, die." But he had Budenny flown out, and replaced him with Colonel General M. P. Kirponos. Then he swiftly detached 28 divisions from other sectors of the front and threw them into the battle.

Three days later, on the 14th, Major General M. P. Tupikov, Chief of Staff to Kirponos, sent a message to Moscow saying that a catastrophic defeat was imminent—that it could not be delayed more than a couple of days. He was not exaggerating. The two claws of the German pincer were within 30 miles of closing, and confused and panicking, some of the Russian forces were trying to leave. Their motorized divisions had just begun rolling through the 30-mile gap, in long columns three abreast, when German reconnaissance planes spotted them. Now Guderian and Kleist stepped up their pace, hoping to close the gap. Two days later, they sealed it; on September 16, their own tanks —one column's vehicles emblazoned with a large white "G," the other's with a "K"—stood side by side at Lokhvitsa, 125 miles east of Kiev. Guderian and Kleist had forged the last link in a giant ring 130 miles wide around Kiev.

On September 17 the Russian defenders received Moscow's permission to withdraw—but it was too late. Inside

The expressionless eyes of mustachioed Marshal Semyon Mikhailovich Budenny, Commander in Chief of the Southwest Theater, give no clue to his jovial disposition. At a prewar stag party that was given when he made an inspection tour of a Bessarabian distillery, he shed his bemedaled uniform and mahogany-handled revolvers to leap into a wine vat with a bevy of naked young women. A favorite of Stalin, he was allowed to escape the German encirclement of Kiev and return to Moscow.

the ring, the trapped Russians fought fiercely—some without weapons—against the Germans. Kirponos was killed in the defense of the city, as was Tupikov. Lacking a central command, the remaining troops fell into confusion. Halder noted in his diary on the 17th that "the encircled enemy units are ricocheting like billiard balls within the ring around Kiev." Hundreds of thousands tried desperately to escape through the wall of tanks and infantry; those who made it—and only a few did—had to wander through the forest, futilely dodging German pursuers. Those who fell inside the city met a macabre death: in their ears rang the voice of Stalin, as recordings of his speeches, meant to encourage acts of bravery, rang out from loudspeakers that had been strung in the trees.

Not many Russian histories deal in detail with the defeat—partly because the debacle ensued from bungling by the High Command. The most compelling account of the

Russian soldiers' fate comes not from official records at all, but from a short story called "Through the Night," by Leonid Volynsky, who survived the battle. The hero—one of the Russian soldiers who tried to break out of the ring—makes his way with three companions along a road lit by the flames of two or three thousand burning tanks, trucks and cars. At length he is captured by the Germans, herded in with thousands of others like himself, and forced to watch while those identified as Jews, commissars and Communist Party members are pulled out of the ranks. "They were taken by tens and led to the side, behind a tree," Volynsky wrote. "There the first 10 men dug themselves a common grave, then a short volley from a submachine gun rang out, and the next 10 headed off to fill up the grave with dirt and dig a new one. So it continued until the end. All died silently, except one who suddenly fell with a heart-rending scream. He crawled on the ground toward the feet of the soldiers, pleading not to be killed. One of the SS men kicked him in the face, and knocked his teeth out, and he was hauled off to the execution ground, his bare feet dragging through the dust."

For 10 days such scenes were repeated inside and outside the ring surrounding Kiev. When the fighting finally ended on September 26, the Russian toll was appalling. Four Soviet armies had been annihilated, and two more had been almost destroyed. One million men were killed, wounded, taken prisoner or unaccounted for.

The Germans claimed to have captured 665,000 Russians, 3,718 guns and 886 tanks. Stalin himself, although officially silent, counted the losses of men and matériel a severe blow. He gloomily told British Ambassador Sir Stafford Cripps: "All that Lenin created—we have lost forever."

Hitler was jubilant, and smug in the conviction that he had been right—and who of his generals could argue with him now? His armies had torn a 200-mile gap in the Russian defenses. The whole of the Ukraine lay open to them now, including the Donets basin, where 60 per cent of the Soviet Union's coal, 75 per cent of its coke, 30 per cent of its iron and 20 per cent of its steel were produced. Beyond that rich prize lay the Caucasus, with its oil deposits.

Field Marshal von Rundstedt's Army Group South wasted no time in going after these. On October 24 his Sixth Army under Field Marshal von Reichenau captured the great industrial city of Kharkov, where Russian tanks were being produced. Five days afterward the Eleventh Army under General Erich von Manstein smashed into the Crimea; by mid-November it had occupied the entire peninsula except for the city of Sevastopol. On the 20th, Kleist's 1st Panzers took Rostov, a major port on the Don, just 25 miles from the point where the river empties into the Sea of Azov.

Meanwhile, Guderian and his colleagues in Army Group Center got the orders they had wanted so badly. The shooting had hardly ended in Kiev when Hitler issued a new directive that was to thrust them toward Moscow. "At last the preliminary conditions have been achieved to enable us to carry out the final powerful blow which is going to lead to the annihilation of the enemy before winter," it stated. "Today begins the last, the great, battle of this year." Called Operation *Typhoon,* the undertaking was to begin October 2; as always, Hitler expected a swift knockout.

What has come to be known as the Battle of Moscow actually consisted of several battles. The action extended over a period of months, across a front 250 miles wide and 180 miles deep, and involved dozens of cities and villages that were strung in two broad concentric semicircles lying to the west of Moscow.

For the monumental assault, Bock's Army Group Center was assigned the lion's share of the German forces in Russia. To be sure, the divisions were now understrength; the panzer formations were short of tanks and the men themselves were tired from the heavy fighting that they had endured in the detour to the south. Nevertheless, the forces came to a formidable total of 69 divisions. Returning to Bock's command from their detour into the Ukraine were Guderian with his panzer group—soon to be designated the Second Panzer Army—and Weichs with his Second Army. And removed from the north—Leningrad having been left to starve under siege—was the 4th Panzer Group, under the command of Colonel General Erich Hoepner. In addition there was to be heavy air support from the Second Air Force under Field Marshal Albert Kesselring, who had some 1,500 planes at his disposal.

Against these forces the Russians set 15 infantry armies with more than half a million men. But a pitiful lot they appeared to be, for the Red Army had been so heavily

drained of men that the commanders now had to make do with what they could get. Some of the soldiers were illiterate and unable to read instructions. They were also ill-equipped. One typical battalion of 675 men had only 295 rifles, 120 hand grenades, nine machine guns, 145 revolvers and pistols, and 2,000 Molotov cocktails at its disposal. Everything seemed to favor another German triumph—even the "sparkling fall weather" that the meticulous Halder noted in his diary.

The German plan was to capture the Soviet capital by quickly knocking out the fortified outlying cities and towns

In a belfry high above the ancient city of Kiev—called the Jerusalem of Russia—two German soldiers pull the heavy ropes of a steeple bell to celebrate the capture of the Ukrainian capital. After the city fell, the Germans found 10,000 Russian mines in churches, museums, hotels, telegraph offices, stores, houses and the railroad station. Those that the Germans did not find set off fires that blazed for five days.

that served as communications centers for the Russian armies that were defending Moscow, and then pursuing the Russians right into the capital. Two big targets along the way—Vyazma, situated between Smolensk and the capital, and Bryansk, located roughly halfway between Kiev and Moscow—were to be attacked at the same time. The 3rd and 4th Panzer Groups were charged with converging on Vyazma and encircling the Russians who were defending it, and Guderian was given the assignment of going after the forces at Bryansk.

Guderian was the first to advance. The excursion to the Ukraine had put him at a distance of more than 150 miles from the army he was rejoining, and he had to move quickly if his panzers were to do their job. On September 30, getting a two-day jump on his fellow commanders to the north, he performed the formidable feat of swinging his 16 divisions a full 90 degrees left.

Advancing to the northeast from the Ukraine, Guderian covered 50 miles on the first day and nearly 100 more during the next three, capturing in his advance the city of Orel, an industrial center that manufactured canned food and felt boots. So unprepared were the Russians for this sudden blow that Guderian's tanks rolled into town right in the path of a streetcar that was laden with civilians who were going home for their noonday dinner.

The only less-than-satisfactory note Halder made in his diary as the drive on Moscow rolled along was the observation on October 7 that the "Second Panzer Army is hampered in its movements by bad weather"—rain mixed with melting snow. But Halder did not consider that development sufficiently worrisome to linger over. On the same day, Guderian, looking ahead with less optimism, requisitioned from headquarters a supply of winter clothing for his men; he was told not to make further "unnecessary requests" of this sort.

There seemed every reason to believe that Operation Typhoon, like the campaign in the Ukraine, would be over soon. In one week's time Hoepner tore the Russian line in two between the strongholds of Vyazma and Bryansk, two of Guderian's panzer divisions converged on Bryansk, and Colonel General Hermann Hoth's 3rd Panzers encircled Vyazma. On the 14th, Hoth crossed the Volga at Kalinin—cutting the all-important Leningrad-Moscow railway—and

took up a position 70 miles northwest of Moscow. To the Germans it looked as though nothing stood in the way of yet another victory.

Inside Moscow, it seemed ominously so to the Russians as well. Measures that had been taken earlier to safeguard the city suddenly seemed insufficient to hold up against the German advances. When Stalin called General Georgy K. Zhukov back from Leningrad and put him in command of the capital's defenses, he ordered: "Organize the Western Front quickly and act!" Zhukov did just that. He made a quick study of the capital's defenses, promptly assembled 90,000 new reserves, and deployed them along the 150-mile Mozhaisk line, so called for one of its key strong points, a city 60 miles west of Moscow. Meanwhile, workers' battalions were mobilized inside the city, one for each of the 25 districts into which the city was divided.

Other measures seemed to betray the Russians' uncertainty as to whether Moscow could survive the German attack. The government began evacuating factories producing essential material, along with certain state offices such as the state mint and the secret police. The diplomatic corps received sudden instructions to move to Kuibyshev, 500 miles to the east. The university shut down, and so did the Academy of Science and the museums.

While this was happening, the government-controlled press began for the first time to let the people in on the seriousness of the nation's plight. On October 7, Pravda and other publications reported the Germans' advances on Vyazma and Bryansk. On the 8th they announced the fall of Orel (which had actually occurred on the 3rd). On the 10th, Pravda somberly stated that "the land of the Soviets, our people and their great achievements are in danger." On the 14th all the city's newspapers ran banner headlines—a startling innovation—warning of the attack; "the savage foe," one said, "is rushing toward the heart of the country." On the 16th, just after Hoepner's 4th Panzer Group had broken through the Russian line near Mozhaisk, the newspapers reported, without naming the location, that the defenses had been breached. Pravda wrote ominously that "the mad fascist beast is threatening Moscow".

Such words would be unsettling enough in any society; in Russia, where most government affairs took place in secret and news was carefully guarded, they were terrifying. Muscovites were accustomed to hearing almost nothing but positive statements from their officials, and since the beginning of the war they had learned to interpret all news in the worst possible light. From returning wounded soldiers and from the ever-flourishing grapevine they knew that the fall of Kiev, which the government had described as merely a scene of heavy fighting, had been attended by astronomical casualties; they also knew when Orel fell. Now, in the crescendo of grave announcements throughout the second week of October, they leaped to the conclusion that Moscow's fall was imminent.

On October 16 the city was overtaken by a mass panic, and the population started to flee. In a matter of hours all roads to the east became clogged with massive traffic jams as official cars, horse-drawn wagons and pedestrians vied with one another to get out of town. The railroad stations were mobbed, and the tracks were congested with cars; it took the train carrying the evacuating diplomatic corps five days to travel the 500 miles to Kuibyshev.

Inside the city, buses and taxis vanished, and the subway ran only irregularly. Shops and abandoned households were looted by Muscovites grabbing what they could. One observer later remembered the ludicrous sight of men running along the street festooned with strings of sausages; another recalled seeing a truck overturned as people fought for its cargo of canned goods. Some shopkeepers willingly gave away food and other merchandise, feeling it was better to hand over their stocks to fellow Muscovites than to allow them to be seized by the invading Germans. There was no one on hand to reestablish order, for the police had ceased to function.

Party official V. P. Pronin was expected to speak on the radio, but the broadcast was repeatedly postponed over the course of two days. When he finally did make an announcement on October 18, it was to order all remaining citizens to stand fast—and to bring the reassuring promise that more than 200 booths and stores would be opened to guarantee the distribution of food. The same day, the newspaper *Izvestia* quashed the rumors that top officials were leaving, announcing instead the government's "irrevocable decision" to defend Moscow "to the last drop of blood." Another official, A. S. Shcherbakov, broadcast that Stalin was at his post in the Kremlin. On the 19th, Stalin decreed a state of siege in the capital. A curfew was imposed from midnight to 5 a.m., along with martial law; anyone caught inciting disorder was to be executed. Now roadblocks went up to prevent any more citizens from leaving, and a special force of the NKVD came in to restore order.

The announcement of Stalin's presence in the city and the institution of martial law stemmed the panic and calmed the people's fears. New life returned to the capital, and a quickened spirit of determination took hold of those who had stayed. They threw themselves into the feverish business of defense in the days that followed—building miles of trenches, antitank ditches and barbed-wire barriers in and around the city.

As perilous as their predicament was, the Muscovites had less reason to fear a German attack than they thought. The Germans were encountering serious trouble, and not least of their problems were the Russian roads—and the lack of them. To accommodate the 69 divisions that Hitler had sent in the direction of Moscow from Smolensk, Leningrad and Kiev, there were only three major roads. That meant that most of the infantry had to march across open country, with the horse-drawn artillery lumbering behind. The roads themselves were poor. One vital paved section leading north from Orel to Tula crumbled under the weight of Guderian's panzers. The drive slowed down while engineers and work crews patched the highway.

Bad enough in the best of times, the roads—and the dirt tracks that passed for roads—customarily became impassable during the autumn months. The early October rains that Halder had so nonchalantly noted in his diary were the beginning of a downpour that lasted for days and turned the tracks into oozing quagmires and the fields into seas of jelly three feet or more deep. The mud sucked up guns and baggage, drew boots off the soldiers and halted vehicles. Trucks and wagons sank to their axles in it, horses to their bellies. Even in places where the tanks could roll and the men could march, the advances they made gained them little reward, for supplies of all kinds became mired in the rear. For want of fuel the tanks stalled; for want of ammunition the guns fell silent; for want of food the troops went hungry. One infantry commander reported to Guderian on October 29 that his men had not received any bread since October 20.

As if the gluey roads were not enough to have to contend with, the Germans soon ran into trouble of another kind. On the road to Tula, Guderian had his first disturbing encounter with the T-34, a lethal new tank that the Russians had been testing throughout the summer; in October they unleashed it with stunning effect. Suddenly the proud German panzer leaders found their weapons outclassed. The T-34 had sloping armor plates that deflected German shells and wide tracks that nimbly rolled over the roughest terrain; and to increase its deadliness, it had a powerful 76mm gun that could cripple a German panzer with a single shot. At the battle of Mtsensk, outside Tula, panzer casualties outnumbered Russian casualties for the first time. "The Russians' tanks are so agile, at close ranges they will climb a slope or cross a piece of swamp faster than you can traverse the turret," wrote one of Guderian's men after seeing the T-34 in action. "When they hit one of our panzers there is often a deep long explosion, a roar as the fuel burns, a roar

Armed with heavy shovels, a hastily assembled work force of Moscow women and elderly men gouge a huge tank trap out of the earth to halt German panzers advancing on the Russian capital. In the feverish effort to save the city, more than 100,000 citizens labored from mid-October until late November digging ditches and building other obstructions. When completed, the ditches extended more than 100 miles.

too loud, thank God, to let us hear the cries of the crew."

German headquarters seemed oblivious of all problems, although the generals repeatedly filed reports of the mounting opposition and worsening weather. On October 28, Hitler sent instructions to Guderian's Second Panzer Army that "fast-moving units should seize the Oka River bridges to the east of Serpukhov"—an objective that was still more than 75 miles away. "There were no fast-moving units any more," Guderian ruefully wrote years later. His troops could scarcely manage a speed of 10 miles a day now. Kluge's

Chief of Staff, General Günther Blumentritt, who was mired in the mud just 40 miles southwest of Moscow with the Fourth Army, wrote: "All the commanders are now asking, 'When are we going to stop?' "

Not until they reached Moscow, Hitler insisted.

By the middle of November temperatures had dropped enough to congeal the mud; although the cold promised new miseries for the shivering men, it brought the officers at headquarters the cheering news that tanks and trucks could roll. At that prospect, Halder on November 13 gathered the

School-aged Russian tots perch on a pile of logs and watch with interest as German officers' cars and motorcycles splash through the autumn mud. When the mud was so deep that it halted vehicles altogether, the logs made useful corduroy roads; hundreds of miles of these log roads had to be constructed before the rainy season was over.

chiefs of staff of the field commands at Orsha, headquarters of Army Group Center, ostensibly for the purpose of inviting them to consider what to do next.

With few exceptions they favored digging in for the winter. Liebenstein, pleading on behalf of Guderian's Second Panzer Army, exclaimed that this was not the month of May; the swift progress of the spring could not be duplicated in cold weather. Most of Guderian's fellow officers took a similar view. An important exception was Field Marshal von Bock, the leader of them all. At the outset of the Russian campaign Bock had been charged with taking Moscow. Since July he had endured too many postponements from on high; time and again he had been obliged to yield up his troops and his tanks to the adventures in the north and the south. Now that his turn had come and the goal seemed near, he was of no mind to quit. In any event, Halder had arrived at the meeting armed with a new Hitler directive ordering a resumption of the Moscow drive. "It is the Führer's wish," he said summarily.

And so the Germans pushed on. The plan this time was for Guderian's Second Panzer Army to take Tula and its airfield, then move north and loop around behind Moscow. In the north the Ninth Army and the Third Panzer Army—which had been taken over from Hoth by General Georg-Hans Reinhardt—would cross the Moscow-Volga canal and swing south for Moscow. In the center, the Fourth Army and the 4th Panzer Group would make a frontal attack on the city.

It was an ambitious plan, a lot to ask of men who were hungry, cold, ridden with lice and sick with fatigue. "I cannot imagine how we can have things straight by next spring," Guderian wrote in a letter to his wife. With his men he could not afford such candor. "A big effort now, if we press on, will save far greater suffering in the year to come," he told them in a desperate effort to keep them going.

But the effort was in vain. In this second push, one battalion reached the suburban village of Gorky; another blew up the railroad station of Lobnya, a short 10 miles from the city limits. Bock, riding at the front of the Army, got close enough to his goal to see the spires of the Kremlin in his field glasses.

That was the closest the Germans were to get to Moscow. All through November the plight of the troops had been growing worse. When the first shipment of winter coats had arrived for the Third Panzer Army, it had included only a single overcoat per gun crew, though the temperature had been well below freezing for weeks. At Fourth Army headquarters, where there were no overcoats at all, an expected consignment of food had brought two trainloads of frozen wine in broken bottles.

Ever since the meeting at Orsha the generals in the field had been sending written appeals to Hitler asking for permission to dig in; all had been denied, and as late as December the Führer was ordering that the generals forge on. But by that time the troops could take no more. In two terrible months of fighting since the launching of Operation *Typhoon*, the German front had advanced scarcely 100 miles while the Army had suffered nearly a quarter of a million casualties. Tank strength had been reduced by two thirds. One by one the commanders took it upon themselves to make their own decisions in spite of directives from headquarters.

On the night of December 5, Guderian withdrew his advance units to a line just south of Tula, where the land was suitable to defense. On the same night Hoepner's Fourth Panzer Army and Reinhardt's Third, just northwest of the capital, suspended their attacks. "The Führer's order," Guderian's Chief of Staff Liebenstein wrote with dismay, "does not correspond in any way with reality. Despite all claims and reports, it has not been understood by those above that we are too weak to defend ourselves."

For the first time in World War II, aggressive German officers, so long on the offensive, were now thinking in terms of defense. Hitler—who had himself failed to reckon with the weather, the terrain, the will of the Russian people and the limits of his own resources—put the blame for the failure that now confronted him on the generals whose advice he had refused to heed. Before December was over, he was to vent his fury by relieving Guderian and Hoepner of their commands, together with others, including Brauchitsch, Rundstedt and Bock—more than 30 generals in all. But like it or not, he was faced by the truth: the attack on Moscow had run down.

As for the Russians, they were already exploiting German weaknesses, and shifting from defense to a counterattack of their own.

THE AGGRESSORS' ORDEAL

A winding procession of German infantrymen retreats through a howling blizzard on the broad plains near Moscow under the watchful eye of a friendly dog.

GENERAL WINTER TAKES COMMAND

The German High Command expected a victorious conclusion to the war with Russia by the last mild days of autumn, 1941. But in October when the first snow fell on the vast plains west of Moscow, the tank-led invaders were still short of victory. Then came "General Winter"—as first the Russians and then the Germans came to call it—and the Army was wholly unprepared for it.

In the early autumn, rain had turned the roads into a muddy morass that had glued German supply trucks axle-deep for weeks. Then the thermometer plunged, and the trucks soon had to be chipped from the frozen mud with pickaxes. On many days the wind caused temperatures to drop to the equivalent of —40° F. Water froze in the boilers of railroad engines, oil froze in trucks, grease froze in guns, and the mechanized German Army had to seek horses to hitch to its tanks.

Wounded foot soldiers often died where they fell, not from their injuries but from shock and frostbite. Many more froze to death inside hospital trains stalled in snowdrifts. Soldiers watched one another for signs of frostbite; nevertheless, nearly 113,000 cases occurred. Supplies dwindled. Infantry companies sent out patrols to forage for food—which usually consisted of frozen potatoes dug from frozen ground. An occasional horse provided meat. Warm coats and boots were at a premium. Many men went through the winter in cotton pants and summer uniforms. West of Moscow on one mid-December day, the frozen legs of 73 dead Russian soldiers were sawed off below the knee, put in ovens and thawed until their felt-lined boots could be slid off and given to 73 German soldiers. Moscow radio then delightedly announced that captured German soldiers were found attired in women's fur coats, woolen jackets and even silk underwear.

The agony of the winter campaign was recorded in the diary of Wilhelm Prüller, a conscript from Vienna and an ardent Nazi who became a first lieutenant in the motorized infantry. Quotes from his diary accompany many of the German photographs in this essay.

As the snow piles up, bundled German troops shovel their way through a yard-high drift. Under such snow the earth often froze four feet deep.

Horses and men retreat past a Russian village. Wilhelm Prüller, one of the officers who managed to survive the awful winter with the German Army, wrote on December 7, 1941: "Yesterday we had 32 degrees below zero. It will get worse. The villages lying in front of us are burned down now, so that the Russians can't use them against us. Behind us on the hills bunkers will be constructed as a winter defense line. Probably we shall burn down all these villages behind us."

A German soldier and his horse struggle through a snowdrift. "No vehicle can get from here to Shchigry—that's seven kilometres," Prüller noted. "No horse wagons either, because the animals sink up to their rumps in drifts." Nearly 100,000 of the horses used by the Germans died during the winter. The carcasses fed the hungry troops.

Panzer troops use picks and shovels to dig out a camouflaged tank from the 5th Panzer Division, bogged down in the snow despite its cleated tracks.

Retreating from Moscow in December 1941, German troops struggle to free their truck from a snowbank before the Russian advance catches up with them.

A German infantryman puts his shoulder to a horse-drawn wagon in an attempt to dislodge it from a snowdrift on one of the primitive Russian roads.

Slaking their thirst with handfuls of snow, members of a German patrol halt in a forest. Cold-weather uniforms such as the ones they are wearing rarely reached the German troops because Hitler ordered that priority be given shipments of ammunition and fuel.

German soldiers in a trench hover around a
fire to keep from freezing. "In our hole,"
Prüller said, "it was so cold that we stood
round the stove in our fur hats and ear muffs,
gloves, two or three blankets and a fur,
and it was still so cold you couldn't stand it."

Through drifts of snow west of Moscow soldiers approach the front swathed in tablecloths and bedcovers that they stole from Russian homes to provide warmth.

Overcome with exhaustion, a gaunt rifleman collapses against a tree as the German campaign reels under the Russian winter. "Our people are kaputt," wrote Prüller. "You've got to say it; and see why: one hour outside, one hour in the hut, watch, alarm, sentry duty . . . one thing after another. It wouldn't surprise me to see some of them break down."

6

November 7, the anniversary of the outbreak of the 1917 Revolution, was ordinarily the occasion for a triumphant military parade in Moscow's Red Square. But in 1941, with the Germans only miles from the capital, Soviet citizens naturally assumed there would be no parade. To expose soldiers, tanks, guns and equipment in broad daylight in Moscow's famous square seemed mad: on captured airfields a few minutes' flying time away hundreds of German bombers stood ready for take-off at the first inkling of so alluring and vulnerable a target. Yet Stalin, in one of his boldest and most imaginative acts, buoyed the morale of civilian and soldier alike by holding the parade as usual.

Normally, weeks of preparation preceded the display. This time, it was not until November 4, three days before the event, that Lieut. General Kuzma Sinilov, Moscow's newly appointed military commandant, was put in charge of the operation. To make things even more difficult, Sinilov—who was ordered to keep the plan secret—had to wait until 2 a.m. on the morning of the parade before informing his unit commanders that the ceremony would begin six hours later. At the same time, Soviet fighters were put on alert, the crews of Moscow's impressive antiaircraft system told to man their posts with greater than usual vigilance, and medical units, ambulances and stretchers moved into streets near the square—in case the worst should happen.

On November 6, clouds could be seen forming in the skies over Moscow, but there were not enough to signal bad weather, at least the kind that would ground enemy planes. Toward evening, wet snow began to fall. By morning Moscow was in the throes of a classic Russian snowstorm. The marching men would be safe from the enemy; their only problem would be the ice underfoot.

On the eve of the anniversary, as the welcome snow filled the sky, several hundred Soviet leaders gathered underground—with a prudent regard for safety—in the elaborate hall of the Mayakovskaya subway station. Their traditional meeting place, the Bolshoi Theater, had been bombed. They listened raptly to the first of two remarkable speeches that Stalin would give on successive days. Instead of addressing himself to party zealots, as in the past, Stalin appealed to the Russian people and their national pride.

He spoke emotionally of German losses and the German failure to cut the U.S.S.R. to pieces in a savage lightning war,

RUSSIA'S BIG SURPRISE

of the defense of Moscow and Leningrad and of the forging, under fire, of new soldiers, airmen and sailors—"men who will tomorrow become the terror of the German army." He spoke of Nazi imperialism and, with telling effect, quoted some of Hitler's most racist remarks about the "subhuman" Slavs. He referred to the Germans as "these people without honor or conscience, these people with the morality of animals," and declared: "The German invaders want a war of extermination against the peoples of the Soviet Union. Very well then! If they want a war of extermination they shall have it!" Stalin closed with rousing words: "Our cause is just. Victory will be ours!"

Stalin gave his second speech the next morning in Red Square, with the snow swirling and guns booming in the background. It was even more stirring, for he was addressing men bound for the front—men who in a few hours would be killing the invaders or dying from their bullets.

"The war you are waging is a war of liberation, a just war," he said. "May you be inspired in this war by the heroic figures of our great ancestors." The names of famous Russian warriors echoed in Red Square: Aleksandr Nevsky, who defeated the Teutonic Knights in 1242; Dmitry Donskoi, the scourge of the Tartars in 1380; Aleksandr Suvorov, the Russian commander who won a great victory against the Turks in 1787; and Mikhail Kutuzov, who saved Moscow by repelling Napoleon's invasion of Russia in 1812.

Stalin's two speeches, invoking the heroic figures and the greatness of Russia, went straight to the hearts of the Soviet people. The texts were duplicated by the millions, distributed to the troops and dropped on populated areas behind enemy lines. Up to now, many Soviet citizens, especially those who had suffered hardship or lost relatives in Stalin's purge and his contrived famines, had seen the war as a contest between two repugnant ideologies, Communism and fascism. But the events of the past few weeks—the humiliation of frequent defeats, the increasingly inhumane behavior of the German occupying forces, the growing realization that Hitler regarded the Russians as subhuman—had begun to dissuade many potential sympathizers with Germany. It was on these people that Stalin's speeches, playing on ancestral pride and patriotism, had their greatest effect.

Meanwhile, the official Soviet attitude toward the German people was changing. Stalin and his spokesmen no longer expressed sympathy for them as being coerced or misled by a fascist gang. The press and radio became openly anti-German—not just anti-Nazi. The famous novelist Ilya Ehrenburg wrote: "The Germans are not human. Now the word 'German' has become the most terrible swear-word. Let us not be indignant. Let us kill. If you do not kill the German, the German will kill you. He will carry away your family, and torture them in his damned Germany."

As the bold new spirit and bitter determination of the Russian people hardened into a firm resolve to beat back the attackers, the German Army encountered a growing ferocity on the part of Russia's defenders. Outside Moscow, a group of wounded Red Army soldiers crippled 14 German tanks and drove off six more. Their leader, armed with a cluster of hand grenades, threw himself under one tank and blew up himself and the vehicle. Similar acts of heroism were repeated all along the front.

Not only were the Russians resisting fiercely, they were scraping together far more reserves than the Germans had thought possible and massing new troops with an astonishing speed. Where were these reinforcements coming from? What the Germans had not reckoned with was the fact that in a land as big and populous as the Soviet Union there was a never-ending supply of bodies to toss into the fight. As the crisis worsened for the Russians, a massive dragnet was thrown out to gather up all able-bodied men from cities, villages and farms, from streets, factories and fields. Even the walking wounded were dragged back into battle. Zhukov's staff scraped the hospitals at the front for "volunteers"—men on the road to recovery, or men whose injuries were not so severe as to prevent them from fighting.

But Stalin's greatest military resource was his army in the Soviet East. On June 22, when *Barbarossa* was launched, a vital question occupying the Soviet High Command had been Japan's intentions. Would the Japanese strike against the Soviet Union? Or against Britain's forces in Asia—or even the United States? Anxious to protect Siberia from attack, the Soviet High Command had stationed more than 30 divisions, with strong cavalry, tank and air support, to the east of Lake Baikal in Siberia, prepared to face an attack by the Japanese from Manchuria. To the west of Lake Baikal stood a second line force, ready for deployment to either

German soldiers, stripped to the waist, bathe in the snow. In fact the Russian cold was so intense that there were thousands of cases of frostbite amputation.

The ingenious shoes of coiled rope these men wear were too cumbersome to use in action.

At a Christmas party at the front, presents under a tree help to convey an impression of good cheer.

A ROSY VIEW OF THE WINTER WAR

While German soldiers were suffering and dying in the bitter Russian winter, the people back home were being given a somewhat different picture of conditions at the front. Carefully edited photographs made Russia look like a *gemütlich* Bavarian ski resort. Reports filed by special correspondents made light of cold-weather problems, including the Army's critical shortage of winter clothing. A dispatch published in the Berlin newspaper, *Der Angriff,* described the troops' efforts to stay warm as "amusing, because they express an air of improvisation." When pictures began arriving from the front showing coatless Germans guarding Soviet prisoners who wore woolen coats, the Ministry of Propaganda banned their publication.

There was a perfectly good reason for all this, solemnly explained Propaganda Minister Joseph Goebbels at a meeting in November 1941: "It's not practical to mention winter clothing in the press at present, as one normally would in order to placate the people, for the result would be that the soldiers would write to their families and say they had not yet received the winter clothing. Thus a certain lack of confidence in the press would be born."

Hot food—a luxury actually enjoyed by few—is brought forward in containers by two runners.

A makeshift game of ice hockey on a frozen stream suggests that German soldiers were able to take time out from an easy war to play at their favorite games.

the Far Eastern or European theaters. In all, available for use in Siberia were nearly three quarters of a million troops.

In September or October, Stalin received a report from his secret agent in Tokyo, Richard Sorge: the Japanese had decided not to take action against Russia—not, at least, until spring—and, instead, were preparing for war in the Pacific against the U.S. Stalin immediately dipped into his precious hoard of men and equipment in Siberia. Half the strength of the Far Eastern Command was rushed by rail to Moscow's defense—18 divisions in all. Twelve more came from the Trans-Baikal region, one from Outer Mongolia, three from the Amur area, six from the Manchurian border.

Meanwhile, entire new divisions were being formed out of recruits and reserves in the Urals and their training was entrusted to General I. V. Tyulenev, who had been wounded on the Southern Front. A fighting man, he did not relish being consigned to a noncombatant post. But Stalin insisted that there was no more vitally important job than that of creating fresh divisions out of raw recruits. "The situation at the front," he said, "depends entirely on how quickly and how effectively we can prepare our reserves."

Tyulenev was not the only general to receive such a challenge from Stalin. Lieut. General F. I. Golikov was cho-sen by the dictator to command an army in the defense of Moscow. Golikov was pleased by the honor, and thanked him. Stalin then told Golikov that the army did not exist and that the general's task would be to form it and mold it into a fighting force within a few weeks.

When the soldiers who would make up this army had assembled, Golikov was dismayed to find that his regimental commanders "lacked general education," that only a handful of his junior officers had combat experience, and that many of his enlisted men were "of an advanced age."

Golikov found his supply situation even more depressing. On November 1, he cabled the quartermaster general: "We have no sugar, fats, fish, vegetables, hay, tobacco or money. All the time my divisions are growing larger." Winter clothing did not arrive until mid-November, by which time his lightly clad soldiers were suffering from frostbite during training exercises. On November 24, Marshal Boris Shaposhnikov, Chief of the General Staff, telephoned Golikov to say that his hastily assembled Tenth Army must prepare to entrain for the front, where it would be pitted against German Army Group Center.

"So soon?" Golikov exclaimed; but he obeyed. Within a few days his 100,000 men, ill-equipped, inexperienced and

undertrained, were fighting the German forces threatening the southern flank of the Moscow defense system.

Stalin now was not only producing armies out of thin air, but running the war on his own. He did not hesitate to intervene directly in battle, shifting troops, throwing in reserves, and relieving or transferring generals whose performances had failed to suit him. At times he was bullheaded, even irrational. Zhukov described the reaction of the Commander in Chief (or C-in-C, as Zhukov sometimes referred to him) when the town of Dedovsk, only 20 miles or so from Moscow, was reported to have fallen.

"Stalin telephoned me.

" 'Were you aware that Dedovsk has fallen?' he asked.

" 'No, Comrade Stalin, I wasn't.'

" 'A Commander should know what is going on on his front!' the C-in-C burst out angrily. He ordered me to leave right away to personally take charge of organizing a counterattack and recapture Dedovsk."

Zhukov made inquiries and learned that Dedovsk was still in Soviet hands. What the Germans had occupied was an insignificant village called Dedovo. But when he called back to explain the misunderstanding, Stalin cut him short and ordered that not only Zhukov but also Major General L. A. Govorov, Commander of the Fifth Army, and Major General K. K. Rokossovsky, Commander of the Sixteenth Army, start on their way at once to see to it that the "unfortunate village" was recaptured from the Germans "without fail."

This impressive array of top brass arrived at the divisional command near Dedovo and instructed an amazed General A. P. Beloborodov to send a company and a few tanks to capture a handful of lightly defended houses. For various tactical reasons it was not a very wise move but, as Zhukov wrote later: "In this case I was unable to let myself be guided by anything like tactical considerations." He had his orders. The German platoon was thrown out.

Zhukov admitted, however, that in spite of such unreasonable and impulsive acts, "Stalin must be given his due. By his harsh and unscrupulous attitude he was able to achieve the well-nigh impossible."

Everywhere along the front the Russians were assisted in their effort by the onset of winter. As the cold intensified, many Germans, lacking adequate clothing, suffered frost-bite, and their equipment broke down. To the Russians, of course, the bitterly cold weather came as no surprise. They were accustomed to winters that began full blast in November. Many were peasants who had lived in poverty and close to nature. They knew how to improvise against the elements, and were better equipped than the Germans were to defy the wind and snow and live without the protection of conventional cover.

Siberian troops, for example, had little difficulty surviving in the frozen woods. They dug away the snow to ground level, packed it into walls, laid a floor of green fir branches and roofed the shelter with a tarpaulin. All they had to do to stay snug and warm then was to build a stove out of an oil drum and a piece of piping.

Besides being able to withstand the winter far better than the Germans, the Russians also had the advantage of being a great deal closer to their sources of supply. Roads and railways flowed out of the capital to almost every area along the Moscow Front, and the Red Army used them to transport food and equipment.

Taking advantage of the situation, the Russians hit Guderian's 112th Infantry Division southeast of Moscow on November 17 with a mass of troops and T-34 tanks. Each of the German division's regiments had already had about 500 casualties from frostbite alone, and casualties from other causes were high. To make things worse, most of the Germans' machine guns were frozen and would not fire; moreover, their 37mm antitank guns had already proved useless against the tough T-34s. Under the pressure of the Russian attack, troops of the 112th Division broke and ran. It was the first time in the campaign that Guderian's men had panicked, and the panzer leader decided that "the combat ability of our infantry was at an end."

The Soviet leaders were aware that all along the Moscow Front the German advance had slowed down, but they did not realize how badly off the invaders were. On December 5, they launched a series of local counterattacks; their intention was only to relieve the pressure on Moscow by driving back the German forces that in some cases stood only 10 to 20 miles away. But when the Red Army leaned against the front, its commanders found to their surprise that in many places the Germans were prepared to yield ground without a fight. Even Guderian pulled back to a line

General Georgy K. Zhukov, the iron-willed son of a peasant family who became Russia's most famous World War II commander, ponders a map while improvising strategy for the defense of Moscow. Zhukov rose to be a sergeant in the Imperial Cavalry, joined the Red Army and the Communist Party in 1919, and eventually gained prominence by defeating the Japanese in a border war in Mongolia in 1939. Stalin called upon Zhukov to organize the defense of Leningrad, then Moscow, and to conduct the Red Army's counteroffensive in the winter of 1941-1942.

that he merely "hoped" he could hold. He wrote in a letter that "the Russians are pursuing us closely and we must expect misfortunes."

Thus began the Russian counteroffensive—and the German defeat as well.

To the great satisfaction of the Russians, the temperature continued to fall. One officer recalled later that the first thing he did every day was to check the thermometer. The lower the temperature, the more pleased he was. "Lovely weather for the Germans," the Russians would say.

So intense now was the cold and so deep the snow that more and more of the German vehicles became immobilized. Tanks, with their narrow tracks and limited ground clearance, sank deep into the snow and stuck there. Relief trucks and troop carriers could not get through. Red Army men found to their delight that for the first time they were capturing bogged-down German supplies and equipment.

Fleeing the cold, Germans sheltered in farmhouses and villages, a hazardous expedient; the Russians soon realized that any settlement or lone dwelling was sure to hold Germans and managed to surround and attack many of them.

At last the German generals, finding it impossible to hold positions almost everywhere along the line, and suffering great losses in men and equipment, urged Hitler to permit an organized retreat. He refused. On December 8, he did officially call off his eastern offensive "because of the surprisingly early and severe winter," placing his armies generally on the defensive. But he would not permit a retreat from the Moscow area. He did allow a number of limited withdrawals, but some were poorly handled and resulted in heavy losses of equipment. A few commanders—Guderian, for one—seized the opportunity to make substantial pullbacks to more secure positions.

On December 16, Guderian wrote: "I frequently cannot sleep at night and my brain goes round and round while I try to think what more I can do to help my poor soldiers who are out there without shelter in this abominable cold." Russian troops had broken his line at Livny, 70 miles southeast of his headquarters city, Orel; and his 293rd Infantry Division was in full retreat from the east. Although he had already pulled back, he decided that somehow he must persuade the Führer of the need for a further withdrawal to a position that would be easier for the Germans to defend.

As he had done four months earlier, Guderian flew off to Hitler's headquarters at Rastenburg. On the first visit he had been welcomed. This time the Führer received him with "a hard unfriendly expression in his eyes." At past meetings, Guderian had attended as a conqueror, a successful general urging deeper and more ambitious advances. Now he was the general who had retreated without orders. Guderian explained the hardships his men faced: their wretched living conditions, the lack of winter clothing, the enormous casualties from frostbite, the heavy losses of vehicles and guns. If his troops were to hold a position throughout the winter, they must be permitted to complete their pullback.

Hitler would not be moved. "They must dig into the ground where they are," he insisted, "and hold every square yard of land!"

Guderian explained that the ground was frozen to a depth of five feet and could not be dug with the sharpest of tools. "In that case," Hitler replied, "they must blast craters with the heavy howitzers." But they could not, Guderian explained; there were not enough howitzers, shells, or explosives of any kind to gouge out craters along the 25- to 35-mile-long lines that they were trying to hold—even if the ammunition were not needed to fire at the Russians.

A glum Guderian returned to Orel. His mission had been hopeless from the start. Hitler had already, on December 16, vetoed the proposal of Field Marshal von Brauchitsch, his commander in chief, for a partial withdrawal and issued an emphatic general order that the Army was to stand firm and fight, regardless of danger to its flanks or rear.

Guderian arrived at his Second Panzer Army headquarters in Orel on December 21. Two days later his 296th Infantry Division was forced to retreat to Belev, 135 miles southwest of Moscow. Then, on December 24, his 10th Infantry Division lost Chern, 150 miles south of the capital. This provoked an angry telephone conversation with his superior, Field Marshal von Kluge, and it came as no surprise to Guderian on December 26 to be relieved of his command.

By the end of December the Red Army had rolled back the front west of Moscow by as much as 50 miles, liberating Kalinin, Tula, Klin and Solnechnogorsk in the process.

Many German commanders believed, as Guderian did, that it was madness to try to maintain a defense line even

The large map at right shows how the German advance (red line), stalled by winter, fell far short of Barbarossa's goal (broken line) before the Russians counterattacked and drove back the invaders by as much as 150 miles (dotted line). The major Soviet thrust occurred near Moscow (shaded area) where Russian armies (arrows, enlarged section of map) tried to pinch off and crush a large part of the German forces. But they failed, and the Russian Thirty-third Army was surrounded and destroyed.

this close to Moscow. They wanted to withdraw to a line that could be securely held and that provided adequate shelter and communications. Some were ready to disobey, covertly, the Führer's order to stand fast, and hastened to pull back before the Russians could prevent their retreat.

But other units of the Army continued to fight furiously, even as they were forced to give ground. Kaluga, which lay 90 miles southwest of Moscow, was recaptured by the Red Army, but only after days of street battles. The Germans burned many villages before abandoning them, and in others they left grim evidence of their occupation: villagers dangling from gallows in the public square, hanged to discourage partisan activities and to terrorize the populace.

The Russian advance had a salutary effect on the Red Army. Zhukov later noted that it was during the opening weeks of the counteroffensive that his men were transformed from a humiliated, retreating rabble into hard, seasoned warriors, an offensive force of impressive proportions. By first holding the German Army at bay and then forcing it into retreat, the Russians had exploded the myth of the enemy's invincibility. Their victories had a tremendous effect not only on Soviet morale but on foreign opinion. British and American military experts, who only months before had almost unanimously predicted a quick Soviet collapse, revised their low opinion of the Red Army and concluded that the defeat of the Soviet Union was no longer a foregone conclusion.

General Noel Mason-MacFarlane of the British Military Mission in Moscow was by now most impressed by what he had seen. "Seven months of continuous hard fighting in war," he observed, "are worth more than seven years of peace soldiering." Although untried in the beginning, the Soviet officers had found their feet; now, he reported, they were "veterans of modern warfare, strong characters and genuine fighting soldiers." The general was even impressed by the commissars, whom he described as "the chaplains of the Red Army, with a political creed and doctrine in place of religion."

The Red Army's transport amazed him; it was "like nothing on earth," he said. Instead of trucks, sleds drawn by tough ponies hauled soldiers and supplies. What the Army lacked in mechanized equipment, it made up for in manpower. Thousands of men were put to work clearing roads of snow with brooms. "Everything is practical," Mason-MacFarlane said.

Taken to newly recaptured villages, he witnessed "the destruction and the brutality of the Hun," and met old men and young girls who had joined the partisans. The Red Army had been in a bad way in the autumn, Mason-MacFarlane concluded, and there had been signs of impending disaster.

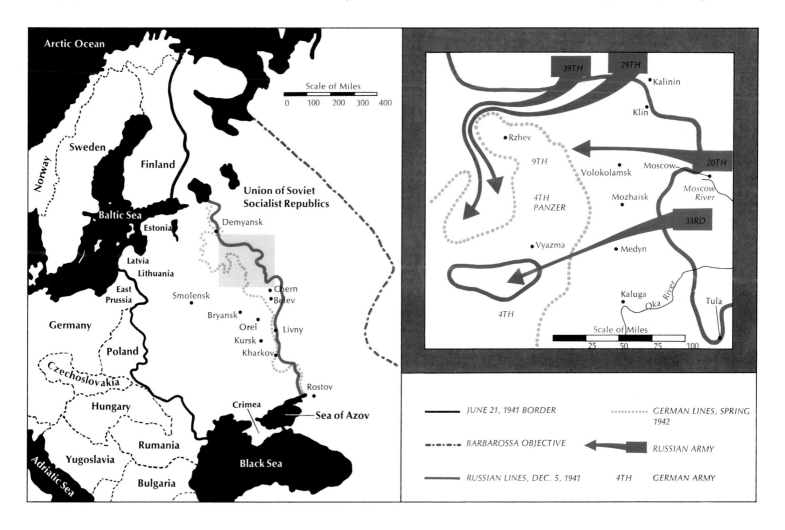

But the tide had turned, confidence had been restored, and Russia was going to carry on fighting.

Not all the Russian successes came in the Moscow area. In the south, Rostov had been recaptured on November 29, and in the north, near Leningrad, the important rail junction of Tikhvin had been retaken on December 9. But for the Russians defending Moscow, there was something marvelous in being able to say that they were the ones who had actually forced the great Guderian to retreat.

Stalin was enormously buoyed. The tone of his communications with Allied leaders changed completely. In September he had written Churchill of the "mortal menace" Russia faced. But by mid-December he could tell British Foreign Secretary Anthony Eden in Moscow that the counteroffensive would be stepped up and continue through the winter. Barely conceding the chance of a German offensive in the spring, he said that the German Army had no large reserve of manpower and that its efficiency was impaired.

A plan was readied calling for the encirclement of the German Army Group Center in the Mozhaisk-Vyazma area west of Moscow. Lieut. General M. G. Yefremov's Thirty-third Soviet Army moved swiftly to force a gap between the Fourth Panzer Army and Fourth Army near Medyn, 80 miles southwest of Moscow. Joined by the First Guards Cavalry Corps as well as by partisans and airborne troops, Yefremov pushed farther to the west until his forces were south of

Russian rockets, the Red Army's surprise weapon in the early part of the war, blast off from truck-mounted rails. Named "Little Kate" for a popular Russian love song, the rocket had a range of four miles, and spread terror by its screaming sound and devastating impact. It was rumored that the rockets cast death rays; the Germans put out a warning that Russian soldiers who fired them would never be taken alive.

Vyazma. Meanwhile, the Russian Twenty-ninth and Thirty-ninth Armies were converging from the north. By February 4, Yefremov had reached the outskirts of Vyazma.

But the Soviet plan was doomed. "The enemy proved to be a harder nut to crack than we believed," Zhukov confessed years later. On January 21 the Soviet High Command withdrew the First Shock Army and Sixteenth Army from the central portion of the Moscow Front and moved them to the northern and southern flanks of the advancing forces. This weakened the westward thrust of the Twentieth Army of Major General A. A. Vlasov (who would be captured in June and would change sides to lead Russian prisoners of war against the U.S.S.R.). Vlasov was to wipe out the German Ninth Army and the Fourth Panzer Army in the pocket being formed by the Soviet pincers. But Vlasov's resources proved inadequate. Spread thin, his army was soon at the mercy of hastily assembled enemy reinforcements.

With the tables now turned, the Fourth Panzer Army and the Ninth Army, saved from the trap before it could close, attacked the Russian flanks. The Soviet Twenty-ninth Army —which had been converging with the Thirty-ninth Army on Vyazma—was now cut off and encircled by the German Ninth Army. Only 5,000 men managed to escape to the south. There they joined other Soviet forces, but were in danger of being encircled again. Yefremov's Thirty-third Army was trapped near Vyazma, together with the First Guards Cavalry Corps, airborne troops and many partisans.

Moscow made frantic efforts to relieve them, but to no avail. Vyazma was 135 miles from Moscow, and the communication line between the beleaguered men and their main base was stretched too thin. Distance, lack of transport and bad weather made it impossible for substantial relief forces or adequate supplies to reach the Russians in the German noose. Yefremov's men received supply drops and some airborne reinforcements, but not enough to save them as they tried to fight their way back to Soviet lines.

The Russian counteroffensive continued throughout February. But the Germans, having recovered from their unexpected defeats of early winter, still held the major inhabited areas that they had seized in their initial advance—Demyansk, Rzhev, Vyazma, Bryansk, Orel, Kursk. They had organized these towns and the surrounding villages and farms into what they called "hedgehogs," installations bristling with fortifications. In addition, the Germans had set up supply dumps in the main transportation hubs, and these resources now stood them in good stead. When stores ran short, airlifts resupplied their fortress cities.

Lacking the artillery to mass against the German hedgehogs, the Russians flowed around them instead with sleds, cavalry and ski troops. Thus the Russians recovered territory—but they soon found it impossible to exploit their gains as long as the bastions behind them remained intact. Whenever they did attack these, they suffered heavy losses.

It was the Germans, now, who occupied sheltered, fortified positions close to their supply lines. And it was the Russians who were out in the cold and the snow. As the Red Army's supply lines grew longer and more vulnerable, their stores of arms, ammunition and food began to run short. By now temperatures had dropped as low as $-50°$F. and the weather was taking a heavy toll of even the Russians.

With their bellies empty, their boots stuffed with straw for warmth, their rifles short of bullets, their horses dropping for want of fodder, their every attempt to pursue an effective offensive balked by the German hedgehogs, the Red Army troops began to falter. In early March the Soviet counteroffensive before Moscow petered out. The Germans had established a firm line of communications and defense 300 miles long from Rzhev through Vyazma and Bryansk to Orel. In late March and early April the Red Army made a final effort, with exhausted troops, to smash gaps in the German line, but without success. General Yefremov failed in his attempt to lead the Thirty-third Army out of the trap near Vyazma. Many of his men were killed, and Yefremov, badly wounded, shot himself to avoid being captured.

But as the front settled into stalemate, the Red Army could take satisfaction in what it had accomplished. Despite the series of terrible defeats it had endured in the early weeks of the war, it had managed somehow to survive, pulling back and regrouping until the German Army was overextended and the Russian winter could take its toll.

Moscow and Leningrad had been saved, and enough reinforcements had been scraped together to enable the Red Army to go over to the offensive. Operation *Barbarossa* had been halted, and the myth of the German Army's invincibility had been shattered once and for all.

THE REBOUNDING RED ARMY

Silhouetted Russian troops, warmly clad for winter warfare, hurdle their frontline trenches and charge German lines southeast of Moscow in December 1941.

A HEROIC EFFORT THAT PAID OFF

In the gray dawn of Friday, December 5, 1941, geysers of snow and red-hot shell fragments erupted in the forests northwest of Moscow, signaling the commencement of the Soviet Union's effort to drive the German Army from the outskirts of the Russian capital. A short while afterward, fresh Siberian troops, who were clad in white camouflage uniforms, swooped forward on skis and the battle was on. In the days that were to follow, the Siberians distinguished themselves. They were fierce soldiers, accustomed since childhood to the rigors of Russia's winters. Kept warm by sheepskin coats, as well as quilted pants, fur hats and felt boots, they could travel almost silently over the snow, and wait patiently for hours in −40° F. (−40° C.) weather before launching an attack at night.

On the 14th of December the Siberians broke through the German line near Klin, a transportation center to the northwest of Moscow, littering the road to the west for 25 miles with the charred and frozen remnants of tanks and men from two panzer divisions. On that day the Siberians killed 3,000 German soldiers.

The Siberians' determination matched that of other Russian troops in the growing counteroffensive. South of Moscow the Red Army's cavalry corps crossed frozen rivers with supply-carrying sleds lashed to saddle horns, and with infantrymen doubled up in the saddles. Tanks pulled armored sleds packed with more infantry. Soldiers fought on the run, carrying sacks of dry bread crusts and raw vegetables, and feeding their horses with straw ripped from thatched roofs. By early winter the Red Army had forced the German lines back 100 to 150 miles.

But not even the Russians were immune to the weather. Near Tula a German unit crept up on a Soviet patrol and found horses and men standing frozen stiff. As winter intensified, Soviet tanks ground to a halt, and deepening snows choked off the flow of supplies provided by horse-drawn wagons, columns of sleighs and parachute drops. Under pressure of the weather, the counterattack slowed down. But Moscow had been saved.

Forced by German bombing to meet in a Moscow subway station, Soviet leaders listen to Stalin on the 24th anniversary of the Bolshevik Revolution.

Red Army units parade through Red Square in the November 7 anniversary review, just minutes before marching directly to the front to defend Moscow.

Red Army soldiers probe the snow for land mines planted by Germans retreating southwest of Moscow near the city of Naro-Fominsk. The fighting here raged for two weeks before the city was liberated by Russian troops.

Russian engineers crawl under German barbed-wire barricades and use wire cutters to clear the way for Soviet ski troops and cavalry. These sappers often risked capture by working in such close proximity to enemy lines.

In a picture from a Soviet documentary film, Red Army infantry troops, their bayonets fixed for close combat, advance cautiously past the bodies of comrades who

fell in an earlier assault. The Russian caption says the soldiers were reoccupying a village but the picture's authenticity has been questioned by some experts.

Russian shock troops equipped with submachine guns and camouflage uniforms attack German positions across a snow-covered field north of Moscow.

Saber-waving Russians from the elite First Guards Cavalry Corps charge through the snow in a field southwest of Moscow. The cavalry tore through a breach in the

Troop-carrying Russian tanks dodge German shells and advance on the town of Klin, which they soon recaptured—an important early Soviet victory.

lines created by Russian infantry to cut off the key road to Smolensk and then remained in the German rear to harass enemy troops for the next six months.

Hands upraised and clutching white flags of surrender, four German soldiers cautiously approach a Russian trench that is manned by camouflaged troops.

A kiss for the liberator is bestowed on a Russian soldier by a villager whose town has just been cleared of Germans.

ACKNOWLEDGMENTS

The editors wish to thank The Bobbs-Merrill Company, Inc., for permission to use quotations from *Stalin and His Generals*, edited by Seweryn Bialer, © 1969 by Western Publishing Company, Inc. The index for this book was prepared·by Mel Ingber. The editors also wish to thank Sadie Alford, Novosti Press Agency, London; Geneva Baker, Quincy, Illinois; Lieselotte Bandelow, Director, Ullstein, Berlin; Terence Charman, Imperial War Museum, London; Cécile Coutin, Curator, Musée des Deux Guerres Mondiales, Paris; Hans Dollinger, Wörthsee, Germany; Ulrich Frodien, Director, Süddeutscher Verlag, Bilderdienst, Munich; General Heinz G. Guderian (Ret.), Bonn-Bad Godesberg, Germany; Dr. Matthias Haupt, Director, Bundesarchiv, Koblenz, Germany; Edward Hine, Imperial War Museum, London; Heinrich Hoffmann, Hamburg; Heinz Höhne, Grosshansdorf, Germany; Colonel P. H. Hordern, Royal Armoured Corps Tank Museum, Wareham, Dorset, England; Dr. Roland Klemig, Director, and Heidi Klein, Bildarchiv Preussischer Kulturbesitz, Berlin; Anna Kruse, Quincy, Illinois; William H. Leary, National Archives, Washington, D.C.; Thomas Oglesby, National Archives, Washington, D.C.; Professor Dr. Jürgen Rohwer, Director, Bibliothek für Zeitgeschichte, Stuttgart; Dr. Paul K. Schmidt-Carell, Hamburg; Jacqueline Schüwy, Novosti Press Agency, Paris; Albert Speer, Heidelberg; R. E. Squires, Imperial War Museum, London; Captain Hans Wolf (Ret.), Koblenz, Germany.

BIBLIOGRAPHY

Accoce, Pierre and Pierre Quet, *A Man Called Lucy*. Coward-McCann, Inc., 1967.

Alliluyeva, Svetlana, *Twenty Letters to a Friend*. Harper & Row, Publishers, Inc., 1967.

Anders, General Wladyslaw, *Hitler's Defeat in Russia*. Henry Regnery Company, 1953.

Armstrong, John A.:
Soviet Partisans in World War II. University of Wisconsin Press, 1964.
Ukrainian Nationalism. Columbia University Press, 1955.

Asprey, Robert B., *War in the Shadows*, Vol. 1. Doubleday & Company, Inc., 1975.

Baldwin, Hanson, *Battles Lost and Won*. Harper & Row, Publishers, Inc., 1966.

Berchin, Michel and Eliahu Ben-Horin, *Red Army*. W. W. Norton & Company, Inc., 1942.

Bialer, Seweryn, ed., *Stalin and His Generals*. Pegasus, 1969.

Billington, James H., *The Icon and the Axe*. Vintage Books, 1970.

Bullock, Alan, *Hitler*. Harper & Brothers, 1960.

Butler, Edwin, *Mason-Mac*. The Macmillan Company, 1972.

Butler, J. R. M., ed., *History of the Second World War*, Vol. 3, *Grand Strategy*. Cox and Wyman, 1964.

Cadogan, Sir Alexander, *The Diaries of Sir Alexander Cadogan, 1938-1945*, edited by David Dilkes. G. P. Putnam's Sons, 1972.

Carell, Paul:
Hitler Moves East, 1941-1943. Little, Brown and Company, 1964.
Hitler's War on Russia. Harrap & Company, 1964.

Cassidy, Henry C., *Moscow Dateline*. Houghton Mifflin Company, 1943

Churchill, Winston S.:
The Second World War. Bantam Books.
Volume III, *The Grand Alliance*. 1974.
Volume IV, *The Hinge of Fate*. 1962.

Clark, Alan, *Barbarossa*. Penguin Books, 1966.

Cooke, Colin, *The Life of Richard Stafford Cripps*. Hodder and Stoughton Limited, 1957.

Dallin, Alexander, *German Rule in Russia, 1941-1945*. The Macmillan Company, 1957.

Deane, John R., *The Strange Alliance*. Indiana University Press, 1947.

Deutscher, Isaac, *Stalin*. Oxford University Press, 1949.

Eden, Sir Anthony, Earl of Avon, *The Reckoning*. Houghton Mifflin Company, 1965.

"Effects of Climate on Combat in European Russia." Department of the Army Pamphlet #20-291, February 1952.

Erickson, John:
The Road to Stalingrad. Harper & Row, Publishers, Inc., 1975.
The Soviet High Command. St. Martin's Press, 1962.

Esposito, Colonel Vincent J., ed., *The West Point Atlas of American Wars*, Vol. 2, *1900-1953*. Frederick A. Praeger, Inc., 1960.

Fischer, George, *Soviet Opposition to Stalin*. Harvard University Press, 1952.

Flower, Desmond and James Reeves, eds., *The Taste of Courage*. Harper & Brothers, 1960.

Fuller, Major-General J. F. C., *The Second World War, 1939-1945*. Meredith Press, 1968.

Garder, Michel, *A History of the Soviet Army*. Pall Mall Press, 1966.

Garthoff, Raymond L., *Soviet Military Doctrine*. The Free Press, 1953.

Gehlen, General Reinhard, *The Service*. World Publishing, 1971.

Gorbatov, A. V., *Years Off My Life*. W. W. Norton & Company, Inc., 1965.

Goure, Leon:
The Siege of Leningrad. McGraw-Hill Book Company, 1962.
and Herbert S. Dinerstein, *Moscow in Crisis*. The Free Press, 1955.

Guderian, General Heinz, *Panzer Leader*, translated from the German by Constantine Fitzgibbon. E. P. Dutton & Company, Inc., 1952.

Halder, Colonel General Franz, *The Private War Journals of Colonel General Franz Halder*, edited by Arnold Lissance. Westview Press, 1976.

Harcave, Sidney, ed., *Readings in Russian History*, Vol. 2, *The Modern Period*. Thomas Y. Crowell, 1965.

Harriman, W. Averell and Elie Abel, *Special Envoy to Churchill and Stalin, 1941-1946*. Random House, Inc., 1975.

Hartman, Tom, *Swastika at War*. Doubleday & Company, Inc., 1975.

Higgins, Trumbull, *Hitler and Russia*. The Macmillan Company, 1966.

Hitler, Adolf, *Mein Kampf*, translated from the German by Ralph Manheim. Houghton Mifflin Company, 1971.

Höhne, Heinz, *The Order of the Death's Head*. Coward-McCann, Inc., 1970.

Howell, Edgar M., *The Soviet Partisan Movement, 1941-1944*. Department of the Army, 1956.

Hyde, H. Montgomery, *Stalin, The History of a Dictator*. Farrar, Straus and Giroux, 1971.

Keitel, Wilhelm, *The Memoirs of Field-Marshal Keitel*, edited by Walter Gorlitz and translated from the German by David Irving. Stein and Day, 1966.

Kern, Erich, *Dance of Death*, translated from the German by Paul Findlay. Collins Clear-Type Press, 1951.

Khrushchev, Nikita S., *Khrushchev Remembers*, edited and translated from the Russian by Strobe Talbott. Little, Brown and Company, (Inc.), 1970.

Kovpak, Major General Sidor A., *Our Partisan Course*, translated from the Russian by Ernst and Mira Lesser. Hutchinson & Co., Ltd., 1947.

Langer, William L. and S. Everett Gleason, *The Undeclared War, 1940-1941*. Harper & Brothers, 1953.

Lash, Joseph P., *Roosevelt and Churchill, 1939-1941*. W. W. Norton & Company, Inc., 1976.

Leach, Barry A., *German Strategy Against Russia, 1939-1941*. Oxford University Press, 1973.

Lenczowski, George, *Russia and the West in Iran, 1918-1948*. Cornell University Press, 1949.

Leningrad. Aurora Art Publishers, 1933.

Liddell Hart, Basil H.:
The German Generals Talk. William Morrow & Company, 1948.
History of the Second World War. Putnam, 1971.
The Red Army, Harcourt, Brace & World, Inc., 1968.
Strategy. Frederick A. Praeger, Inc., 1967.

Macksey, Kenneth, *Guderian, Panzer General*. MacDonald & Jane's, 1975.

Maisky, Ivan M., *Memoirs of a Soviet Ambassador*, translated from the Russian by Andrew Rothstein. Charles Scribner's Sons, 1968.

Manstein, Field-Marshal Erich von, *Lost Victories*, edited and translated from the German by Anthony G. Powell. Henry Regnery Company, 1958.

Maule, Henry, *The Great Battles of World War II*. Galahad Books, 1972.

Mellenthin, Major General F. W. von, *Panzer Battles*, edited by L. C. F. Turner and translated from the German by H. Betzler. University of Oklahoma Press, 1958.

"Military Improvisations during the Russian Campaign." Department of the Army Pamphlet #20-201, August 1951.

Nekrich, Aleksandr M., *June 22, 1941*, edited and translated from the Russian by Vladimir Petrov. University of South Carolina Press, 1968.

Nepomuk, George and Owen John, *Hell's Mouth*. Peter Davies, 1974.

Nettl, J. P., *The Soviet Achievement*. Harcourt, Brace & World, Inc., 1967.

Nicholson, Harold, *The Diaries and Letters of Harold Nicholson*, Vol. 2, *The War Years*, edited by Nigel Nicholson. Atheneum, 1967.

"Night Combat." Department of the Army Pamphlet #20-236, June 1953.

O'Ballance, Edgar, *The Red Army*. Frederick A. Praeger, Inc., 1964.

Poliakov, Alexander:
Russians Don't Surrender, translated from the Russian by Norbert Guterman. E. P. Dutton & Company, Inc., 1942.
White Mammoths, translated from the Russian by Norbert Guterman. E. P. Dutton & Company, Inc., 1943.

Ponomarenko, Lieut.-General, et al., *Behind the Front Line*. Hutchinson & Company, Limited, 1945.

Prüller, Wilhelm, *Diary of a German Soldier*, edited by H. C. Robbins Landon and Sebastian Leitner, and translated from the German by H. C. Robbins Landon. Coward-McCann, Inc., 1963.

Rauch, Georg von, *A History of Soviet Russia*. Frederick A. Praeger, Inc., 1957.

Reitlinger, Gerald, *The House Built on Sand*. The Viking Press, 1960.

Salisbury, Harrison E., *The 900 Days: The Siege of Leningrad*. Harper & Row, Publishers, Inc., 1969.

Schapiro, Leonard, *The Communist Party of the Soviet Union*. Vintage Books, 1971.

Seaton, Albert:
The Battle for Moscow, 1941-1942. Stein and Day, 1971.
The Russo-German War, 1941-1945. Praeger Publishers, Inc., 1972.

Sherwood, Robert E., *Roosevelt and Hopkins*. Grosset and Dunlop, 1950.

Shirer, William L., *The Rise and Fall of the Third Reich*. Simon and Schuster, Inc., 1960.

PICTURE CREDITS

Credits from left to right are separated by semicolons, from top to bottom by dashes.

COVER and page 1: Novosti Press Agency.

THE LAST BLITZKRIEG: 6, 7, 8—Süddeutscher Verlag, Bilderdienst, Munich. 9—Süddeutscher Verlag, Bilderdienst, Munich. 10, 11—Library of Congress. 12, 13—Süddeutscher Verlag, Bilderdienst, Munich; Ullstein Bilderdienst, Berlin. 14, 15—Courtesy Paul Carell, *Der Russlandkrieg.* 16, 17—Süddeutscher Verlag, Bilderdienst, Munich—Bundesarchiv, Koblenz; Library of Congress. 18, 19—Bibliothek für Zeitgeschichte, Stuttgart; © Imperial War Museum, London.

THE THRUST TO VICTORY: 22—Copied by Charlie Brown. 24—Zentralbild, Berlin. 27—Ullstein Bilderdienst, Berlin. 28—Map by Nicholas Fasciano.

RUSSIA'S WILY LEADER: 32, 33—Wide World, courtesy National Archives. 34—United Press International. 35—Wide World. 36—Sovfoto—United Press International; From *Stalin, A Political Biography,* by Isaac Deutscher, published by Oxford University Press, New York and London, 1949. 37—Wide World. 38, 39—Library of Congress, except left, United Press International. 40, 41—United Press International. 42—Emmanuel D'Astier. 44—Emmanuel D'Astier—Fototeca Storica Nazionale, Milan. 45—From LIFE Picture Collection—Wide World. 46, 47—U.S. Office of War Information, National Archives.

MAN BEHIND THE PANZERS: 48, 49—Ullstein Bilderdienst, Berlin. 50—Courtesy General H. G. Guderian, Bonn-Bad Godesberg. 51—Bundesarchiv, Koblenz. 52, 53—Margaret Bourke-White for LIFE, inset, Royal Armoured Tank Corps Museum, Dorset. 54, 55—Süddeutscher Verlag, Bilderdienst, Munich. 56, 57—Courtesy General H. G. Guderian, Bonn-Bad Godesberg (2). 58, 59—Ullstein Bilderdienst, Berlin; copied by Henry Groskinsky, courtesy General H. G. Guderian, Bonn-Bad Godesberg. 60, 61—Bundesarchiv, Koblenz.

THE SHAM RED GIANT: 65—Publifoto Notizie, Milan. 67—Imperial War Museum, London. 68, 69—Dever from Black Star. 70—Ullstein Bilderdienst, Berlin. 73—Photoreporters. 74—Copied by Charlie Brown, from *Napoléon,* published by Lapina, Editeur.

THE FALSE LIBERATION: 76, 77—Farabola, Milan. 78—Ullstein Bilderdienst, Berlin. 79—Süddeutscher Verlag, Bilderdienst, Munich. 80—E. C. P. Armées, France. 81—H. Roger Viollet—Enzo Nizza, Milan. 82, 83—Fototeca Storica Nazionale, Milan. 84, 85—Zentralbild, Berlin—Enzo Nizza, Milan; Farabola, Milan. 86, 87—Novosti Press Agency.

THE PEOPLE STRIKE BACK: 88, 89—Library of Congress. 90—Novosti Press Agency. 91—Farabola, Milan. 92, 93—Fotokhronika Tass; Novosti Press Agency. 94, 95—Novosti Press Agency. 96, 97—Novosti Press Agency; Sovfoto (2). 98, 99—Novosti Press Agency. 100—Bildarchiv Preussischer Kulturbesitz, Berlin. 101, 102, 103—Novosti Press Agency.

THE SIEGE OF LENINGRAD: 106—Map by Nicholas Fasciano. 108—Copied by Charlie Brown, from *The 900 Days,* by Harrison Salisbury. 111—Novosti Press Agency.

A CITY THAT REFUSED TO DIE: 114, 115, 116, 117—Novosti Press Agency. 118, 119—Sovfoto—B. Kudoyarov, Novosti Press Agency; A. Brodsky, Novosti Press Agency. 120, 121—B. Kudoyarov, Novosti Press Agency; M. Trakham, Novosti Press Agency—Novosti Press Agency. 122—Novosti Press Agency. 123—Fotokhronika Tass—copied by Henry Groskinsky, from *The 900 Days,* by Harrison Salisbury. 124, 125—Novosti Press Agency—B. Kudoyarov, Novosti Press Agency; Novosti Press Agency.

AN ARTFUL CALL TO ARMS: 126, 127—Courtesy Mark Sawtelle. 128—Margaret Bourke-White for LIFE. 129—Imperial War Museum, London. 130—Drawing from *History Lesson,* by Kukryniksy—courtesy Mark Sawtelle. 131—Chelsea House Publishers, New York, © 1976. 132, 133, 134, 135—Courtesy Mark Sawtelle.

REACTION IN THE WEST: 139—Margaret Bourke-White for LIFE. 141—Publifoto Notizie, Milan; Library of Congress—Fotokhronika Tass; Burt Thomas, courtesy *The Detroit News.* 142—United States Information Agency, National Archives.

TO RUSSIA WITH LOVE: 146, 147—Fox Photos. 148, 149—Publifoto Notizie, Milan. 150, 151—Hans Wild. 152—W. Eugene Smith from Black Star (2). 153—National Archives—John Florea for LIFE. 154, 155—Publifoto Notizie, Milan; from "Winston Churchill: La Seconda Guerra Mondiale," published by Arnoldo Mondadori, Volume 2, issue 45, page 1443, 156, 157—Library of Congress.

A CONFLICT OVER GOALS: 161—Wide World. 162—H. Roger Viollet. 165—United States Information Agency. 166—Bundesarchiv, Koblenz.

THE AGGRESSORS' ORDEAL: 168, 169—Bibliothek für Zeitgeschichte, Stuttgart. 170—Courtesy Paul Carell, *Der Russlandkrieg.* 171—H. Roger Viollet. 172, 173—Süddeutscher Verlag, Bilderdienst, Munich. 174—Bundesarchiv, Koblenz—Süddeutscher Verlag, Bilderdienst, Munich. 175—Süddeutscher Verlag, Bilderdienst, Munich. 176, 177—Ullstein Bilderdienst, Berlin; Heinrich Hoffmann, courtesy Geneva Baker. 178, 179—Süddeutscher Verlag, Bilderdienst, Munich. 180, 181—Copied by Charlie Brown, courtesy Enzo Nizza, Milan.

RUSSIA'S BIG SURPRISE: 184—Publifoto Notizie, Milan—Bildarchiv Preussischer Kulturbesitz, Berlin; Süddeutscher Verlag, Bilderdienst, Munich. 185—Bibliothèque Nationale, Paris—Ullstein Bilderdienst, Berlin. 186—Courtesy Paul Carell, *Der Russlandkrieg.* 189—Map by Nicholas Fasciano and John Drummond. 190—Mondadori Press.

THE REBOUNDING RED ARMY: 192, 193—Dmitri Baltermants. 194 through 199—Novosti Press Agency. 200, 201—Novosti Press Agency; Arkadij Sajchet from *Fotografovali Válku,* by Daniela Mrázková and Vladimír Remeš published by Odeon, Prague, 1975—LIFE Picture Collection. 202, 203—Novosti Press Agency.

INDEX

Numerals in italics indicate an illustration of the subject mentioned.

A

Art, Soviet, war posters, *126-135*
Arthur, Jean, *153*
Astor, Nancy, and Stalin, 34
Atlantic Charter, 143

B

Bagramian, I. K., and order for counterattack in Ukraine, 66-67
Barbarossa, Operation, *6-19,* 21; begins, 29, 30; date postponed, 26; first date set, 24; map *28;* named, 24; plan, 24-26
Bayerlein, Fritz, 160
Beaverbrook, Lord: meeting with Maisky, 138-139; at three-power conference in fall 1941, 145
Beloborodov, A. P., 187
Berezhkov, V. M.: informed of attack, 31; on meeting with Hitler in November 1940, 23-24
Bialystok salient, 65-66, 68-69
Blumentritt, Günther, on inability to advance during fall 1941, 166
Bock, Fedor von: and attack on Moscow, 162, 167; commands Army Group Center, 65; protests orders on treatment of commissars and civilians, 26; relieved of command, 167; supports attack on Moscow, 159
Boldin, Ivan V., 30, 31, 66, 69
Brauchitsch, Walther von: drops support for Moscow attack, 159; suggests partial withdrawal from Moscow area, 188; supports attack on Moscow, 25, 158
Bridges, building by German Army, 8, *13, 16*
Bryansk: attack on, 163; captured by Germans, 191
Budenny, Semyon Mikhailovich, 160, *161;* commands defense of Kiev, 160; relieved of command, 160

C

Caldwell, Erskine, *153*
Cartoons, commenting on Soviet alliance with Britain and U.S., 140, *141*
Cheremnykh, Mikhail, 128
Choltitz, Dietrich von, on losses in Ukraine, 73
Churchill, Mrs. Winston, on situation in U.S.S.R., 148
Churchill, Winston: and aid to U.S.S.R., 136-137, 138, 139, 144, 148; Atlantic Charter meeting, 143; and invasion of Iran, 143, 144; message to Stalin in July 1941, 140; response to domestic pressure for second front, 144-145; responses to Stalin's requests for second front, 139-140, 144; sends warning of German invasion to U.S.S.R., 21; on Soviet attitude toward West, 138; support for White Russians, 136; told of attack on Leningrad, 104
Clark, Bennett Champ, on German-Soviet war, 137
Colman, Ronald, *153*
Colville, John, and Churchill, 136
Communist Party, British, positions on war, 138
Communist Party, U.S., positions on war, 138
Coy, Wayne, 142
Crimea, invaded, 162
Cripps, Sir Stafford, 21; message to Churchill requesting second front, 144; on mission to U.S.S.R., 139; told of losses at Kiev, 161

D

Dekanozov, V. G., told of attack on U.S.S.R., 31
Demyansk, captured by Germany, 191
Djugashvili, Josef Vissarionovich. *See* Stalin
Djugashvili, Yakov, captured by Germany, 72, *73*
Dvina River: German crossing of, 69

E

Eden, Anthony: meetings with Maisky, 138-139, 144; told by Stalin of progress of counteroffensive, 190
Ehrenburg, Ilya, on Germans, 183
Einsatzgruppen, killing of prisoners of war and civilians, 71. *See also* SS
Estonia: annexed by U.S.S.R., 23; Soviet sphere of influence, 22

F

Fedyuninsky, Ivan I., 20; assumes command of Leningrad, 109; on situation in Ukraine, 66
Finland: invaded by U.S.S.R., 64; portions annexed by U.S.S.R., 23; Soviet sphere of influence, 22
Finland, Army of: attack on Leningrad, 104, 106; invades U.S.S.R., 24, 26
Foote, Alexander, warns of German attack, 21
France, panzer advance across, 57
Fuller, J. F. C., 48

G

Germany: cartoons, 140, *141;* control of Balkans, 26; guarantees Rumanian security, 23; home propaganda about Eastern Front, *184-185;* nonaggression pact with U.S.S.R., 22, 33; policy in Ukraine, 78; proclaims war on U.S.S.R., 8; treaty with Finland, 23; withdraws diplomats' families from U.S.S.R., 21
Germany, Air Force of: and attack on Leningrad, 104, 107, 109, 124; and attack on Moscow, 162; first attacks on U.S.S.R., 30; reconnaissance of U.S.S.R., 21, 26
Germany, Army of: advance through Ukraine, 160-162; aids invasion of Greece, 26; antipartisan operations, *100-103;* Army Groups Center, North and South, and invasion plans, 24-26, 29; attack on Kiev, 160-161; attack on Moscow, 162-163, 164-167; attack and siege of Leningrad, 104-109; commanders disagree about Moscow offensive, 75, 158-160, 167, 189; on defensive, 187-193; development of mechanized warfare, 50, *52-55;* early advances in invasion of U.S.S.R., *6-19,* 31, 68-70, 72-73, 75; Eastern Front stalemate, 191; effects of winter 1941-1942 on, 167, *168-181, 184-185,* 187, 188; Hitler relieves 30 generals of command, 167; Hitler's relationship to High Command, 23; invades U.S.S.R., 30; invades Yugoslavia, 26; losses in advance on Moscow, 167; losses in Ukraine, 73; losses in U.S.S.R. by August 1941, 158; map of battle for Moscow, 188, *189;* map of invasion, *28,* 29; occupation of Ukraine, *76-87;* organizes "hedgehogs," 191; panzer grenadiers, *9, 16-17;* quality of intelligence, 70; reaction to Hitler's orders concerning treatment of commissars and civilians, 25-26; rebuffs counterattack near Moscow 191; retreat from Moscow, *174,* 187-189; retreat in north and south, 190; support for attack on U.S.S.R., 24; transportation problems, 70-71, 164-165, *166,* 167, 170, 173, 188; treatment of prisoners of war, 69; unprepared for winter, 24, 163, 167, 170, 185, 187
Goebbels, Joseph: reads proclamation of war on U.S.S.R., *8;* on Soviet peace feelers

before invasion, 29; on unpreparedness for winter, 185
Golikov, F. I., leads new army of recruits, 186
Golubev, K. D., on situation of Tenth Army, 65-66
Gorbatov, Aleksandr V.: at defense of Vitebsk, 75; on Great Purge, 63; purged, 63; on quality of Army, 64; reinstated, 64
Govorov, L. A., 187
Grant, Cary, *153*
Great Britain: and aid to U.S.S.R., 136-140, 143, 145, *146-148, 150-151, 154-155;* Atlantic Charter, 143; British Communist reaction to war, 138; cartoons, 140, *141;* exchanges military mission with U.S.S.R., 139; invasion of Iran, 143-144; pact with U.S.S.R., 139; posters, *148;* pressure for invasion of France, 144-145; three-power conference in fall 1941, 145
Great Britain, Air Force of, trains Soviet pilots, *142,* 143
Great Britain, Army of: argues against invasion of France in 1941, 145; invasion of Iran, 144; revises opinion of Soviet prospects, 189
Greece, Axis invasion of, 26
Grigoryev, Pyotr P., purged, 63
Gromyko, Andrei, promotes aid to U.S.S.R., *152*
Guderian, Heinz, *48-53, 56-59;* and advance on Smolensk, 74; and attack on Brest fortress, 29; and attack on Bryansk, 163; and attack on Kiev, 160; and attack on Moscow, 162-163, 166, 167; captures Brest fortress from Poland, 29, 56-57; on controversy with Hitler about Moscow offensive, 75, 158-160, 188; on defensive at Moscow, 187-188; development of tank tactics, 53; early successes, 57, 60-61, 68-69; on Eastern Front prospects, 24, 58; halts advance on Moscow, 167; leads troops, *59,* 69; on plans for invasion of U.S.S.R., 58; on prospects for Moscow attack, 167; reaction to Hitler's order concerning treatment of civilians, 26; relieved of command, 167, 188; requisitions winter clothing, 163

H

Halder, Franz: on attack on Moscow, 162, 163; on Guderian's attack on Smolensk, 74-75; 57th birthday, 70; on Hitler's invasion message to troops, 29; on Hitler's meddling in details, 71; on Hitler's plan for Leningrad and Moscow, 106; on Hitler's plan for U.S.S.R., 25; on Leningrad siege, 109; orders troops to continue advance on Moscow, 166-167; on progress after first day of invasion, 67-68; receives orders to invade, 29; on Soviet resistance in Kiev District, 66; support for attack on Moscow, 25, 158-159; support for opening Eastern Front, 24
Harriman, Averell, at three-power conference in fall 1941, 145
Hedgehogs, 191
Hess, Rudolph, British Communists on, 138
Himmler, Heinrich: authority over U.S.S.R., 25; plans for U.S.S.R., 25
Hitler, Adolf: on Eastern Front as war of extermination, 25; and fall of Kiev, 161; forbids retreat from Moscow area, 188; goes to invasion command post, 29; on Halder's birthday, 70; intentions toward U.S.S.R., 21-22, 25; invasion message to troops, 29; meeting with Guderian on Moscow attack, 158; meeting with Molotov, November 1940, 23-24, 26, *27;* opposes direct attack on Moscow, 25; orders advance on Leningrad and Ukraine instead of Moscow, 75; orders advance to Oka River, 166; orders attack on Moscow, 162; orders

D. L.: TO. 947-79

Printed by Artes Gráficas Toledo, S.A.

X

MEGATECH

Cloning

Frontiers of
genetic engineering

David Jefferis

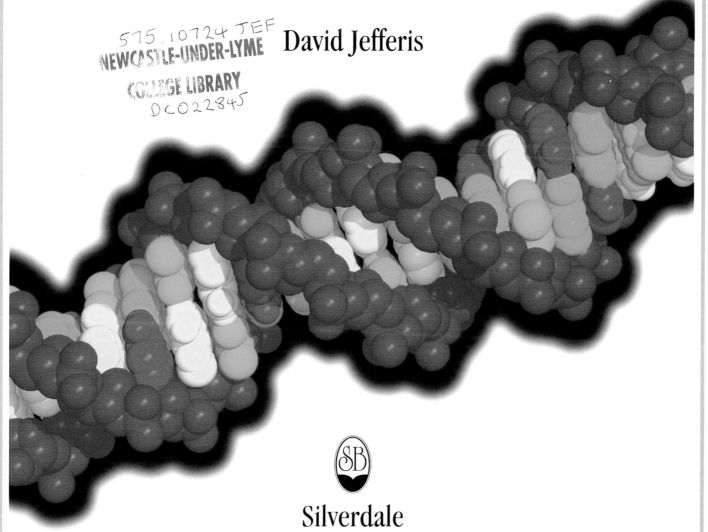

Silverdale

Introduction

Cloning is the creation of a living thing that is identical to, or a 'clone,' of a single parent. Some simple plants and animals reproduce this way. Human clones happen in nature as identical twins. Today, scientists are beginning to make clones to order. Cloning is an area of science called genetic engineering.

Developments in cloning research make newspaper headlines almost every day. The purpose of the research is to change all sorts of living things ('organisms') to provide people with better health, drugs, and food.

The success of genetic engineering, and cloning in particular, reveals a future for humanity which is full of promise, yet which has some frightening prospects, too. Read about both sides of the question in these pages.

Published by Silverdale Books
An imprint of
Bookmart Ltd
Registered Number 2372865
Trading as Bookmart Limited
Desford Road
Enderby
Leicester
LE9 5AD

Edited by
Norman Barrett
Coordinating editor
Ellen Rodger
Consulting Editor
Virgina Mainprize

Technical consultant
Gerard Cheshire BSc
Picture research by
David Pratt

Created and produced by
Alpha Communications in association
with Firecrest Books Ltd.

©1999 Alpha Communications and
©1999 Firecrest Books Ltd.
Silverdale edition published 2000
ISBN 1 85605 550 7

British Library Cataloguing in Publication Data for this book is available from the British Library.

Pictures on these pages, clockwise from far left:
1 Possible human clones.
2 Genetically modified tomato plants.
3 Genetic researcher checks on cloned bacteria.
4 Dolly the cloned sheep.
5 Genes of a fruit fly.
6 DNA profiling.

Previous page shows:
Computer image of DNA.

Color separation by
Job Color, Italy
Printed in Belgium by
Casterman Printers

Contents

Genes and clones

Cloning is one aspect of genetic engineering, the rapidly growing area of scientific research that tries to change and control the design of living things.

To understand cloning, you need to know about the smallest parts of living things. In every one of the billions of tiny cells that make up the body, there are groups of chemicals called 'genes.' Each gene is a set of instructions that controls how a protein is made. There are thousands of different proteins. They carry out the work of the body, from breaking down food for energy, to helping brain cells communicate with each other.

Genetic engineering can remove some gene instructions from one cell and place them in another. A plant may be given genes to resist disease carried by insects. An animal may have genes added to help it stay healthy.

▲ *The hydra is a small animal that lives in ponds. A baby hydra grows on the side of its parent. Soon it breaks away to live by itself. The two hydras have exactly the same genes, so they are clones.*

A clone is a living thing that has exactly the same genes as its parent. In sexual reproduction, genes from both male and female parents are mixed to create children that have genes from both their father and mother. A clone has the genes of only one parent, so it is identical to the parent. Many plants, and some very simple animals, reproduce by cloning. However, genetic engineering has now made it possible to clone more complex animals, such as frogs, sheep, and cows.

▲ *Genes are in the dark stripes of these hugely enlarged curly objects called 'chromosomes.' These are chromosomes of a housefly.*

▼ *To grow a new banana tree, a farmer simply cuts off a new shoot and plants it. The new banana has identical genes to its parent plant, so it is a clone.*

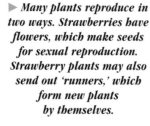

▶ *Many plants reproduce in two ways. Strawberries have flowers, which make seeds for sexual reproduction. Strawberry plants may also send out 'runners,' which form new plants by themselves.*

▶ *Researchers in Scotland created a cloned sheep in 1996. The animal, named Dolly, was a big step for genetic engineering. It was the first clone of such a complex animal. Read the story of Dolly on page 14.*

It took researchers nearly 300 tries before they succeeded with Dolly

Tʜe secrets of genes, and how to control them, were once a complete mystery. The invention of the microscope in 1608, helped scientists find out what living things are made of, and how they work.

Mice were cloned in 1998 by researchers based in Hawaii

◀ *The sea anemone normally lays eggs, but can also reproduce by cloning. An adult anemone splits in two, and the two halves slowly move away from each other. When they have grown to full size again, they split once more. In this way an entire colony may be formed, every anemone a clone of the original animal.*

???

Are there drawbacks to cloning?

Reproduction without mixing genes has one big problem. Because all cloned living things are the same as their parent, they share the same strengths and weaknesses. If disease strikes and one clone is infected, they all could be infected.

With sexual reproduction, the variety of genes in any group of plants or animals usually means that some will escape the disease.

5

Life changes

▲ *Charles Darwin's ship set off in December 1831 on a long mission to map the coast of South America. Collecting plant and animal specimens was an important part of the exploration.*

The science of genetic engineering has its roots in the experience of farmers who have been breeding animals for thousands of years.

Genetic engineering is a new science, yet it is not so different from the breeding done by farmers for thousands of years. Even though no one knew why a particular cow gave very creamy milk, farmers discovered that breeding from the best milkers gradually improved a herd.

▲ *Charles Darwin (1809-82) was one of the pioneers of evolution theory. His grandfather, Erasmus, had earlier suggested that living things adapted to changes in their environment.*

◄ *Farm and domestic animals have long been bred to suit human needs.*

Other animals – horses, pigs, sheep, dogs, and many others – have also been improved by selective breeding. Farmers know that by planting seeds from their best plants, they can have tasty fruit or bumper crops.

It was not until the first fossil-hunters found remains of long-extinct creatures such as dinosaurs that the idea of living things changing naturally over time began to be accepted.

Charles Darwin was one of a group of scientists and others who found that living things could change over time, without the assistance of humans. During a five-year voyage (1831-36) as ship's naturalist on the HMS Beagle, Darwin visited the Galapagos Islands in the Pacific Ocean, 600 miles (965 km) from South America.

Darwin found fossil remains of extinct animals and collected plants and animals that no one had ever seen before. Among these were 'Darwin's finches,' thirteen different types of the same bird. Each type lived on its own island and had a different shape and size of beak.

▲ *An early edition of Charles Darwin's famous book 'On the Origin of Species.'*

◄ The Galapagos Islands have many unique and interesting creatures, including these giant iguanas.

▼ The finch below uses a twig to dig out insects from holes in a tree branch. No wonder Darwin found finches so fascinating!

Darwin had an idea, or theory, to explain why the birds were different. He thought that one type, or species, of finch had once flown from mainland South America to the islands. Isolated on the separate islands, their descendants gradually changed, or evolved, to suit conditions on each particular island. Some birds developed sharp beaks for opening seeds, others acquired larger beaks for eating insects.

For many years, Darwin developed his ideas on how this process of change might work. Finally, in 1859, he published his results in a book called On the Origin of Species. It showed that life on Earth seems to have evolved from earlier forms.

What is natural selection?

Darwin's theory was that conditions in the wild 'selected' creatures that could survive best.

Plants or animals best suited to their environment had the best chance of survival.

If the environment changed, only plants and animals that could cope would survive. Darwin thought that at one time all the finches on the Galapgagos Islands were the same type. Over thousands of years, the birds on different islands slowly changed, or evolved, depending on the conditions on each island.

Darwin concluded that eventually such gradual changes could lead to entirely new species.

Genetic dawn

▲ *Gregor Mendel's work laid the foundations of genetics despite his research being ignored for many years. He gave up his experiments in 1868, when he became abbot of the monastery.*

Mendel used pea plants for various experiments

The man who set the scene for genetics was an Austrian monk called Gregor Mendel. He bred plants for many years in a monastery garden, where he studied them carefully.

Gregor Mendel was born in 1822, at Heinzendorf in Austrian Silesia (now in the Czech Republic). When he was 25, he became a priest at Brunn monastery and went off to Vienna University to train as a teacher. He returned to the monastery, and in 1856, he started an eight-year series of breeding experiments with plants. His aim was to see how different features were passed from parent plants to their offspring.

Mendel decided to study plant characteristics, such as tallness and shortness, color of seeds, and smooth or wrinkled seeds. He fertilized plants by taking pollen from flower to flower, just as insects do in the wild. He found definite patterns in the young plants that grew from these seeds and decided that plants must have what he called 'particles of inheritance.'

Soon, Mendel could predict how many plants would be tall, how many short, and so on.

▲ *Creating splendid new or mixed (hybrid) varieties has been the aim of keen gardeners for centuries. Today's commercial flower growers tempt buyers with large, brightly colored blooms that last a long time.*

◄ *Bonsai, the art of miniature trees, started in Japan centuries ago. Tiny trees result from the careful pruning of roots. Even so, their seeds do not change. If you plant a bonsai's seed in open ground, in a few years you should have a full-size tree.*

◄ *Gregor Mendel's monastery was built in eastern Europe, in what is now the Czech Republic. Mendel was a monk of the Augustinian order. Brunn (white cross on this map) has since been renamed and is now called Brno.*

▲ *For his experiments, Mendel pollinated test plants by hand. In the wild, bright colors and scent attract insects, which take pollen to other plants. This method mixes genes between plants at random and is good for keeping a species strong and healthy. It is not so good if a grower wishes to develop precise color or other characteristics.*

Mendel was correct with his theory of 'particles,' which today are known as genes. He thought that each plant had a pair of particles for each characteristic, one from each parent. Mendel suggested that some characteristics, such as tallness, were more powerful, or 'dominant.' Others, such as shortness, were less powerful, or 'recessive.' Even so, the recessive genes did not disappear. They could come back in later generations of plants.

Mendel gave genetics a good start, but his work was overlooked at first. His work was published in the Brunn Natural Scientific Society's journal in 1865, but it was not until 1900, 16 years after his death, that Mendel's achievements were recognized.

What is a polygene?

Mendel had a fairly simple task in his experiments, because his work with plants involved just single genes.

A polygene is more complicated. It is a group of genes that works as a team and may control things such as the color of skin or body weight.

Single genes in a polygene can be studied, but, like the runners in a relay race, it is the result of the group's action that counts.

Exploring the cell

Like bricks that make up a wall, cells are the basic units of all living things, from tiny bacteria to giant oaks, from sea slugs to human beings.

▲ *Robert Hooke's studies covered a number of subjects, from fleas to leaves, but his microscopes did not give huge enlargements in comparison to today's powerful microscopes.*

Before Mendel's experiments, scientists, using microscopes, had explored the world of the very small. English physicist Robert Hooke was among the first to use the microscope for serious scientific work. The instrument had been invented by Zacharias Jansen, of Holland, in 1608, before Hooke was born in 1635.

Hooke published a book called Micrographia, which means 'small drawings.' In 1665, he showed that a thin slice of cork was made of "a great many little boxes." He called them cells, after the compartments of a bee honeycomb, which he thought looked similar.

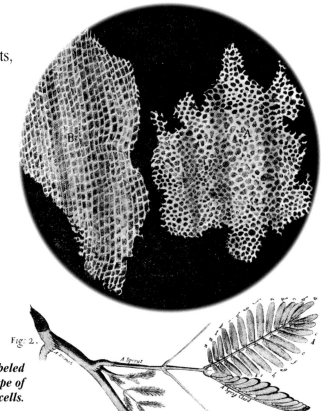

▶ *Right, one of Hooke's carefully labeled drawings, a twig and leaf. Above, the type of closeup view his microscope showed of plant cells.*

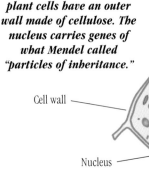

Robert Hooke lived long before cameras were invented, so he made drawings of specimens, including this flea

Other scientists joined in to investigate the invisible world that the microscope revealed. In 1831, Robert Brown from Scotland discovered that plant cells have a small object inside. He called this center of the cell, the nucleus.

Soon, three German scientists added new findings to the study of cells. In 1838, Matthias Schlieden saw that other plants were also made of cells. A year later, Theodor Schwann put forward the 'cell theory.' Schwann thought that animals are also made of cells. He was convinced that each cell is a living thing, and that complex organisms such as humans are made of many cells, acting as a group. Scientist Carl von Siebold went back to basics. He saw that some of the tiniest organisms are made of just a single cell, which also has a nucleus.

▶ *Unlike those of animals, plant cells have an outer wall made of cellulose. The nucleus carries genes of what Mendel called "particles of inheritance."*

Cell wall

Nucleus

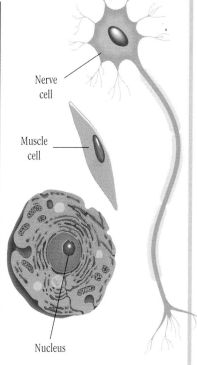

Nerve
cell

Muscle
cell

Nucleus

▲ *Cells come in all shapes and sizes. They carry out different jobs in the body. Complex plants are also made up of many different types of cells. They all have a nucleus containing genetic material.*

◄ *Electron microscopes can magnify more than a million times, They can produce images of a tiny universe invisible to the naked eye.*

With these discoveries, the secrets of the cell were being unlocked. Further research involved cell division, which is the process by which living things grow.

How do cells divide?

Cell division or 'mitosis,' is the way an organism grows. The nucleus splits in two, and two new 'daughter' cells result. Each cell is the same as its parent. As this process repeats, the organism gets bigger.

Male and female sex cells divide in a process called 'meiosis.' When male and female sex cells join together, genetic material from the nucleus of each is mixed. The result is an offspring with a mixture of each parent's characteristics.

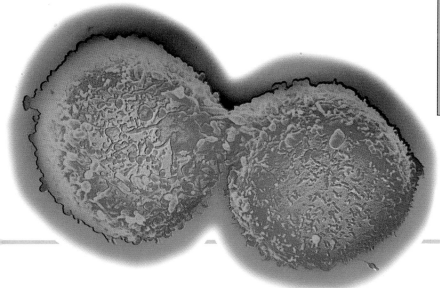

◄ *A cell at the moment of division. The very bright colors shown here are not real. The cells are colored to show details in the picture.*

The plan of life

▲ *James Watson (left) and Francis Crick revealed the shape of the DNA molecule in 1953.*

I nside the nucleus, or core, of every cell are the things that control how living organisms work – chromosomes, DNA, and genes.

To the pioneer researchers in genetics, investigating the nucleus was like exploring a new world. Inside this world, they found tiny, thread-like chromosomes, which contain genes, or what Gregor Mendel called 'particles of inheritance.'

▼ *Computerized view of the spiral shape of DNA.*

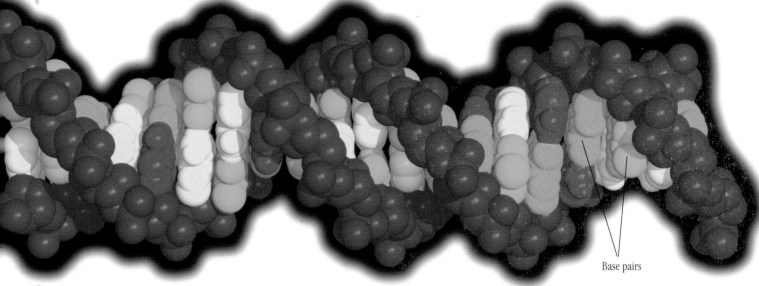

Base pairs

A chromosome is made mostly of the molecule DNA, short for 'deoxyribonucleic acid.' DNA molecules are the message carriers for thousands upon thousands of chemical patterns, or sequences. These patterns are the genes, which together make up the plan of life.

DNA consists of two strands, which form a spiral called a 'double helix.' Like a ladder, the strands are joined by rungs, known as 'base pairs.' These base pairs, or genes, are the various code messages that define each living thing. Gene sequences provide the instructions for everything in nature, from the blue of a kingfisher's feathers to the length of an elephant's trunk.

▶ *Inside the nucleus of each cell are the genetic instructions that rule life. DNA in the chromosomes carries these instructions as patterns of gene sequences.*

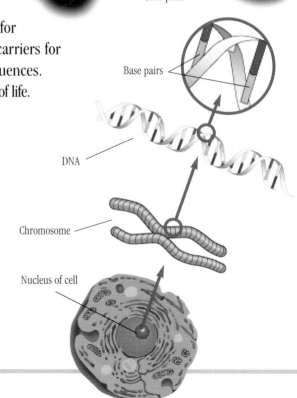

Base pairs

DNA

Chromosome

Nucleus of cell

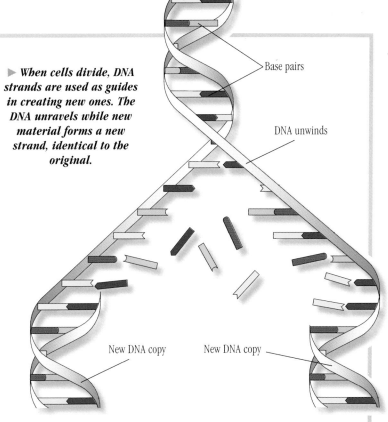

▶ *When cells divide, DNA strands are used as guides in creating new ones. The DNA unravels while new material forms a new strand, identical to the original.*

Base pairs

DNA unwinds

New DNA copy   New DNA copy

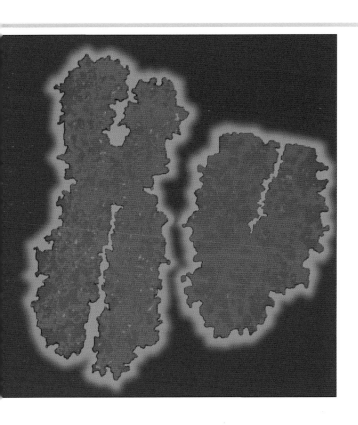

▲ *There are 46 chromosomes in each human cell. The 23rd pair, shown here, control whether you are a boy or a girl. Males have an 'X' and a 'Y' chromosome (above). Females have two 'X' chromosomes.*

D NA is a very effective message carrier. Just as the 26 letters of the alphabet can be arranged to make millions of different words, the genes in DNA can carry a large amount of information. In a human cell, each DNA molecule has about three billion base pairs, or genes, paving the way for countless genetic instruction groups.

If the DNA strands in just one human cell were stretched out in a line, they would measure about 36 inches long (91 cm). There are billions of cells in the human body!

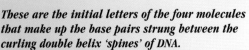

Human chromosomes, shown enlarged about 2500 times

▼ *The color of eyes, blonde or brunette hair, fair or dark skin – these and all other characteristics are controlled by the genes. Originally, they come from the sex cells of parents. Each parent gives its child half of the genetic material that makes the child unique.*

What is CGTA?

These are the initial letters of the four molecules that make up the base pairs strung between the curling double helix 'spines' of DNA.

Different groupings of these molecules – cytosine, guanine, thymine and adenine (CGTA) – control the chemical processes inside a cell.

Using this basically simple system, DNA is in charge of the elements of life itself.

Dolly the clone

The year 1996 saw a scientific breakthrough that few people had expected so early. It was the cloning of a sheep, an animal much more complex than simple plants or bacteria.

To create the sheep, a team of scientists from Scotland, led by researcher Ian Wilmut, took a single cell from the udder of a female sheep. They joined this to an unfertilized egg cell from another sheep, having first removed all genetic material from the egg. The joined cells grew into an embryo, which was then put into the womb of a third sheep. From there on, pregnancy and birth were normal. When born, the lamb (named Dolly) was also perfectly normal, except that she had no father. She was exactly like the sheep from whose udder the cell had been taken.

▲ Lamb number 6LL3, named Dolly, made big news. Scientists dealt with 2000 telephone calls, nearly 100 reporters, 16 film crews and over 50 photographers.

Sheep A

Sheep B

Udder cell with DNA taken from sheep A

DNA removed from egg cell of sheep B

Cells joined together

Embryo grown in test tube

Embryo placed in womb of sheep C

Sheep C

Dolly born as sheep A's clone

◄ How to clone a sheep. It looks simple here, but researchers worked for years to achieve success. The process used for Dolly is called 'nuclear transfer,' or NT. A cell from one animal is fused (joined) with an egg cell from another. All the genetic material has been taken away from the egg, so the embryo that starts growing has only one sort of DNA. It is a clone.

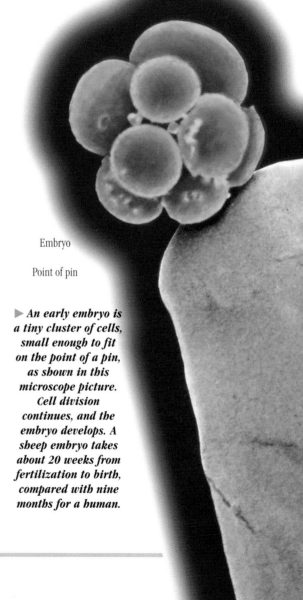

Embryo

Point of pin

▶ An early embryo is a tiny cluster of cells, small enough to fit on the point of a pin, as shown in this microscope picture. Cell division continues, and the embryo develops. A sheep embryo takes about 20 weeks from fertilization to birth, compared with nine months for a human.

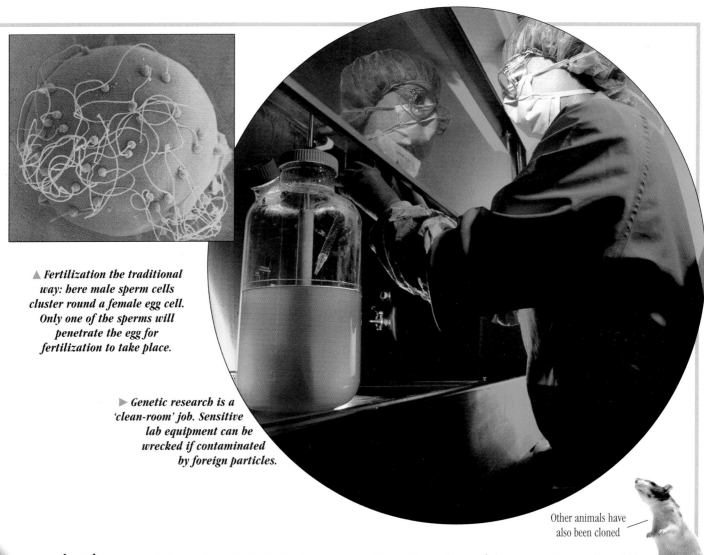

▲ *Fertilization the traditional way: here male sperm cells cluster round a female egg cell. Only one of the sperms will penetrate the egg for fertilization to take place.*

▶ *Genetic research is a 'clean-room' job. Sensitive lab equipment can be wrecked if contaminated by foreign particles.*

Other animals have also been cloned

The unusual thing about Dolly's cloning was that the udder cell was fully grown. Normally, adult cells are 'differentiated.' This means that, as an embryo develops, cells specialize, forming udder, nose, foot, or other body parts. For cloning to work, Ian Wilmut's research team had to make the cell 'young' again. Part of the procedure was to almost starve it. This process made the egg cell believe it was meeting a young cell, and so the growth process was begun. Why the near-starvation plan worked is not fully understood.

Clones of more animals have been made since Dolly, including mice and calves. Dolly gave birth to a lamb, Bonnie, in 1998. Bonnie seemed normal, which encouraged the research team to consider using their 'nuclear transfer' method in other ways. Future plans include modifying pigs' organs to use as 'spare parts' for humans who need new hearts, livers, or other organs.

???

What is fertilization?

This is the word for the meeting of male and female sex cells during reproduction.

In humans and other mammals, a male sperm joins with, or fertilizes, a female egg. This fertilization begins a new life.

Genetic material from the sperm and egg mix to create a new set of DNA instructions. The fertilized egg cell divides and grows, and soon an embryo (unborn infant) is growing in the female's womb.

Cracking the code

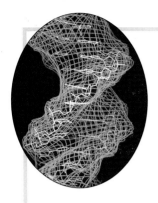

Discovering all the secrets of DNA is an international project, involving scientists across the world. Scientists are sharing the results of their research into the nature and make-up of chromosomes.

The genome is the name for all the genes in any species, or type, of plant or animal. Finding out about human genes is the aim of HUGO, the Human Genome Organization. It is a worldwide project which links together more than 1000 scientists in 50 countries.

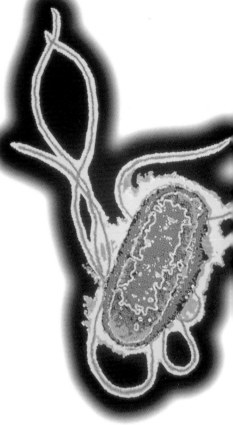

▲ *E.coli, the food-poisoning organism, is enlarged in this image produced by an electron microscope.*

▲ *DNA patterns vary between people, and a way of showing this is in DNA profiling. It is a useful technique in investigating crimes. By matching the DNA in the hair, blood, or skin cells, with those taken at crime scenes, scientists can tell if a suspect is guilty.*

There are about three billion genes in human DNA, although only 50,000 to 100,000 seem to be actively involved in sending messages. No one yet knows what the rest are for. Progress on the genome project has been rapid, and by 1998, over 6000 genes had been identified.

These discoveries included genes that may cause epilepsy, drug addiction, and brain damage. Identifying a gene sequence is only the first part of the story and is probably the easy part. The difficult task that follows each discovery is to find out how the gene works in the body.

What is a mutation?

Sometimes genetic instructions are damaged or are not copied perfectly from adult to offspring. Such a change in the genes is known as a mutation.

Most mutations are too small to be noticed. Others cause dramatic changes. This is how evolution can work in 'sudden jumps.' The 'sudden jump' idea was first suggested by Dutch botanist Hugo de Vries, back in the 1800s.

◄ *A two-headed turtle is not the sort of creature you meet every day, even on the Galapagos Islands. It is a mutant, with damaged genes.*

Mutants were a feature of 1950s science fiction stories. In the movie 'Them,' giant ants resulted from genetic changes caused by atomic bomb radiation

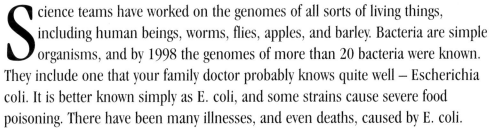

Science teams have worked on the genomes of all sorts of living things, including human beings, worms, flies, apples, and barley. Bacteria are simple organisms, and by 1998 the genomes of more than 20 bacteria were known. They include one that your family doctor probably knows quite well – Escherichia coli. It is better known simply as E. coli, and some strains cause severe food poisoning. There have been many illnesses, and even deaths, caused by E. coli.

Discovering the genomes of different organisms has revealed that all living things use variations of DNA and has shown how closely linked the life forms are on our planet.

◄ *Giraffes, snakes, eagles, and other living things all have DNA coding to pass on their genes to offspring.*

Cloning people

Experimenting with human beings is the next step in cloning. Some genetic researchers have pointed out that there are many problems with cloning people.

▲ *Cloning researchers point out that even perfect-looking 'natural' babies may have many genetic defects. These can result in illnesses that show up only later in life.*

Cloning is not that unusual. Gardeners have been cloning plants for centuries, without knowing anything about the science involved. Genetic engineers have also been cloning living things for many years, but experiments have been mostly on simple organisms such as bacteria.

▶ *The movie 'Gattaca' showed a future in which the natural-born hero fights to survive in a world filled with cloned humans and genetically perfect super beings. In a world such as this, normal humans could become slaves to these new bosses.*

▼ *Tiny samples of blood from a blood bank, or stray hairs with roots in a comb may provide enough cells to create a clone.*

Dolly the sheep changed things because she was the first clone of such a complex creature. The experiments were mostly made for money-making purposes. If you have one valuable animal, perhaps a sheep with fine-quality wool, you can clone a flock of exactly the same sheep. Doing these experiments with humans raises many difficult questions.

Most experts think that this type of cloning technology is too dangerous for use with humans. However, it is only a matter of time before someone tries it out.

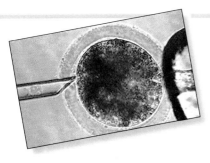

▲ *Cloning technology is a very delicate science. Special micro-size equipment has been developed to deal with tiny cells.*

▶ *Bacteria containing cloned DNA are inspected in a laboratory. Methods used to clone Dolly the sheep were used with other creatures, too. By 1998, researchers had succeeded in cloning other complex organisms, including mice and calves. Experts believe a human could be cloned soon.*

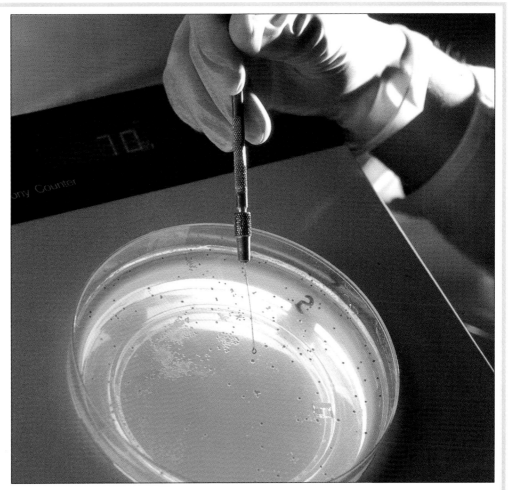

If you had a clone, would it be an identical twin? The answer is: yes and no. Like identical twins who are separated at birth, the clone might look and behave somewhat like you, but it would not be you. Like you, the clone would be an individual and would act as an individual, even if it was raised in a similar environment.

People outside the medical world are also interested in human cloning research. One group believes that humans were cloned by extraterrestrial visitors in prehistoric times. Other work includes the cloning of family pets. If your pet dies, you could pay to have it recreated as a clone. In 1998, a U.S. millionaire paid a research team $5 million to try to clone his dog!

◀ *Pet cloning is a possible for the future, but will a parrot clone talk as well as its parent?*

Danger – clones ahead?

Cloning is a new technology, and many people say it is best to take a breather before rushing ahead too fast, especially with humans.

Certainly, there are many things to find out. For example, no one knows exactly how the aging process works. If you were cloned at the age of 40, your clone might be born with 40 years of genetic damage, or have a lifespan cut short by that amount.

There are still many questions to answer, so further research and experiments with human cloning are best carried out with great care.

Organ transplants

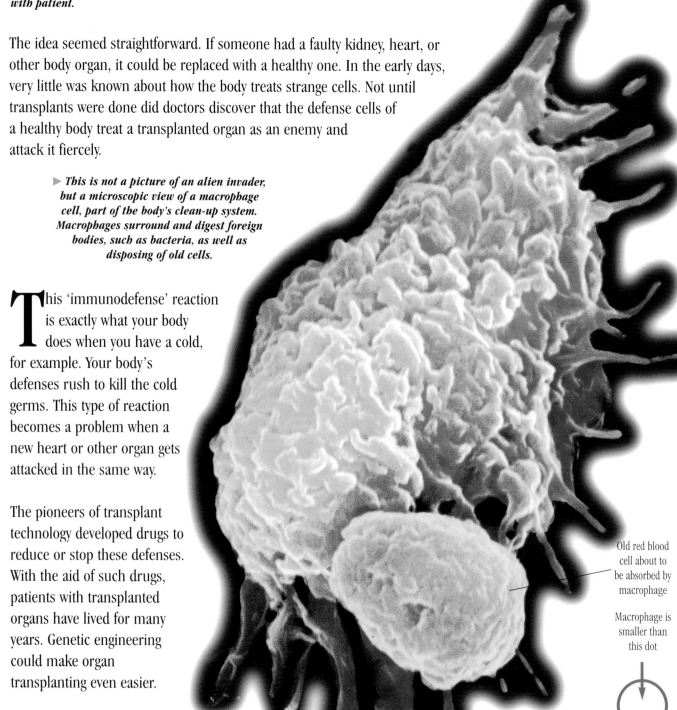

▲ *Dr. Christiaan Barnard, 1960s heart transplant pioneer, with patient.*

T he first transplants of human organs such as the kidney date back to the 1950s. In the 1960s, Dr. Christiaan Barnard broke new ground with heart transplant surgery in South Africa.

The idea seemed straightforward. If someone had a faulty kidney, heart, or other body organ, it could be replaced with a healthy one. In the early days, very little was known about how the body treats strange cells. Not until transplants were done did doctors discover that the defense cells of a healthy body treat a transplanted organ as an enemy and attack it fiercely.

▶ *This is not a picture of an alien invader, but a microscopic view of a macrophage cell, part of the body's clean-up system. Macrophages surround and digest foreign bodies, such as bacteria, as well as disposing of old cells.*

T his 'immunodefense' reaction is exactly what your body does when you have a cold, for example. Your body's defenses rush to kill the cold germs. This type of reaction becomes a problem when a new heart or other organ gets attacked in the same way.

The pioneers of transplant technology developed drugs to reduce or stop these defenses. With the aid of such drugs, patients with transplanted organs have lived for many years. Genetic engineering could make organ transplanting even easier.

Old red blood cell about to be absorbed by macrophage

Macrophage is smaller than this dot

▶ *Pigs, whose organs are used for human transplants, are known as 'transgenic' animals. The pigs are raised on laboratory farms where they are kept in totally virus-free conditions.*

One idea is to use pigs as donors, because their internal organs are similar in size to human organs. By adding human genes to pig cells, scientists hope to create organs which human bodies will not reject. Researchers are concerned, however, that certain pig diseases could be passed on to humans.

Another transplant possibility may be tissue engineering. A small piece of tissue from a transplant patient or a relative, is used as a building block for growing cloned cells. Skin and cartilage have been grown this way, but growing more complex organs is still quite difficult. Some researchers have been trying to grow a liver. They hope to create tissue that is genetically engineered to be accepted by a body's defenses. The result may be 'cell banks,' in which replacement organs are grown to order.

Researchers fear that using animals as organ donors may pass animal diseases on to humans

▼ *Body parts may one day be grown to order. In this futuristic view, the structure of a heart (seen on the video screens) has been made in plastic materials. This plastic heart is seeded with cloned muscle, blood vessels, nerves, and other cells. As the cells divide and the new heart grows, the plastic gradually dissolves, and its remains are carried away by pumps.*

??? Where do organs come from?

Transplants are now very common. Figures for 1996, for example, show that 20,000 operations were carried out in the United States alone.

Spare organs are sometimes donated by living donors. A close relative may give a kidney. Most transplant organs, however, result from someone's misfortune, usually a fatal accident. A person who is dead, but with organs in good condition, makes a perfect organ donor. In some countries, people may carry a 'donor card' giving permission for their organs to be removed after death.

There is a trade in organs in India, where about 2000 people a year sell one of their two kidneys because they need the money.

Gene therapy

▲ *The first steps in public health care included building sewers. In 1870, a boat trip through the new sewer system of Paris was a big attraction!*

Experts believe gene therapy is a big leap forward in the treatment of disease. With this new medical technology, perfect genes can be inserted into human cells to correct diseases that might otherwise be incurable.

So far, there have been three big steps in treating disease. The first was public health works, such as providing clean water supplies and efficient disposal of toilet waste. The second was anesthetic surgery, which allowed a wide range of operations. The third was the vaccines and antibiotics that let doctors treat many diseases spread by microbes. Gene therapy is a fourth step.

Many illnesses are the result of one or more genes not working properly. The faulty genes cause cells to make the wrong amount or type of protein, leaving the body open to all sorts of illness. The idea behind gene therapy is to deliver a gene into a patient's cells to cure a disease.

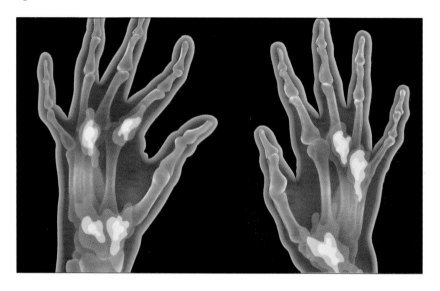

▲ *The crippling condition of arthritis could be relieved by gene therapy.*

An early gene therapy patient was a young girl from the United States, Ashanti DeSilva. Ashanti inherited a defective gene from both parents, giving her a condition that left her body unable to fight infections. She was very ill and left home only to visit doctors.

When Ashanti was four years old, gene therapy was tried out as a cure. On September 14, 1990, a medical team took out some of her white blood cells, inserted normal genes into them, and then returned the cells to her body.

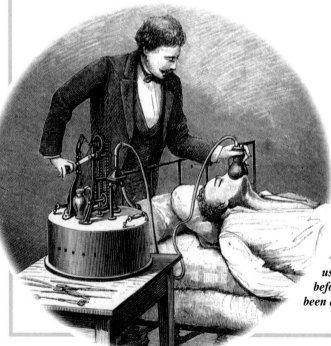

◄ *The second big step in treating disease. A doctor uses anesthetic gas to make a patient unconscious before an operation in 1885. Without it, surgery had been a grim and painful experience.*

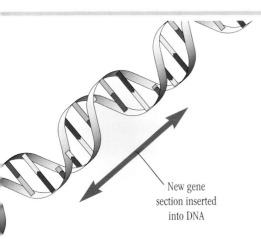

New gene section inserted into DNA

▶ *In the future, gene therapy may mean injections of genes directly into the bloodstream. The genes could be aimed at target cells (cancer cells, for example) while ignoring others. Once there, the new genetic material would order the patient's body to make a helpful protein to kill the dangerous cells.*

▲ *New genes are joined to DNA inside a cell. Cells carrying the repaired DNA are then ready to be returned to the body.*

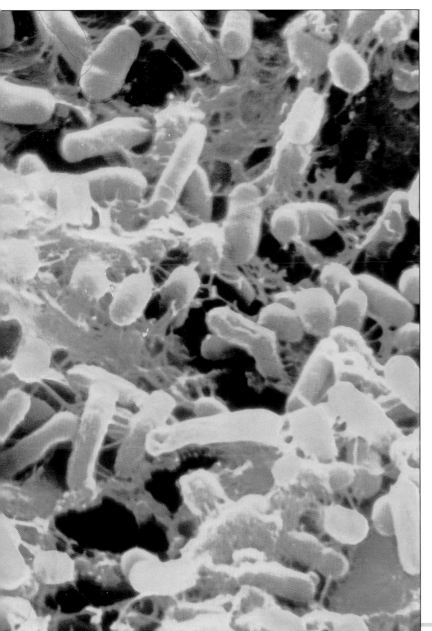

Over the next few months, Ashanti received more 'corrected' genes, and her health started to improve. The new genes had turned on her immune system, allowing her body's natural defenses to go to work and fight microbes from the outside world. Ashanti needs 'booster' treatments from time to time, but the gene therapy proved a great success.

Through the 1990s, other patients have been given gene therapy for other disorders. Many specialists are convinced that this treatment will become a normal medical practise.

◀ *Bacteria, such as these shown enlarged over 4000 times, are typical body attackers. The body's white blood cells, the 'antibodies,' are a defense force designed to destroy the invaders.*

Can genes cure diseases?

The potential is there to cure diseases and disorders. There are 5000 or more types of single gene disorders.

Cystic fibrosis is an inherited lung disease that kills most sufferers before they are 30 years old.

The gene that causes this disease was located in 1989. Four years later, a possible cure was tried out, with corrective genes breathed in through a nose spray. The tests were encouraging and work continues.

Genetic farming

▲ Young 'Flavr Savr' tomato plants. This genetically modified food was first put on sale in 1994. The changes allowed fruit to ripen without softening.

In the 1960s, a 'green revolution' produced bumper crops by introducing new types of plants and herbicides to kill insect pests. Now genetic engineering is changing farming and food production around the world.

Today, genetic engineers are working on a new green revolution. Crops are being designed to have a better chance of survival against pests.

Some of these improvements will help farmers, but the big food companies may benefit most. They are moving fast to control the complete chain of food production, from seeds planted in the soil to the breakfast cereal in your bowl.

► Genetically modified crops promise good yields, with fewer chemical sprays needed to eliminate pests, but some people still say traditional ways of growing are better.

▲ Genetic foods have become big business. For example, Europe buys up to 40 percent of the U.S. soya bean crop, of which nearly one-third is genetically modified.

One genetically engineered product is the 'terminator' seed. This super-seed is disease-resistant and can produce bumper crops. However, farmers must buy a new supply every year, because the seed grows only once. Seeds cannot be harvested and saved for future use. For the seed company, 'terminator' seeds mean greater sales. For the farmer, it means spending more on seed.

Across the world, about $400 billion is spent on food production every year. In 1995, about $450 million was spent on genetically engineered seed, a sum that may grow 15 times or more by 2005. Not everyone agrees that genetically changed foods are without problems. Some people think super-seeds may end traditional farming methods.

▶ Genetically modified fruit and vegetables are already on supermarket shelves. This group shows just a few planned changes to familiar foods.

Herbicide-resistant corn is already grown. Healthier cooking oil that uses low-fat corn is now being developed

Genetically altered broccoli is a cancer fighter

Genetically modified cheese suitable for vegetarians is available now. It uses a special enzyme, rather than rennet, which comes from calves' stomachs

Flavr Savr tomatoes have been in grocery stores since 1994. Further work could produce fruits that help fight cancer

High starch potatoes do not absorb as much fat when cooked in oil

An antifreeze protein from a cold-water fish may allow strawberries to be grown in cold climates

Bananas could in the future contain a vaccine against the liver disease hepatitis B. Slower ripening could improve taste

◀ ▶ A growing human population in the 21st century will make better food production important. Climate change may cause drought (left). Accidental fires may ruin crops (right).

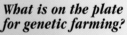

Some experts believe there may be unknown dangers with genetically changed crops. Switzerland, Austria, and Luxembourg are among the countries that turn away products that include genetically modified organisms (GMO). "It's a risk that even the best scientist cannot predict," warned one scientist in 1998. The deadly disease BSE, or mad cow disease, which resulted partly from feeding ground-up meat remains to cattle, is a reminder that experts can make mistakes.

Despite these fears, genetic engineers may come up with some very tempting ideas. On the planning list are 'nutraceutical' products that are a cross between food and medicine. They include tomatoes that can protect against bowel problems, and vegetables with extra vitamins.

What is on the plate for genetic farming?

Food companies interested in GMO, or genetically modified products, spend a great deal of money persuading people that the new technology is safe.

People who object to the products do not have as much money to spend, so they compete by staging demonstrations and meetings, hoping to catch the attention of the world's news media.

Examples include protesters in Ireland uprooting GMO test crops, and Germans preventing the planting of some GMO sugar beets. In Britain, one action group visits supermarkets and marks packages of GMO food with a big 'X.'

Into the future

Genetic engineering will be one of the most important areas of scientific progress in the future. What does the future hold for genetic engineering?

▲ *Genetically improved and cloned people might be living in the 21st century.*

Cloning technology has already moved ahead by leaps and bounds. It took only two years after Dolly the sheep was created for researchers to clone other mammals. Research in human cloning is progressing, too. Soon, this type of genetic engineering could be an option for people who cannot otherwise have children. However, many people are worried about the problems this new technology will bring.

▶ *In the future, genetic weapons may be more dangerous than nuclear bombs. Scientists could create diseases that are more deadly than the Black Death of the Middle Ages. Just a teaspoon of the worst plague germs could wipe out most of the people in a major city.*

For other fields of genetic engineering, the future is a whole new frontier. Gene therapy has already helped many people fight disease. Researchers are also investigating the possibility of using some animals as organ donors for humans.

By genetically engineering plants, seed companies have already created 'super-seeds' that grow plentiful crops but also change traditional ways of life. Genetic engineering could create flowers that have strange new color patterns and plants that are altered to produce oil for vehicle fuels.

◀ *By 2020, a flower-show winner may be the GMO 'super-stripe' rose, a possible outcome of early-1990s Dutch experiments, when petunias were grown with petals covered with rings and splashes of color.*

In 1998, a gene was found that may unlock the secrets of aging. Lifespans vary widely in nature – bristlecone pines live 5000 years or more, but an adult mayfly may last just one day. Humans vary in lifespan, too. The oldest recorded person (Jeanne Calmet, right) lived for 122 years. Some researchers believe that one day people may lead an active life to this sort of age, instead of today's more usual 70-80 years.

Huge tusks and shaggy coats mark out mammoths from their elephant relatives

Mammoths became extinct over 10,000 years ago, perhaps because of hunting by humans

◄ Woolly mammoths may be brought back to life using cloning technology. Pandas, tigers, and other endangered species may also be rescued from extinction this way.

▲ The future? A young 'mammophant' (left) with its elephant mother.

It may be possible to bring some prehistoric animals back to life. Researchers plan to find a frozen woolly mammoth in icy-cold Siberia. They will use DNA from a mammoth sperm cell to fertilize the egg of a distantly related modern elephant. By painstakingly adjusting the genes through several generations, it is hoped eventually to have an almost 'pure bred' mammoth.

While this is not quite so dramatic as the dinosaurs of the Jurassic Park movies, wildlife parks of the future may have some interesting 'new' animals.

Can cloning save animals?

Maybe, says Professor Chen Dayuan. He is a Chinese scientist eager to save the rare giant panda, of which there are fewer than 1000 left in the wild.

Professor Dayuan plans to insert cells from an adult panda into another animal's egg from which the DNA has been removed. That animal (probably a dog) will go on to give birth to a baby panda.

In New Zealand, the disappearing Auckland Island cattle breed was saved from extinction in 1998. By similar methods as were used to clone Dolly the sheep, a cloned calf was born.

Time track

A list of some important dates in genetic research, from the work of pioneer botanists to the first transplant of a human organ.

▲ *By the 1990s, plants were genetically modified for all sorts of reasons.*

1608   Zacharias Jansen from Holland invents the microscope, an instrument that reveals the universe in miniature. For the first time, people can see the details of tiny living things, such as insects and plants.

1665   English scientist Robert Hooke publishes Micrographia, the first book based on observations made using a microscope. In the book, Hooke tells how he looked at a slice of cork and saw that it was made of "many little boxes." He calls them cells, and scientists will show later that all living things are made up of cells.

1735   Botanist Carl Linnaeus from Sweden publishes System of Nature. The book sorts living things into plant and animal kingdoms. Linnaeus also starts the two-part Latin naming system still used today. An example is Homo sapiens. 'Homo' is the family of man, while 'sapiens' is our particular type and means 'thinking.'

▲ *Alfred Wallace was an English naturalist who came up with ideas similar to Charles Darwin's. The two lectured together in 1858.*

1822   Gregor Mendel born. The modern science of genetics dates from his work in the gardens of the monastery at Brno, in what is now the Czech Republic. After experimenting for many years, he forms his laws of inheritance. These enable researchers to predict what characteristics – height, color, and so on – can be expected in new generations of living things.

1831   Charles Darwin from England sets out as ship's naturalist on HMS Beagle, on a mission to survey the coast of South America. During mainland visits on the five-year voyage, Darwin finds many fossils, showing that some animal species die out while others continue to breed and flourish. On the isolated Galapagos Islands, far out in the Pacific Ocean, Darwin discovers groups of finches with different-shaped beaks, a puzzle he is determined to solve.

1831   Scottish botanist Robert Brown investigates cells with a microscope and sees that they all have a tiny speck inside. He labels this object the 'nucleus,' a Latin word meaning 'little nut.'

1838   German botanist Matthias Schlieden studies many plants and sees that they are all made from cells.

1838   Karl von Nageli, a Swiss botanist, sees how a cell divides into tiny strands, later called 'chromosomes.'

1859   Charles Darwin's On the Origin of Species is published. He claims that living things may change naturally, according to changes in their environment. Darwin also suggests the idea of evolution from simpler forms of life millions of years in the past. Many people are upset by this and by Darwin's suggestion of apes as human ancestors. Religious teachings have said that life on Earth was created only a few thousand years ago, with humanity being the highest form of life.

1865   Gregor Mendel's studies are published in the journal of the Brno Natural Scientific Society. It is largely ignored until it is rediscovered in 1900 by Hugo de Vries, from Holland. De Vries also puts forward the idea of evolution moving in sudden jumps, by 'mutation.'

1907   Experimental work is begun by American Thomas Hunt Morgan. He produces the first 'chromosome map,' showing the location of genes. His tests use fruit flies because of their simple genetic structure and rapid breeding.

1932   First electron microscope made by two German engineers Ernst Ruska and Max Knoll. It uses beams of electron particles instead of light rays.

1953   American James Watson and Francis Crick from England determine the shape and structure of the DNA molecule, shown as a 'double helix,' or double spiral. DNA is the carrier of the genetic code common to all forms of life on Earth.

◄► *In 1838, Matthias Schlieden found that all plants are made of cells. At left a cactus, at right a convolvulus.*

1960s   Organ transplants started by Dr. Christiaan Barnard in South Africa. His work reveals problems created by the body's natural defenses, notably the rejection of foreign tissues.

1960s   The first 'green revolution.' Crops are bred for better growth. New chemicals designed to kill crop-wrecking insects are mostly successful, but many insects develop resistance to chemicals.

1973   Two U.S. researchers, Herbert Boyer and Stanley Cohen, experiment with 'recombinant DNA.' They slide out sections of DNA from different bacteria, rejoining them to form a new strand of DNA.

1980   First patent granted on a living thing – a microorganism designed to digest waste created by spills from tankers at sea or from offshore oil rigs.

1988   Special type of mouse patented for use in research projects.

1990   Gene therapy used to treat a patient with a poor immune defense system. Injections with undamaged DNA boost the body's ability to resist disease and let the patient lead a normal life.

1990   Human Genome Organization (HUGO) involves thousands of scientists across the world. Its aim is to map out all the genes in human DNA by 2005. It is estimated there are 80-100,000 of them.

1994   First genetically modified food, the 'Flavr Savr' tomato, goes into supermarkets. Modifications allow the tomato to ripen on the vine without softening. The modified fruit are also less likely to be damaged when being transported.

1994   Second green revolution begins, with genetically modified organism (GMO) crops being planted.

1994   First 'genetic crime.' Two men are caught by police after stealing cells from a U.S. laboratory and trying to sell them for $300,000. The cells contain a gene that could be useful in helping combat failing human kidneys.

1996   Dolly the sheep cloned by a team based in Edinburgh, Scotland. They strip a cell of its genetic material and put fresh DNA into it, resulting in a clone. Dolly is the first mammal to be cloned.

1997   Researchers at the University of Bath in England, create headless tadpoles. Possible future uses for the technology include tissue banks, where spare organs can be grown as replacements.

1998   Scientists at the University of Hawaii create 22 mouse clones, using similar methods as those used for Dolly the sheep. The researchers also create clones of the clones, and say they could produce up to 200 mouse clones a day.

1998   Experiments with cell-repair genes show that it may be possible to extend the human lifespan by 40 percent. Researchers say that people could still be active and largely free of the diseases of old age.

1998   A disappearing breed of New Zealand cattle is cloned by 'nuclear transfer,' the same method as used for Dolly the sheep in 1996. This marks the dawn of cloning to save endangered species. Other ideas include bringing back to life extinct animals, such as the woolly mammoth.

Beyond 2000
The Human Genome Organization completes the map of human chromosome.

Pigs raised in laboratory conditions used as organ donors. This follows the earlier use of pigs to supply heart valves.

First human clones.

Tissue banks become common, with organs grown to order in the laboratory.

Genetic screening for defects becomes a standard check for pregnant mothers.

Active human lifespan of 120-150 years becomes possible as researchers find out the secrets of cell repair and many diseases of old age.

'Alpha humans' are created, with reduced number of genetic defects, superior intelligence, and resistance to disease.

Human genetic modifications and cloning become common.

▲ *In 1980, a microorganism was created to help clean up oil spills.*

▲ *The microscope was invented in the early 1600s. This model dates from the 1870s.*

Glossary

A n explanation of technical terms and concepts.

▲ *Fossil remains of an ammonite, an ancient sea creature.*

Amino acids
Units that make up all the proteins in living organisms. Green plants can make all of these organic acids they need. Animals must eat nutrient-rich food to provide all the amino acids necessary for building tissues.

Arthritis
Painful inflammation of the joints. It is usually a condition that comes with age.

Bacteria
Single-cell organisms that reproduce by dividing. Many types cause diseases, but other bacteria, such as the those that change milk to yogurt, are very useful.

Cell
Smallest living unit. Some simple organisms are single cells. Most plants and animals are made of many cells of different shapes and sizes. Typically, a cell consists of a watery, jelly-like substance called 'cytoplasm,' surrounded by a membrane that gives the cell its shape. Various things enter through this cell wall, including oxygen and food. Waste products pass the other way. Tiny chemical factories in the cell, called 'organelles,' produce enzymes and other substances useful to the body (see Enzyme).

Cell division
In simple organisms, a cell, including the nucleus, divides by splitting in half. In complex organisms, a process called 'mitosis' ensures the genes are shared. 'Meiosis' is the way male and female sex cells – sperm and eggs – are formed.

Chromosome
Microscopic threads inside the nucleus of a cell that carry DNA and genes. Humans have 22 pairs of chromosomes plus a pair that determine sex. We all have the same number of chromosomes, but our slightly different genes make us individuals.

Clone
Living creature made from a single cell without sexual reproduction. The new organism is genetically identical to the parent. In humans, a 'natural' clone is an identical twin, where the egg has split after fertilization, separating into two embryos that have the same genes.

DNA
Abbreviation for deoxyribonucleic acid, the molecule that makes up chromosomes and genes. It is shaped as two long spiral threads, coiled around each other.

Egg
Sex cell made by a female animal. After fertilization, the egg (or ovum) divides into more cells to become an embryo. In birds, developing chicks feed on the yolk until they are big enough to hatch. A female mammal's egg is not laid like a bird's. A developing embryo gets its food from the mother's body until birth.

Electron microscope
Type of microscope with strong magnifying power. A beam of electrons is fired on a subject, then focused by a powerful magnetic system. The result is shown on a video screen, and photographed.

Embryo
Name for the early stages of a fertilized egg, as it divides and grows. At eight weeks, a human embryo is barely an inch (25.4 mm) long, though it has the beginnings of arms, legs, and eyes. In later development, an embryo is usually called a 'fetus.'

Enzyme
A substance, made of protein and produced by a cell, that speeds up various processes. A typical cell may have up to 100,000 different enzymes, needed for various jobs. Examples of these include enzymes that convert food to simple

➡ KINGDOM	*Animalia*	Animals
➡ PHYLUM	*Chordata*	Animals with backbones
➡ CLASS	*Mammalia*	Mammals
➡ ORDER	*Carnivora*	Meat eaters
➡ FAMILY	*Felidae*	Cats
➡ GENUS	*Panthera*	Panthers, group of similar species
➡ SPECIES	*Tigris*	Tiger

◀ *How to classify a species, using the system first developed by Carl Linnaeus (1707-1778). Organisms are placed into smaller and smaller groupings, down to species. A species is a group of animals that can breed with each other over several generations. Species may evolve or change over time, if their genes adapt to a changing environment. Mutations may also create changes.*

◀ *Panthera tigris.*

substances for digestion. Other enzymes link simple substances together to form more complex ones.

Evolution

The theory that existing species developed from earlier forms of life. 'Natural selection' is a part of evolution theory. It means that creatures change in ways that best suit survival in particular environments. Creatures not suited to the environment will die. Evolution can also happen through mutation (see Mutation).

Extraterrestrial

Literally, 'out of the Earth.' Normally used to describe life (even simple organisms) on other planets.

Fertilization

Meeting of sex cells, such as male sperm and female egg during reproduction. When sex cells join together, DNA from each is mixed, and egg cells divide and grow to form an embryo.

Fossil

Hardened, or 'petrified,' stone-like remains of a living thing that died millions of years ago. Fossils of many prehistoric plants and animals have been found, from sea creatures (see picture top left, opposite) to giant dinosaurs.

Gene

Coded message stored along the DNA of a chromosome. Gene sequences provide the pattern for life – from the size of your foot, to the color of your hair.

Gene therapy

Medical treatment that injects perfect genes into the cells of a patient to 'switch on' the patient's own defective genes.

Genetic engineering

Changing the genes of a living thing in the laboratory. Genes are taken from one set of genes to another using enzymes that act as 'scissors' to cut up a DNA molecule.

Genome

All the genes in a cell. Each type of living thing has its own genome, ranging from simple ones in flies to the complex ones in humans and other mammals.

GMO

Short for genetically modified organism. A GMO might be anything from a strain of disease-resistant wheat to a mouse that has been genetically engineered for laboratory tests.

Hydra

Small freshwater creature with a tube-shaped body and mouth surrounded by tentacles. Hydras reproduce 'asexually' – by budding. The young are clones of the parent hydra.

Immune system

Body defense against infections. 'Antibodies,' produced by white blood cells, attack invading bacteria and viruses.

Mammal

Animal that is warm-blooded, gives birth to live young, and feeds its babies with mother's milk. Examples include sheep, cows, cats, dogs, and humans.

Molecule

Group of atoms arranged in various ways. A molecule of water is made of two hydrogen atoms and one of oxygen. DNA molecules are very complex, ranging from 100,000 to 10 million atoms, depending on the organism.

Mutation

Sudden change in a gene. Most mutations are harmful in some way and result in early death, but some may be useful and get passed on to new generations.

Nucleus

The life center of a cell, containing DNA. Genetic instructions carried by the DNA control the way the body works.

Protein

Organic compound found in living things, made from chains of amino acids. There are thousands of proteins, each with a different job. Body parts such as muscles are made almost entirely of protein.

Rejection

Non-acceptance by the body of organs transplanted from another person or an animal. The body's immune system treats the new tissue as an invader.

Species

A group of living things that can breed among themselves (see table on opposite page) and have young that can do the same. Some species are close enough to each other to breed, but the young cannot continue to reproduce. A mule is an example of this. It is an animal that results from fertilization between a donkey and a horse but cannot have young itself.

Transplant

The transfer during special surgery of a healthy organ, such as a heart or kidney, from one body to another.

Virus

Tiny organism that usually causes disease in animals and plants. A virus invades a cell, turning it into a virus production center. Then the cell bursts and dies, releasing the new viruses to spread to other cells. Viruses are parasites that need a host cell in which to live.

Womb

Another word for the female uterus, the part of the body in which an embryo develops.

▲ *There is a great variety of life on earth. Yet, all species are thought to have a common ancestor that thrived nearly four billion years ago, when the first lifeforms developed.*

Index

Acknowledgements
We wish to thank all those
individuals and organizations that
have helped us create this
publication:

Photographs supplied by:
Alpha Archive
A. Barrington Brown
Bruce Coleman Collection
Cellmark Diagnostics
Celltech Ltd.
Chris Bjornberg
C.C. Lockwood
Columbia TriStar Films (UK)
Corbis UK Ltd
D. Phillips
Dr. Gopal Murti
Dr. Linda Stannard, UCT
Dr. Yorgos Nikas
Eurelios
Institut Pasteur/CNRI
James Holmes
J.C. Revy
Mary Evans Picture Library
Mary Plage
Maximilian Stock Ltd.
New Scientist
Peter Menzel
Professor K. Seddon and Dr. T. Evans,
    Queen's University, Belfast
Catherine Pouedras
Hans Reinhard
Science Photo Library
Kim Taylor
Telegraph Colour Library
The Kobal Collection
Topham Picturepoint
L. Willatt, East Anglian Regional
    Genetics Service

Digital art created by:
David Jefferis
Gavin Page/Design Shop

Further assistance from:
Michael Gerr and his pigs